HOLLYWOOD ON THE POTOMAC

How the Movies View Washington, DC

Published in the United States by:
The Friends of SE Library, 403 7th Street, SE, Washington, DC 20003.

ISBN 978-0-578-11021-9

Book design by:
Karen Falk Marketing Communications

First Edition. Printed in the United States of America.

Some critics say that people complain about the movies because the movies do not reflect reality. It is this writer's suspicion that more people lament the fact that reality does not reflect the movies.

– Leo Rosten, Screenwriter, humorist

Movies are fun, but they're not a cure for cancer.

– Warren Beatty, actor

HOLLYWOOD ON THE POTOMAC

How the Movies View Washington, DC

TABLE OF CONTENTS

III. Tracking Shot – The Nineties......114

IV. Quick Cuts – The Last Decade......168

Selected Short Subjects......234

FOREWORD

Images are perceptions that convey the reality of a time and place. Whether impressed upon the brain through the words of a poet or a novelist, a biographer or a historian, those images–authentic or not–stay with us, creating memories, frequently shaping our attitudes and outlook.

More powerful than the written word, however, are the visual images, things we have actually seen or vicariously experienced in paintings or through the eye of the camera. And when those images move, they have a more profound effect, for good or ill.

In promoting the history and culture of Washington, DC, and Capitol Hill, the Friends of Southeast Library sponsored a film series in 2011, presenting movies that were partly filmed in our neighborhood. Introduced by film critic and historian Mike Canning, the series presented Hollywood's view of the nation's capital, from the idealism of *Mr. Smith Goes to Washington* to the sharp wit of *Born Yesterday* and the paranoia of *Seven Days in May*.

This book grew out of that series and documents an important part of the city's history. Mike discusses the complex relationship of the movie industry and the way it portrays our city to the world, and he catalogues the movies about Washington since the start of talking pictures, a period that roughly parallels the history of Southeast Library.

No city can provide more recognizable images than the Capitol, the Library of Congress, the Washington Monument, the Lincoln Memorial, or the White House. And no city can provide a locale for such a range of stories–from *The Exorcist* and *The Day the Earth Stood Still* to *A Man Called Peter*, *All the President's Men* and *Charlie Wilson's War*. Although Hollywood frequently fakes locations, there is really no substitute for the real thing: Washington, DC.

Many of the films cited herein, along with the books that inspired some of them, are available on DVDs from your library.

–Neal Gregory, President,
Friends of Southeast Library

HOLLYWOOD ON THE POTOMAC

INTRODUCTION

This volume offers a comprehensive look at significant commercial feature films of the Sound Era (1930-2011) which treat Washington, DC as either subject, background, or as incidental material. The book is intended for fans and students of both movies and politics, and especially those who, like the author, combine the two interests. While it is most specifically addressed to Washingtonians curious about how their town has been depicted in this country's most popular art form, it is also addressed to the general reader.

Since it is published by a Capitol Hill-based enterprise, the book's coverage of movies made on or about Capitol Hill (especially films treating the U.S. Congress) is given special emphasis. It is hoped, also, that this survey of Washington movies will offer readers useful and intriguing tidbits of the city's history and lore.

A total of 58 films are given full treatment in mini-chapters. Each chapter contains basic credits and cast, a synopsis, and background or production data on the film. In some instances, this writer's personal assessment of the film is included in a "Comments" section. Elements of a film (especially filming locations) that highlight the District or, specifically, Capitol Hill, (which is also a residential neighborhood) are indicated in "DC/Hill Notes." For additional entertainment value, individual chapters also carry a section on "Goofs," which shows specific film errors–both fundamental and trivial–in presenting Washington's geography or practices. *(Note: The 58 films cited above will not carry their year of release throughout the text.)*

"Goofs" recognizes what local moviegoers have long noted: Hollywood so often gets DC *wrong*. Commercial movies, of course, as entertainment vehicles, drive with a certain license. Dramatic or comedic effects that get people in their seats is the point, after all, and not a hidebound accuracy. Still, if you live in DC and see these films, you know that one peek at the phone book or asking some random guy on the street would offer accurate information.

An attentive reader might ask: what are the criteria for the films described in these mini-chapters? The judgement to include a film or not is wholly mine, based on a combination of what I think is pertinent city content, historic or cultural interest, and significant or distinctive use of Washington locations. Just because a movie "takes place" in Washington, DC was not, for me, a compelling reason to give it full treatment. For readers who think I have dropped the ball or ignored some singular, exciting picture, just let me know (I'm reachable through my website: www.mikesflix.com).

Some of the films cited here are well known, even famous; many are obscure and have been little seen. The former merit, and receive, fuller treatment, while the latter will at least be acknowledged. Those pictures with only a minor or tangential Washington tinge will be treated collectively in the round-up section: "Selected Short Subjects."

Almost all of the listings can be seen via video rental services (DVDs or streaming) or purchased. The single exception will be noted.

– Mike Canning (2012)

HOLLYWOOD ON THE POTOMAC

How the Movies View Washington, DC

POLITICS AND FILM

I. Through the Camera Lens Darkly: the Pol in Movies

How many times have you seen it? The glowing image of the Capitol dome, backlit by a setting sun, or that same dome glowing ivory from a morning sun, with the Washington Monument stalwart behind it?

Such is the standard "establishing shot" of myriad movies, a ready shorthand which tells any audience in the world they are now in Washington, D.C. That shot–also called the "postcard shot"–is used so often and so readily, since the bulk of motion pictures about Washington are set here and because it is our national capital and seat of government, with that dome as the steadfast symbol of our political life. It is no surprise, either, that politics and government are the subject or backdrop of many of the titles highlighted in this survey of Washington movies.

An old bit of conventional wisdom in the movie business is that politics (like baseball) "is poison at the box office." Yet that hasn't stopped filmmakers who thought they had good material from producing feature films about our national politics over the years. In recent years, in fact, movies featuring political figures and themes have proliferated, many featuring the Presidency, but with the Congress, too, receiving its cinematic innings. For one who has long lived on Capitol Hill and who loves politics–and who also happens to review movies–a survey of how American cinema has treated both politics and the town which hosts its primary players might offer some intriguing insights into Washington, DC history itself.

In reviewing products of commercial entertainment, any perceptive observer must realize that Hollywood films are rarely *realistic* portrayals of our national politics. In his comprehensive study of U.S. political films, *Reel*

Politics, professor Terry Christensen states that such movies "seldom point out fundamental defects in the system, and they rarely suggest that social problems can be solved by collective or communal action. They simplify the complex problems of a complex society and solve them quickly and easily so we can have a happy ending."

Further, popular art forms like the movies typically presuppose a pointed conflict which can be tidily resolved–they are mostly "dramas" after all. This means that whole untidy–or unobserved–spheres of basic political or governmental activity, such as preparing reports, committee meetings, inter-agency actions, bureaucratic relationships, the nitty-gritty of campaigns, inter alia, have been effectively absent from films.

In the Congress alone, the whole legislative "process" itself, with its arcane language and fits-and-starts, is difficult to dramatize. Likewise, its committees, where veteran Hill watchers say the real business of Congress is conducted, have figured little in congressional cinema. The fact is that real committee work makes unpromising material for fiction films.

It really could not be otherwise. In reviewing American motion picture history, writer/critic James Monaco reminds us that "the homogeneous factory system of the studios...most subtly reflected (or inspired) the surrounding political culture. Because Hollywood movies were mass-produced, they tended to reflect the surrounding culture–or, more accurately, the established myths of the culture–more precisely than did the work of strongly individual authors." One long-standing premise of that culture deems much of our national politics as basically deceitful and politicians as barely redeemable.

Such a dismissive outlook on politics, and especially the Congress, is hardly new. A number of observers have remarked that "Congress-bashing is almost as old as the Federal Government itself," while historian James Sterling Young found that, even when our republic was new, Americans had "a culturally ingrained predisposition to view political power and politics as essentially evil."

Sourness about politics has not been confined, of course, to the average citizen. In the political science literature, negative views have been chronicled regularly among academics, within the national news media, and certainly among campaign hopefuls–the latter ever ready to boost their own reputations at the expense of our own political institutions by "running against Washington." Individual congressmen are continually disassociating themselves from Congress.

Reflecting these broadly-held societal attitudes, movies typically show politics as a corrupting process, an enterprise for dunces or villains. These are popular dramas, after all, that need villains to get their comeuppance in the third act. These are entertainments filtered through a popular sensibility and duly mirrored by a pliant Hollywood which desires to serve its audience. This overall surly view of politics has long encouraged filmmakers and script writers, as audience surrogates, to feel superior to their political characters and to portray them as typically inept, roguish, or corrupt.

If a motion picture politico is *ever* redeemable, it has been only because he (it is only rarely a she) is that rare worthy who is a combination of naif and "White Knight," able to appeal directly to The American People (read: the movie-attending public) because he is essentially one of them. He thus reflects the legion of solo cinematic heroes–all those rogue cops, one-man armies, Lone Wolves, and Men in White Hats that have appeared in thousands of standard cop flicks and war movies and Westerns.

The American popular movie hero is, above all, an *individual* who acts alone, who goes against the grain, who challenges the organization--one guy versus The System. He must vanquish–not just disarm–his opponent, and he sees any compromise as unmanly. Yet, of course, compromise is the very lifeblood of politics. Ergo: politicians as a class are nothing but evil double-dealers, base betrayers of principle. Thus has show biz ever viewed--and condemned–political biz.

A qualification can be made here that more presidents (if not cabinet members) are depicted as positive in American films than are members of Congress. Presidents, after all, can be more readily grasped as an individual, one of those plucky loners fighting against a faceless organization, defying an inchoate bureaucracy, or besting a vile terrorist. Think Harrison Ford, brows knit, fighting off Russian thugs on *Air Force One* (1997). Collectives, like the "Congress" (writ large) or government departments lack individual traits and personalities and, thus, typically can represent only baneful presences.

II. The Capital and Hollywood: A Convergence?

Besides just treating politics and politicians more, it could be said that Hollywood is also becoming more *like* Washington. Our politicians could be said to behave more and more like actors–and vice versa (consider Ronald Reagan as exhibit number one)–and our politics morph more and more into show business.

The contemporary performer and politician probably have more in common now than ever before. Even the movies themselves recognize this, witness a character in a James L. Brooks film, *I'll Do Anything* (1994), who, in expressing a litany of grim similarities between Hollywood and Washington, sums them up as both known for the "same spiritual bloodletting."

American politics have become, especially in the last decades, much more a public affair, less played out in private chambers and "smoke-filled rooms" and more often running a political video race. Especially with the expansion of television coverage, "playing to the crowd has become much more rewarding than playing to the club," as Greg Easterbrrok noted years ago.

Politicians appear, more and more, to bear the attributes of thespians. To begin with, many of them–as always–are still lawyers, very often of the performing, courtroom type who showed a bent for debate or public speaking when young and were rewarded for it, much as actors' egos were early salved with applause. But even beyond this glib, public persona, politicians must "look good" on TV, they must memorize and deliver lines, they must declaim on issues, they must work all the media for the best possible PR, they must *perform* constantly for their public-cum-audience. In lieu of agents, they have media advisers.

More and more Hollywood stars, meanwhile, like Warren Beatty, Charlton Heston, Barbra Streisand, Tom Selleck, Robert Redford, Arnold Schwarzenegger, Tim Robbins, Tom Hanks, etc., have become identified with our partisan politics, especially during campaign seasons. The two coasts may even be moving closer together in some kind of psychic tectonic drift. After all, in recent years, the Congress has welcomed into its ranks the likes of Sonny Bono, Fred Dalton Thompson, and Fred Grandy. More are likely to follow.

A whole book, intriguingly titled *Hollywood on the Potomac*, has been devoted to pictorial evidence of this convergence. The volume, by Jason Killian Meath, shows hundreds of photos of politicians, mainly presidents, interacting with movie stars and celebrities, mostly in standard encounters like state dinners, award and charity events, or film premieres. While much of the material is made up of standard publicity shots, Meath cumulatively adds to the case of elected officials needing and using Hollywood glamour and stars associating themselves with individual politicians and worthy causes.

Politicians have been moving towards Hollywood style much faster than Hollywood seems to be moving towards Washington style. The strongest parallel may come down to a fundamental characteristic of both the politician and the performer: the need for the public's approval, the need for applause.

Meath, cited above, adds a useful parallel to the convergence idea. He notes that both kinds of celebs come to live in the same kind of bubble. He remarks: "...both the commander-in-chief and the captains of the box office get in their limousines, pass by legions of press on their doorstep, and read reviews from their demanding public."

Long-time political practitioner and observer Elliott Richardson, quoted by Hedrick Smith decades past in his inside-Washington book *The Power Game*, had another apt metaphor to apply to the city's power figures. "Washington is really, when you come right down to it, a city of cocker spaniels," said Richardson, a cabinet member in the Nixon and Ford Administrations. "It's a city of people who are more interested in being petted and admired than in rendering the exercise of power." Rather like movie stars.

III. The Rest of Washington on Screen

Two other significant spheres of government activity should be mentioned that have long been featured in feature films within a Washington context: the military and the intelligence services, i.e., the soldier and the spy. Both these categories, of course, engage in work that is inherently dramatic and leads to finales with impact. War and espionage have been two of the life-bloods of popular culture for a century or more. Moreover, the activities of war-making and spying provide perfect set-ups to highlight that necessary man of action, the Lone Ranger.

A modest listing of some of the major films in these categories with a Washington setting would include: *No Way Out, Gardens of Stone, A Few Good Men, True Lies, Breach, and Fair Game*–among others. All are described fully in this volume.

Although I have highlighted films about politics, not all significant DC movies revolve wholly around them. There are major DC films which treat journalism and the media (*Broadcast News, Wag the Dog, Shattered Glass, Thank You For Smoking, Talk to Me, State of Play*), crime (*Suspect, The Pelican Brief, Along Came a Spider*), suspense and horror (*The Exorcist, Enemy of the State, National Treasure*), science fiction and fantasy (*The Day the Earth Stood Still, Earth vs. the Flying Saucers, Chances Are, Minority Report, Night at the Museum*), and even romance (*Houseboat, St. Elmo's Fire, Random Hearts, How Do You Know*).

These, and others like them, will have their own treatment in this book.

IV. The Future?

This survey of DC films confirms the considerable contrast there has always been in this popular art between the typical one-dimensional Hollywood view of Washington and the more complex, multi-dimensional reality that is this capital city. One critic, Jonathan Alter, recognized this when reviewing the movie *True Colors*, but his remarks can be read more broadly. He wrote: "Much of the real Washington is too dramatic for filmmakers to handle... Perhaps (it doesn't) square with those misty Capitol-dome shots." He added that movie men missed "the truly juicy stories because they impose character and theme rather than letting them grow out of the fertile subject they have chosen."

Alter has a point. People who truly know the city well believe that its inherent and diverse human comedy, its "real" business, could rightly be a natural source for Washington drama rather than the contrived Tinseltown version (always given the right script, of course).

In their 1995 study *Congress as Public Enemy*, political scientists John Hibbing and Elizabeth Theiss-Morse, after listing the reasons for long-standing negative views of our national legislature, lament that the "citizens' big failure is that they lack an appreciation for the ugliness of democracy." Yet the movies can be of little help here since, as mass entertainment, they will inevitably favor ripe pulchritude over messy process, individual heroes over collective actions. Further, Hibbing and Theiss-Morse warn—in a comment all too pertinent today—that "If we fail to teach the American public that... debate and compromise are not synonymous with bickering and selling out, operational support (for the Congress) will never be forthcoming." Just so, but that dramatic "bickering and selling out," as we will see in this survey, is exactly what much of the popular arts, including motion pictures, have emphasized for decades—genuine debate and real compromise don't stand a chance in comparison.

It still would take some doing to make congressional procedures ring with the more overt drama that Hollywood favors. Perhaps one can, straining very hard, imagine a compelling scene where the perky but pugnacious freshman Congresswoman from Ohio (Reese Witherspoon) locks horns with the handsome but hustling Senator from Michigan (Tom Hanks) in a House-Senate conference committee wrestling with the intricacies of an agricultural subsidies amendment.... But perhaps not.

Given that Hollywood's view of Washington has always mirrored, and will continue to mirror, the mass sentiments of the American public, it is unlikely that a more genuine, more comprehensive treatment of our city will ever prevail on America's screens, except in some very rare, isolated cases. For those of us who value our Capital City, we can only be grateful for those occasionally rare cases.

LOCATION, LOCATION, LOCATION

No, this section does not discuss that most crucial aspect of real estate in the Nation's Capital; it is addressed to the vagaries of shooting a film in that same capital. The fact is, Washington is not an easy target for filmmakers, and it takes patience, tenacity, and skill to get the city right.

The principal dilemma for shooting in Washington, DC is the complex structure of varying–and sometimes competing–governmental jurisdictions. There are principally three: Executive, Congressional, and local, the first covering the presidency, the cabinet departments, and the executive branch agencies, the second concerning the area of the Capitol grounds (including its multiple office buildings), and the third covering the District's lands distinct from federal properties. To complicate matters further, within the Executive element is the National Park Service, responsible for myriad monuments and green spaces throughout the city.

Thus, to shoot anywhere in and around the Capitol–which is the most desired shot for almost all filmmakers–authorities on the Hill, like the Speaker's Office, or the Architect of the Capitol, must give their blessing, and it's not easy in coming. After all, lawmakers think their work is fairly important and should only be subject to disruption for very good reasons, a Hollywood movie not being high on the list of priorities. One of the city's long-time and best known location managers, Stuart Neumann, asserted that Capitol Hill was the most difficult film location in the world.

If you want to incorporate the Washington Monument or Lincoln Memorial into your picture (and many do), you need to convince the National Park Service which is concerned about keeping these sights and others like them open and accessible to their principal public, the American people. The Park Service has also argued that movie companies, as commercial ventures, should have no special access to what is federal property belonging to all. As a DC location manager, Patrick Burn recently described it: "The National Park Service doesn't allow you to shoot anything that the regular public won't do" (i.e. like running in a reflecting pool...).

Adding to the layering of official jurisdictions is the relatively new Federal Protective Service (FPS), the federal police force of the Department of Homeland Security. FPS is responsible for the security of thousands of federally owned and leased buildings, many of them in the District.

Shooting in and around the regular streets of the city is easiest overall, but there are still limitations and restrictions. And even on the regular streets of the city, there are other jurisdictional questions, like which police force do you have to clear with—the city has more than a dozen of them!

Did I even mention the White House?–forget about it.

Officials, like those at the DC Office of Motion Picture and Television Development, as well as city boosters and general movie fans, would like more Hollywood filming in the District. After all, it can bring in dollars and jobs, as well as additional tourist interest and potential civic promotion. A major Hollywood production can spend up to half-a-million dollars in one day. But DC has usually lacked the financial incentives that other cities, like Baltimore, and even Richmond, have typically offered to film productions.

Also, when you can offer professional film crews and technicians ample studios, varied urban settings, a common language, and, especially, financial incentives or a favorable exchange rate for your dough (as Canada has over the years), it is no surprise that major studios are constantly looking to shoot their version of Washington in towns like Baltimore or Vancouver.

* * * *

Complicating the use of Washington as a location for films is the big bugaboo of this century: security.

Once upon a time, a much more innocent time, access to Washington's inner sancta was much easier. These were the years, particularly between 1945 and 1960, when there were many fewer movies made on location and outside the Hollywood studio system. When, however, they did consider shooting in DC for a film, the doors were rather open. Of course, the Senate and House chambers and the White House have **always** been off-limits (the nation's official business must not be disturbed, after all), but other areas could be negotiated.

When the film itself looked to cast a positive light on government practices, filming access might be readily granted. One early example was the extensive coverage of the FBI, including its internal operations within the Justice Department, during the shooting of *The House on 92nd Street*. The latter was a 1945 docudrama which showed just how effective the Bureau could be in tracking down Nazi spies, a most positive message to send viewers as World War II came to an end. It even incorporated secret footage the FBI took of Nazi officials moving into and out of the actual German Embassy in Washington. Some years later, *The FBI Story* (1959) offered a paean to the Bureau and was granted full access.

In the hit comedy *Born Yesterday*, the filmmakers went out of their way to use imagery from the city. Sequences inside the Capitol and highlighting the DC's major monuments and institutions (see page 32) underscored the film's theme of gaining civic consciousness, exemplified by the character of Billie Dawn, winningly played by Judy Holliday.

Another good example of ample access in this period was *Washington Story*, a narrative that offered a basically affirmative view of a Congressman and his labors. The Architect of the Capitol at the time liked the script and gave permission to the filmmakers to shoot extensively in the Capitol, including scenes in the Rotunda and Statuary Hall.

Judy Holliday got to Washington and the Capitol one more time in *The Solid Gold Cadillac* (1956). She, an outspoken shareholder of a New York company, goes to Washington to see a defense contractor, and it shows her walking up the steps of the Capitol on the Senate side.

Ample interiors and exteriors of the Capitol were also on view in *Advise *and Consent.* Though it didn't paint the best picture of individual legislators, the film basically presented the Senate as an institution in a positive light, and extensive location shooting in and around Capitol Hill gives the film a resonance that is still attractive after 50 years.

One kind of watershed was crossed in 1976 when the maverick actor-director Tom Laughlin, who had a major success with his independent "hippy-western" *Billy Jack* (1971), came to DC to film his version of *Mr. Smith* called, imaginatively, *Billy Jack Goes to Washington.* As in the earlier Capra classic, Billy Jack is a naïve westerner who is accidentally named a senator so he can be easily manipulated by political bosses.

Laughlin's film, however, goes off any number of rails, and apparently the director and his team were extremely arrogant and did actual damage in and around the Capitol. According to an informed location manager, "(Laughlin) was so rude to Congressional authorities that they refused any filming on the grounds" thereafter.

It was also reported at the time that when Laughlin was denied entry to shoot inside the Lincoln Memorial (as was done in the earlier *Mr. Smith*), he left town denouncing the government's bureaucracy." He claimed there was a "White House plot" against him and also accused the National Park Service and others of "specific incidents of harassment."

Now, in Billy Jack's wake, the large area around the Capitol, called the Capitol grounds, or in some parlance, the Capitol jurisdiction, is effectively off-limits. The trauma of 9/11 certainly contributed to additional security concerns at the site, but it was the dramatic attack within the Capitol itself in July 1998 (where Capitol Police officers were gunned down by a madman) that was the first major trigger for shutting down access to the building. The area known as the Capitol grounds has been extended over the years to where it now extends out to 3rd Street on the east, to First Street to the west (running in front of the Grant Memorial), down south to C Street, SE, and up north to the Union Station Plaza.

The limitation on shooting the Capitol up close and personal has resulted in filmmakers who want the Capitol background (most of them do!) to usually settle for shooting at the Grant Memorial on First Street west of the Capitol (the edge of an area called Union Square). This site is the dividing line between what constitutes the Capitol grounds and the Park Service's territory, allowing an unfettered look at the dome. A number of examples are cited in this book.

For outsiders watching these films, it might appear that the Grant Memorial is a most important site to discuss serious political matters. In reality, however, almost no one doing business at the Capitol would walk here; the Memorial is mainly a tourist attraction from which to watch birds in the reflecting pool or on whose steps you can take decent class photographs.

Even the allowance extended to the Grant Memorial has been put in question at the time of this writing. In December 2011, Congress slipped into an appropriations bill an extension of the Capitol Police's authority, closing off the Memorial. As reported in a front-page article in *The Washington Post* (January 31, 2012), "the DC film community (was) horrified to learn...that Congress had quietly lifted control over this easternmost patch of the Mall from the US Park Service, which is known as the film-friendly agency, and given to the Capitol Police, which is not."

As Crystal Palmer, director of the DC Office of Motion Picture and Television Development, has said: "Security trumps everything." Still, at the time of this writing, the prospect of the new limitation on Capitol filming was still on hold and could be reconsidered.

Exceptions to these limitations on the use of the Capitol grounds have been rare. In 1978, the film *F.I.S.T.*, starring Sylvester Stallone as a Hoffa-like Teamsters' boss, there is a scene of a truckers' protest near the Capitol in the 1950's. The production was able to create a mass mobilization of vehicles just north and west of the Capitol. The makers of *The Seduction of Joe Tynan* were able to shoot a school bus turning off First Street, NE, and just onto the Capitol Grounds, a move that would probably be prohibited today.

Another film, *First Monday in October* concerned the Supreme Court, and Court officials allowed shooting around the perimeter of the building but not inside. Another significant exception was granted in 1993, when Robert Redford's production of *Quiz Show* (1994) was allowed to shoot on the steps of the House side of the Capitol, an exception specifically made for Redford after he came to Washington to make an in-person appeal to then-Speaker Tom Foley. There have been no up-close Capitol shots since.

Even when a master like Alfred Hitchcock needs a shot of that singular dome, he can't avoid messing with it. In his classic *North By Northwest* (1959) the single Washington sequence opens with a shiny refection of the Capitol in the nameplate of the "United States Intelligence Agency." Trouble is that, from the subsequent shot showing the Capitol's West Front from a large picture window, it appears the Agency is located smack on the Mall, around 4th Street, an ideal spot for a super-secret spy operation.

Thirty-five years later, that shot gets a wacky reprise in *Forrest Gump* (1994), when Forrest's friend Jenny is showing him around the DC headquarters of the Students for a Democratic Society and the Black Panthers. Again, a window reveals a full frontal view of the Capitol's West Front, placing those radical bastions also in the middle of the Mall!

Though it lies within the Capitol Jurisdiction, the Library of Congress, in particular, the original, splendid Jefferson Building, has been seen more often in commercial films. Its authorities have been more liberal in allowing film crews outside and inside its walls. Early films featured it, such *Mr. Smith Goes to Washington, Born Yesterday,* and the espionage thriller *The Thief* (1952). Significant 1970's Washington movies, like *All the President's Men* and *The Seduction of Joe Tynan,* highlighted it also.

Beginning around the late 1970's, however, there was almost no use of the Library, perhaps because of the bad taste left after an incident during the filming of *All the President's Men* (q.v.). In more recent years, more productions have begun again to shoot in the Jefferson Building. Now with more recent films like the two *National Treasure* thrillers and *J. Edgar* featuring its Main Reading Room, the Library has again become a steady supporting player in DC movies.

One noteworthy refusal to shoot within the Capitol was a turn down to Stephen Spielberg when he was filming the period piece *Amistad* (1997). Since the film takes place in the years 1839-41, Spielberg wanted to use the site of the original Supreme Court in the basement of the Capitol, where a famous trial of slaves from the ship Amistad was actually held. Though the actual site might have made for great cinema (not to mention educating millions of Americans on this intriguing sliver of history), the director was refused permission, apparently because of the disruption the filming might cause in the building. A special reconstructed set had to be used instead.

* * * *

The White House is, as indicated above, basically off-limits to film companies, but it is, of course, often featured in movies. The standard exterior establishing shots, taken from park property, are behind the Ellipse (looking from the south) and below Lafayette Park (viewing from the north). Movies have never been shot inside the Presidential Mansion or even on the grounds, but the gates have at least been seen.

A few times, the Pennsylvania Avenue side has been used, amply in films like *Seven Days in May* and *The Pelican Brief,* and minimally in others like *The Hunt for Red October* (1990) and *Absolute Power.* That street area of the Avenue even served as the sight of a roller hockey game at the finale of the 1996 comedy *The First Kid.* Even films–like *Thirteen Days*–that have the White House as their basic setting have to make do with replacements (a favorite stand-in is the State Capitol in Richmond) recreations, or digitally-created versions of the building.

The inside of the White House has been re-created, both good and bad, dozens of times on Hollywood studio sets. When the sitting president is sympathetic to the film project, the filmmakers are at least allowed to visit, sketch, and even photograph the building so the production company can construct a realistic set. Such was the case with several pictures cited in this volume. The 1964 Cold War thriller *Seven Days in May* was allowed such access and produced a worthy replica of the office. Likewise, the mistaken identity comedy *Dave* and the romantic drama *The American President* were able to use on-the-ground intelligence about the Oval Office to re-create it convincingly on screen. In 1997, the production people for *Murder at 1600* constructed their own version in a Toronto studio.

Over the years, the studios keep asking, perhaps naively, to film in the real White House. The production team for *All the President's Me*n (q.v., Coblenz) thought they had a promise to shoot in the building in 1975, but it was later withdrawn. According to one veteran DC location manager, a number of Hollywood producers during the Reagan years thought they had a special "in" because they knew the actor president (" I used to work with Reagan," they would say)–but no dice. In an April 1997 *New York Times* article, Hillary Clinton's spokesman at the time, Neel Lattimore, addressed the question and said "we're as gracious as we can be, but the answer is no." The fact is, the building is an historical property not a set. "Besides," Lattimore, added, "using it would put all those set designers out of business, and we're for jobs."

*　*　*　*

There are probably as many Washington movies actually shot elsewhere as there are movies using actual locations here. Most often the stand-in cities are Baltimore, Richmond, or a number of Canadian options. Again and again throughout this book, you will see references to these other filming locations. The reasons are the restricted access and security concerns mentioned above, along with–and perhaps most importantly–dough. The stand-in cities offer building and housing stock that can mimic Washington, professional crews and studios at good rates, financing incentives, and–in the case of Canada–a very favorable exchange rate.

In the case of Canada, Hollywood began looking at shooting there in the 1970's, when the Canadian dollar dropped below parity with the US dollar. That favorable exchange rate continued for decades, reaching a low point in January 2002, when each Canadian dollar was worth about 62 cents. Only in September 2007 did the Canadian dollar again reach parity with the US dollar. Among the films highlighted in this book, half-a-dozen major studio efforts over the last 20 years, films like *Suspect, Along Came a Spider, Shattered Glass, The Sentinel, Breach,* and *Talk to Me,* did principal photography in Canadian cities.

In the case of Baltimore, the city and the state of Maryland have often budgeted film incentive money to encourage filmmakers to shoot there, figuring they will earn back more than their investment from the monies the production company puts into the local economy during its filming. Virginia, too, through its Virginia Film Office, can offer some film incentive money, as well as historical and picturesque settings. Some of its government buildings, like the State Capitol and legislative buildings, provide adequate substitutes for federal DC.

Such location shoots, if extended, can truly pay off for a jurisdiction. In just one case, for example, the Virginia Film Office reported in a 2000 release that the three-month shoot for the film *The Contender* generated $6.5 million for the state. One recent estimate indicates that a feature film crew can spend up to $500,000 a day on location.

The January 2012 *Washington Post* article cited above also reported that Maryland had increased its film incentive budget to $7.5 million, multiples of what the District has been able to offer in recent years. A similar piece from the *Washingtonian* magazine (February 2012) noted the lack of the city's underwriting of prospective Hollywood productions, saying the last time the D.C. Office of Motion Picture Development was able to budget incentives was in 2007 when a total of $1.6 million was used to attract three features.

One of those three films was James L. Brooks' *How Do You Know* (released in 2010). In the same *Washingtonian* piece, Brooks was quoted as saying the District is "the most difficult" city to work in. "I shot all of *Broadcast News* there, and it was glorious," he said. By 2009, he added, it was much harder. He shot for three weeks and had to adjust his filming almost block by block in the city because of the usual jurisdictional and security concerns.

*   *   *   *

Given the jurisdictional haggles, security restrictions, and the lack of financial incentives, it might seem a wonder that ***anything*** is shot in DC, but, of course, there are no sets or studios that can finally substitute for the look of the Real Thing on the big screen. The fact is that some major sites—mostly under National Park Service jurisdiction—are used repeatedly because they offer one of those iconic views that so many movie productions want.

One good example is the Memorial Bridge over the Potomac River that runs between the entrance to Arlington Cemetery and the Lincoln Memorial. The Memorial side view has been used in countless films because it's available, and because it has a real visual payoff. Another way to get the

Memorial in the background is to film in the roadway leading up to the Memorial, called the Potomac Parkway. That drive has been used several times in DC movies, most significantly in *Breach* and *Burn After Reading*. Beyond the bridge itself, the Lincoln Memorial and its reflecting pool have been featured in numerous films over the years, beginning with *Mr. Smith*. Other films using this icon include *A Man Called Peter*, *The FBI Story*, *D.C. Cab*, *In the Line of Fire*, *The Firm* (1993, which uniquely showed the Memorial after a snowfall), *Dick*, *Burn Before Reading*, and more recently, *Night at the Museum: Battle of the Smithsonian*.

The Memorial and its reflecting pool were featured perhaps most famously in *Forrest Gump*, where Forrest both addresses a giant anti-war rally on the steps of the Memorial and from there runs into the pool to embrace his girl Jenny. Also, in the silly spy-romp *Get Smart* (2008), agent Maxwell Smart literally "walks" on the water of the pool to gain access to a secret underground passageway.

Another major DC icon that has been used is the Jefferson Memorial, one of the capital's most delectable sights, and its companion Tidal Basin, both of which can be wonderfully picturesque. The Memorial and the Tidal Basin appear in a number of films cited in this volume, including *Born Yesterday*, *Houseboat*, *Protocol*, *Broadcast News*, and *Murder at 1600*. This Memorial also gets a nice close-up in the classic thriller, *Strangers on a Train* (1951), the only film of Alfred Hitchcock that has a Washington, DC setting.

The Washington Monument also figures in countless films, but usually in a brief, random establishing shot. The Monument has not figured as a major plot point in Washington movies, perhaps because it boasts no intricate, architectural elements to emphasize. Still, its stairwell made up of hundreds of steps could have made a great chase scene for an Alfred Hitchcock thriller.

The National Mall, also under the Park Service, has been used on a regular basis. After all, it offers those iconic buildings at its ends, but it also has a distinctive look and sweep all its own. It's a good place for a senatorial chat (*Advise and Consent*) or a congressional job (*Random Hearts*). Some of the Mall's major occupants also figure in movies, like the Smithsonian Castle, the Air and Space Museum, and the National Gallery of Art. As of this writing, Hollywood directors or production designers have not yet discovered the inimitable Hirshhorn Museum and Sculpture Garden or the new National Museum of the American Indian.

* * * *

An interesting special location case is the Washington area's subway system, the Metro. Opened in 1976, the Metro, under the Washington Metropolitan Area Transit Authority (WMATA), early on allowed shoots to take place at the entrances to stations in various parts of the system but for many years no filming was allowed *inside* the stations. This made for the standard "goof" in Washington movies of a film's protagonist running (almost always running) down into a genuine subway location but ending up on a platform and entering a train car in the Baltimore system! Such a sequence would always get a laugh out of Washington natives.

After 30 years, however, Metro's rigid rule has been relaxed, and recently, in films like *The Invasion* (2007) and *State of Play*, the interiors of stations—right down to the platforms—are shown. Restrictions still exist, of course. For example, WMATA script approval is required to film in the system, and filming, understandably, has to be done at off hours. Still, this essential artery of the city's life is now filmable, a bit of an exception to what has been a history of restrictions.

DC's individual neighborhoods, as distinct from its celebrated landmarks, get much less screen time in feature films. Georgetown, for its history, prestige, and period look, has appeared most often, and it is cited in a number of the films in this volume. Capitol Hill, which shares some of Georgetown's appeal, is also a contender. This book specifically highlights all those movies which have used the Hill as a location. There are, of course, whole massive chunks of the city which have never been featured in the Cinema of DC.

Feeling that Washington does indeed have a lot more to offer the professional filmmaker in terms of attractive, picturesque locations, director Palmer and her staff at the D.C. Office of Motion Picture and Television Development try to do what they can, within a limited or non-existent budget, to entice those filmmakers to look down the less-traveled roads in DC. They have even taken Washington's mayor—for the first time—on jaunts to Los Angeles and New York to pitch the city as worthwhile film location.

One device they have instigated recently is their "One City Location of the Month," where a intriguing (and less well-known) neighborhood, site, or structure is highlighted and described on the Commission website. Palmer accentuates the positive, as in a recent radio interview, when she said that, in filmmaking terms, "DC is similar to Paris, London, and New York," and offers "a good local workforce" for movies.

If you scout through the listings of the selected "One City Locations" over the last year, you can only agree that there is so much more for the Hollywood crowd to discover, if they could just get over their obsession with the Capitol.

Soft Focus – Mr. Smith through the Sixties

This survey considers only films of the Sound Era and, the fact is, Washington, DC was not the principal setting for any significant silent films, with the possible exception of D. W. Griffith's *The Birth of a Nation* (1915) which did include some scenes of the Lincoln Administration and a famously racist depiction of the Reconstruction-Era Congress. Years later, Griffith followed it up with the sound film *Abraham Lincoln* (1930), a straightforward biography with Walter Huston playing the Great Emancipator.

Huston shows up again as the lead in the strange (to today's eyes) *Gabriel Over the White House* (1933), a depression-era product which posits political reform in the person of an almost fascist president (Huston). Though assumedly taking place in Washington, the only DC material was newsreel footage of a presidential swearing-in (on the East Front of Capitol), followed by historic footage of a real inaugural parade. Another film of the era, *The President Vanishes* (1934), features a president who pretends to be kidnapped for political ends.

There were occasional movies in the early sound era which starred congressional characters (like *Washington Masquerade* and *Washington Merry-Go-Round* (both from the landmark campaign year 1932), but congressional movies truly begin with Frank Capra's *Mr. Smith Goes to Washington*, the classic fable of the unsophisticated Little Man taking on Big Corruption and the opener to our survey.

The World War II years produced a spate of films, like *The More the Merrier,* which treated the problems of a wartime capital, busting at the seams (see also **Selected Short Subjects** and photo insert). With films of this earlier era, farce is the more gentle farce of the day, the satire is more silly than biting, and requisite punches are pulled, understandable when all films were essentially rated "G" and intended for the whole family.

The Cold War certainly contributed to a more somber political mood in the country, and filmdom's product it reflected on screen. For example, at the peak of the Red Scare, Hollywood dutifully mirrored the fears of many Americans with a spate of anti-commie productions, like *Big Jim McLain* (1952), which had John Wayne as a stalwart Congressional staffer of the

House Un-American Activities Committee busting foreign leftists (seen today, the film is likely to bring on fits of unintended hilarity). Even science fiction, as in *The Day the Earth Stood Still*, had overtones of the Cold War and the growing threat of nuclear weapons. A new seriousness, laced with cynicism, began to emerge by the 1960's also, with taut dramas that questioned current political forces like *Advise and Consent, Seven Days in May*, and *The Manchurian Candidate* (1962).

Washington movies weren't all doom and drama, of course. There was still time for inspiration (*A Man Called Peter*), as well as some froth (*Houseboat*).

1 MR. SMITH GOES TO WASHINGTON

 1939. Columbia Pictures
125 minutes, black & white.

Director: Frank Capra.

Screenplay: Sidney Buchman
from a story by Lewis R. Foster.

Cameraman: Joseph Walker.

Editing: Al Clark and Gene Harlick.

Musical Score: Dmitri Tiomkin.

Principal Cast:

James Stewart	Jefferson Smith	Guy Kibbe	Gov. Hubert Hopper
Jean Arthur	Clarissa Saunders	Eugene Pallette	Chick McCann
Claude Rains	Sen. Joseph Paine	Beulah Bondi	Ma Smith
Edward Arnold	Boss Jim Taylor	Harry Carey	President of the Senate
Thomas Mitchell	Diz Moore	H.B. Warner	Sen. Fuller

Synopsis: A classic Hollywood fable of the Little Man taking on the Political Bosses and winning by dint of persistence and pluck. Youth leader Jefferson Smith, a guileless naïf handpicked by a state political machine in an (unamed) Western state, stumbles into the Senate to fill an unexpired term. Bedazzled by the capital, he spends his first day in office avidly seeing its historic sights. To keep him out of trouble (and out of the Senate's real business), his handlers guide him to craft a piece of benign legislation. But, when he does, innocently sponsoring a boy's camp in his district, he runs up against both Washington cynicism—in the forms of his tough cookie secretary, Saunders; the sarcastic Hill journalist, Diz Moore; and Jeff's own flawed hero, Senator Joseph Paine—and in the person of a pitiless political boss, Jim Taylor. It turns out his camp legislation conflicts with a plan of graft Taylor has in mind for the same land, a plan which Paine is to introduce as a contending bill.

The disheartened Smith is ready to quit when Saunders, who has now fallen for him, urges him to fight for his legislation, using the form of a Senate filibuster to block the Taylor scheme. All Smith has going for him in a dramatic finish on the Senate floor are a great heart and the rules of the body, outlined by Saunders from the gallery and aided by rulings from the avuncular President of the Senate. Jeff's Boy Rangers back home, aroused by their upstanding leader, act as democracy's saviors by publicizing his cause back home in their club paper. When Taylor's gang stoops to attacking even the Rangers' efforts and swamps the state with its own propaganda, Smith is ready to concede his defeat, but he faints on the Senate floor, and the remorseful Paine unsuccessfully attempts suicide before denouncing himself and the Taylor machine.

Production Notes: Though director Capra tried mightily, Congressional rules then (and now) would not allow him to shoot inside the Senate chamber, so he spent $100,000 to have a crack design team of 125 men recreate a duplicate chamber in Hollywood over several weeks complete in every detail. In his biography, *The Name Above the Title*, Capra extols his art director, Leslie Banks, and his team:

> *From ancient blueprints dug out of the Capitol's catacombs, and thousands of photographs, (Bank's) department of magicians was asked to conjure up, in one hundred days, exact replicas of what had taken one hundred years to build. In reconstructing the Senate chamber, seen by countless eyes and hallowed by a thousand traditions, even the omission of historic scratches on a desk might betray the imitation.*

This wonderful, to-scale replica, which one magazine called "complete to the last acanthus leaf and arabesque," is one of the finest sets Hollywood ever produced and has since been revived for other film productions featuring Congress (see photo insert). When Smith wanders into it for the first time with awe on his face, his impression was certainly matched by millions of American filmgoers who had never entered the Senate chamber. Much of the authentic Washington flavor of *Mr. Smith* was aided by Capra's technical advisor on the film, James Preston, who had been a long-time superintendent of the Senate Press gallery (itself effectively reproduced in the film).

The Senate filibuster had long been maligned by congressional reformers as the last refuge of parliamentary scoundrels, yet, in *Mr. Smith*, this floor device is used to heroic effect (see photo insert). To achieve the appropriate level of hoarseness for Stewart as he drones on during his filibuster, Capra and company resorted to swabbing Stewart's throat with a "vile mercury solution" twice a day. "The result was astonishing," Capra wrote, "No amount of acting could possibly simulate Jimmy's intense pathetic efforts to speak through real swollen chords."

Background: The day of the Washington premiere, October 16, 1939, was declared "Mr. Smith" Day in DC. Capra cracked: "Natives said nothing like it had hit the national Capital since the British sacked the White House." The evening started with cocktails and dinner at the National Press Club in honor of Jim Preston, allowing women into the closed club for the first time in its history.

The premiere was at the DAR's Constitution Hall in DC. Many in the audience were displeased, some walked out, and the prominent Senator Burton Wheeler, seated with Frank Capra, gave the director the cold shoulder. Film historian Daniel Fineman noted that Roosevelt's Ambassador to Great Britain, Joseph Kennedy, urged that the movie not be released in Europe because it would destroy morale. Fineman added that many in the film industry worried that Mr. Smith's depiction of political corruption would be misused by the Axis powers. The other Hollywood studios were so alarmed that they offered Columbia Pictures $2 million to "can" the film.

A more serene assessment of the film came from then-Senator Harry Truman of Missouri. In a letter to his wife, Truman notes that he went to the DAR, along with cabinet members, advisors and a "lot of other Senators." His own review was crisp, but accurate: "It makes asses out of all Senators who are not crooks. But it also shows up the correspondents in their true drunken light too."

Comment: The film is well worth revisiting to see its memorable cast, beginning with the winning Stewart, for whom the film was a breakthrough to true star status (he was nominated for an Academy Award as Best Actor). Jean Arthur, with her soft fog horn voice, is ideal as Saunders, as is Rains as the elegant yet reptilian Senator Paine. Thomas Mitchell personifies the cynical but decent journalist-as-lush, while Edward Arnold wholly incarnates the blustering Boss Taylor. Harry Carey brings crusty charm to the President of the Senate, while Guy Kibbee is a quivering mess as Taylor's "bought" governor. The parade of sardonic secondary characters usually present in a Capra picture round out the singular cast.

While full of cynical asides, this picture may be the most optimistic ever made about the Congress. Politics, by nature corrupting, is here redeemed by the pure of heart. While it tells a tale of political corruption and venality, *Mr. Smith* ultimately celebrates the institution of the U.S. Senate as superior to the compromised men who make it up.

As *The New York Times* reviewer of the time, Frank S. Nugent, saw it: "Although he is subjecting the Capitol's bill-collectors to a deal of quizzing and to a scrutiny which is not always tender, (Capra) still regards them with affection and hope, as the implements, however imperfect they may be, of our kind of government." The comedy, he added, is "a stirring and even inspiring testament to liberty and freedom...." More contemporarily, academic Terry Christensen thinks Capra's intent is to show that "there is a problem because something isn't working properly, but the problem is minor, caused not by faults in the system or its institutions, but by bad men...."

Belying the conventional line that movies about politics are "box office poison," the picture was second only to *Gone with the Wind* in 1939 box office receipts and was nominated for 11 Academy Awards, winning the Oscar for Best Original Story.

DC/Hill Notes: Though almost all of *Mr. Smith* was shot at Columbia Pictures, some second unit location shooting was done in and around Washington to use as background footage for a sequence early in the picture when Smith discovers Washington by tour bus. To produce the "montage effects," DC footage was projected onto a screen with actors photographed in front of it. The most significant local footage was shot at the Lincoln Memorial, where we see Smith in awe of the president's statue and the famous lines from Lincoln on the side walls. In another part of that early montage sequence, we see Smith visit the Library of Congress, where he admires both the Great Hall of the building and passes before our founding documents, which at the time were still housed in the Library prior to the existence of the National Archives, where they now reside (a similar scene takes place in *Born Yesterday,* q.v.).

Goofs: Upon arriving in DC, Jeff Smith looks directly out of Union Station's front door to see a glowing Capitol dome, but the doorways are nothing like the real ones, and the dome, which should be obscured by the Columbus Fountain, is in plain view (this is clearly a process shot).

Smith's Senate office looks out onto the Capitol dome but with a fountain in front of the window at an impossible angle.

The "President of the Senate," never identified as the Vice President, seems to always be in the chair during sessions. Yet Senate insiders know that the presiding officer of the Senate revolves constantly, with junior senators called on most often to preside.

Quote: From *Mr. Smith:* Jeff, speaking on the floor of the Senate during his filibuster:

> *There's no place out there for graft, or greed, or lies, or compromise with human liberties. And, uh, if that's what the grownups have done with this world that was given to them, then we'd better get those boys' camps started fast and see what the kids can do. And it's not too late, because this country is bigger than the Taylors, or you, or me, or anything else. Great principles don't get lost once they come to light. They're right here; you just have to see them again!*

2 THE MORE THE MERRIER

1943. Columbia Pictures, 104 minutes, black & white.

Director: George Stevens.

Story and Screenplay: Robert Russell and Frank Ross; screenplay by Russell, Story, Richard Flournoy and Lewis R. Foster.

Cameraman: Ted Tetzlaff.

Editing: Otto Myer.

Music: Leigh Hairline.

Principal Cast:

Jean Arthur	*...... Connie Milligan*	*Frank Sully*	*......... FBI Agent Pike*
Joel McCrea	*...... Joe Carter*	*Donald Douglas*	*...... FBI Agent Harding*
Charles Coburn	*...... Benjamin Dingle*	*Clyde Fillmore*	*...... Sen. Noonan*
Richard Gaines	*...... Charles J. Pendergast*	*Stanley Clements*	*...... Morton Rodakiewicz*
Bruce Bennett	*...... FBI Agent Evans*	*Ernest Hilliard*	*...... Senator*

Synopsis: Retired millionaire Benjamin Dingle arrives in wartime Washington unable to book a hotel. He answers an ad for a roommate and talks young Connie Milligan into letting him sublet half of her tiny apartment. Dingle then encounters Sergeant Joe Carter, who needs a place before he is shipped overseas. Dingle rents him half of his half. When Connie learns of this arrangement, she orders them both to leave, but she is also attracted to Joe, even though she is engaged to the insufferable hyper-bureaucrat Charles J. Pendergast. Dingle later meets the unctuous Pendergast and immediately decides that decent Joe would be a better match for her.

After Dingle reveals secrets from Connie's diary to Joe, she again demands they both vacate the apartment. After a nosy teenage neighbor reports Joe as a suspected spy, he is taken in for questioning and Connie along with him. When Dingle and Pendergast show up to vouch for them, it is revealed that Joe and Connie live in the same apartment. Dingle then urges the couple to marry to avoid a scandal–then have it annulled. They wed for convenience but realize it is truly for love.

Background: The film was one of director George Stevens best film comedies, one whose reputation has grown since its release during wartime. He won the 1944 New York Film Critics Circle Award for Best Director for this film and was also nominated for an Oscar for his direction. For Stevens, it was also his last Hollywood project for five years; after finishing the picture, he accepted a commission into the Army Signal Corps to produce war documentaries. Interviewed years after shooting the film, Stevens indicated "we had fun on that picture, " adding, "I don't usually have fun on a picture because I've usually got a little too much writing to do." This time, however, things "just folded in nicely."

Charles Coburn won an Academy Award for his marvelous portrayal of Benjamin Dingle, but as a "Supporting Actor," even though it was clearly a principal role. *The More the Merrier* also won Oscar nominations for Best Picture, Best Actress (Arthur, her only nomination), Best Writing (Story), and Best Writing (Screenplay).

Comment: Though entirely filmed on Hollywood sound stages, *The More the Merrier* merits mention in this compilation of Washington movies because it is simply one of the best comedies "set" in the city and because it uses that setting to comment on a then timely subject, i.e., the housing shortage in World War II-era Washington (see photo insert).

The film contains one of the funniest, yet quietly fervent petting scenes in movie history, when Connie and Joe (Arthur and McCrea) arrive at the steps of their apartment building before departing for their separate bedrooms. Arthur's biographer, John Oller, said the scene is "justly regarded as among the sexiest comedy sequences ever filmed." His description:

> *They...sit down, whereupon Joe, as McCrea later described it, begins "copping feels" while Connie half-heartedly resists (the scene was improvised, according to McCrea, when he and Arthur began playing around between takes to ease her nervous tension). As Joe continues to nuzzle her, Connie, practically gasping for air between words, gamely tries to switch the subject*

to her engagement to Mr. Pendergast. But eventually Connie embraces her fate, grabbing Joe's face in her hands and giving him a long, passionate kiss.

The venerable *New York Times* movie reviewer Bosley Crowther gave the film a rave when it premiered in May 1943, saying it was "as warm and refreshing as a ray of sunshine." But he couldn't help getting in a typical New Yorker's lick at DC, wrapping up his notice by cracking: "It even makes Washington look attractive—and that is beyond belief." Harumph.

Goofs: The newspaper mentioned in the movie is the fictitious "Washington Sun," though a number of years later an African-American newspaper by that name was founded in the District.

Connie's apartment building, where she advertises her room for rent, is located at 1708 "D" Street, NW, and is shown to be in a sunny residence which looks out on the "Government Printing Office." In reality, that address would place it in the American Red Cross Building overlooking the Corcoran Gallery.

Postscript: *The More the Merrier* was remade in 1966 as *Walk, Don't Run*, starring Cary Grant (his last film). The latter, however, had nothing to do with Washington but was set in Tokyo during the 1964.

3 BORN YESTERDAY

1950. Columbia Pictures, 103 minutes, black & white.

Director: George Cukor.

Screenplay credited to Albert Mannheimer, adapted from the Broadway play by Garson Kanin.

Cameraman: Joseph Walker.

Editing: Charles Nelson.

Original Musical Score: Frederick Hollander.

Principal Cast:

Judy Holliday............ Emma "Billie" Dawn
Broderick Crawford .... Harry Brock
William Holden .... Paul Verrall
Howard St. John .... Jim Devery
Frank Otto .... Eddie
Larry Oliver.............. Cong. Norval Hedges
Barbara Brown........................ Mrs. Hedges
Grandon Rhodes .... Sanborn

Synopsis: Crass junkman Harry Brock comes to Washington, D.C. with his brassy mistress, ex-show-girl Billie Dawn, and his crooked lawyer, Devery, to buy some political influence for his businesses. His lawyer urges Harry to marry Billie on the grounds that a wife cannot testify against her husband—in case he's indicted for bribery. Harry is disgusted with Billie's lack of class (though he has none of his own) and hires journalist Paul Verrall to tutor her to become more "couth."

Billie blossoms under Paul's tutelage, turning out to be brighter than expected, and she begins thinking for herself. The two fall in love. Meanwhile, Devery persuades Harry to sign over many of his assets to Billie to hide them from the Feds. When Harry needs to get them back, he runs up against Billie's new-found wisdom and independence. She and Paul use her newly-attained intellectual leverage to escape from Harry's control, and she promises to give him back his property little by little as long as he leaves her and Paul alone.

Background: Garson Kanin's comedy became a smash Broadway hit in 1946 with Judy Holliday becoming a star in the role of Billie Dawn. Columbia Pictures' Harry Cohn bought the rights to the play for $1 million, a record for a film property at the time. Cohn initially balked at having Holliday—whom he delicately called "that fat Jewish broad"—recreate her role (Columbia star Rita Hayworth was tapped for the lead but begged off after her marriage to Prince Aly Khan). Cohn later relented on Holliday, however, to his great good fortune, after seeing her shine in a Tracy-Hepburn hit *Adam's Rib*. Broderick Crawford took on the Harry Brock role instead of the Broadway Brock, Paul Douglas. According to a biographer of the director, George Cukor, Cohn felt Douglas was too sympathetic an actor and thought the "repugnant Crawford would encourage the audience to root for William Holden," the romantic interest.

The first draft of the screenplay was originally entrusted to Albert Mannheimer and was later touched up by the Epstein twins, Julius and Philip. Cukor turned it down flat, feeling it had left out excellent material from Kanin's original play. Cohn then convinced Kanin to work out the adaptation himself (though eventual screen credit went to Albert Mannheimer). Cukor praised Kanin's work in transferring the stage work to a new medium:

> *Garson solved that by moving the action around very convincingly without destroying the unity of the thing. (The script) moved all over Washington... and Washington became a real dramatic personage in the story. I remember on location seeing the Jefferson Memorial and having been moved by it, and I said, "Let's photograph that." It wasn't just the physical photography of it, but something of the way I felt about it came across on the screen.*

Production Notes: To help facilitate shooting, Cukor (who had directed Holliday the year before in *Adam's Rib*) decided to rehearse the story as if it were still a stage play. For two weeks, the cast worked on their lines while a construction crew built a mini-theater on one of Columbia's soundstages. It was there that the principals gave six full performances in front of live audiences so Cukor could better time the pacing of the script's jokes.

Born Yesterday was a major box office success and was nominated for five Academy Awards: Best Picture, Best Actress, Best Director, Best Screenplay (with Mannheimer cited), and Best Black-and-White Costume Design. Judy Holliday won the Oscar for her definitive interpretation of Billie Dawn.

DC/Hill Notes: The film used a great deal of primary photography in DC, appropriately enough because the Billie Dawn character (Holliday) was being instructed in government and culture by her tutor Verrall (Holden). It shows the two of them walking on the East Front steps of the Capitol, (see photo insert) then strolling in the Rotunda, where the camera pulls up to view the Apotheosis of Washington on the dome's ceiling.

While they are touring the Library of Congress, Billie sees the draft of the Gettysburg Address in the Great Hall, then she shows Verrall the Constitution, the Declaration of Independence, and the Bill of Rights where they were located at the time– before their transfer to the National Archives (just as was shown in *Mr. Smith Goes to Washington,* q.v.). The pair are also shown at the Neptune Fountain in front of the Library.

Billie's education continues at a Watergate concert– on the famous Potomac barge which faced the steps of the Lincoln Memorial, at the National Gallery, where they roam the halls then sit before a large Manet, and at the Jefferson Memorial, where Billie reads the inspiring words of Jefferson.

Goofs: When Brock is shown around his luxury suite at the Statler Hotel on 16th and K Streets, NW (now the Capitol Hilton), it has a close-up view of the Capitol dome. This is obviously a process shot, since viewing the Capitol is impossible from the site.

Explaining to Billie the founding documents at the Library, Paul says that the country's governing principles are based on "these three pieces of paper." Yet the Declaration of Independence, the Constitution, and the Bill of Rights were all written on vellum, stretched and treated animal skin.

Postscript: *Born Yesterday* was remade in 1993, with Melanie Griffith, Don Johnson, and John Goodman as the three leads (Griffith and Johnson were married at the time). For most observers, it was one of those disasters that result from attempting to remount a classic. The film was a critical bomb and did little business. Unlike the original, the film used few DC locations (they filmed a scene in the Library of Congress) and offered some egregious substitutes, such as the LA County Museum of Art standing in for the National Gallery and an airport in Burbank pretending to be a DC one.

The remake offers a bit of inside Washington: the characters of the Secretary of the Navy and his wife are played by retired *Washington Post* editor Benjamin C. Bradlee and his real-life wife, former *Post* reporter Sally Quinn. The film provides one bit of prophecy: Fred Dalton Thompson, who plays Senator Hedges in this version, went on to be elected Senator from Tennessee the following year (1994).

4 THE DAY THE EARTH STOOD STILL

FROM OUT OF SPACE....
A WARNING AND AN ULTIMATUM!

THE DAY THE EARTH STOOD STILL

MICHAEL RENNIE · PATRICIA NEAL · HUGH MARLOWE

SAM JAFFE · BILLY GRAY · FRANCES BAVIER · LOCK MARTIN

JULIAN BLAUSTEIN · ROBERT WISE · EDMUND H. NORTH · 20th century fox

1951. 20th Century Fox, 92 minutes, black & white.

Director: Robert Wise.

Screenplay by Edmund H. North, based on a story by Henry Bates.

Cameraman: Leo Tover.

Editing: William H. Reynolds.

Music: Bernard Herrman.

Principal Cast:

Michael Rennie	*Klaatu*	*Sam Jaffe*	*Prof. Jacob Barnhardt*
Patricia Neal	*Helen Benson*	*Francis Bavier*	*Mrs. Barley*
Billy Gray	*Bobby Benson*	*Lock Martin*	*Gort (the robot)*
Hugh Marlowe	*Jim Devery*	*Frank Conroy*	*Mr. Harley*

Synopsis: A gleaming flying saucer lands in Washington in the middle of the Ellipse. An alien, Klaatu, emerges and is shot by a nervous soldier, but Gort, a powerful robot from the space ship, saves him and defends the ship with powerful rays. Klaatu restrains the robot and is then hospitalized, but he escapes in order to learn more about this planet. He secretly lodges at a boarding house where Helen Benson, and her son Bobby live. The boy takes Klaatu on a tour of the city and–at the alien's request–they visit the home of the leading American scientist, Professor Jacob Barnhardt. Klaatu warns him that the people of the galaxy have become concerned for their own safety after human beings developed atomic power.

Barnhardt agrees to arrange a meeting of scientists at the ship and suggests that Klaatu give a demonstration of his power, whereupon Klaatu neutralizes all electric power on earth. He also reveals to Helen that he is the visiting alien. The 30-minute world blackout creates a manhunt for Klaatu, who is shot again but revived inside his spaceship by Gort, aided by Helen. Before departing, Klaatu addresses the world's assembled scientists, explaining that man's penchant for violence has caused concern elsewhere in the universe. He warns that if mankind threatens to extend its violence into space, that robots like Gort will destroy Earth, adding, "The decision rests with you."

Background: Producer Julian Blaustein was the impetus for this film allegory on both the Cold War and the threat of nuclear weapons. He reviewed many science fiction short stories and novels looking for a storyline that could address these issues as contemporary metaphors. 20th Century Fox approved the project, and Blaustein hired Edmund North to write the screenplay based on elements from a short story by Harry Bates, "Farewell to the Master."

Claude Rains had been first choice for Klaatu but was busy performing in a play, so Englishman Michael Rennie, then a new contract player with 20th Century Fox, was hired. As Prof. Richard Keenan characterized him, "Rennie's face has the gaunt yet kindly quality suggestive of a modern Christ," though the picture, Kennan noted, stopped short of a possible accusation of sacrilege, which would have been the studio's concern in those more censorious times. As Kennan elaborates how the script fudged the problem:

> When...Barnhardt asks him if his power is truly unlimited, Klaatu is quick to point out that unlimited power is "reserved to the almighty spirit." Later, in the scene where Helen Benson witnesses his resurrection, Klaatu makes it clear that he has been "restored for a certain period." Answers such as these were sufficient to satisfy the censors.

Production Notes: Principal outdoor photography for the film was shot on the 20th Century Fox sound stages and on its studio back lot, now located in Century City, Los Angeles. The spacecraft set was designed by Thomas Little and Claude Carpenter, working with the noted architect Frank Lloyd Wright on the design. The saucer itself looked substantial enough but was actually made of plaster of paris and silver paint over a wooden framework. According to one commentator, it measured 350 feet around, was 25 feet high, and cost $10,000. It was flimsy enough that "it almost took off from the studio back lot during a gale."

The robot Gort was played by the seven-footer Joseph "Lock" Martin, who the filmmakers discovered working as an usher at Graumann's Chinese Theater in Los Angeles. He worked cautiously and only in 30 minute segments within his metallic suit.

To give the film the true documentary flavor of the time, clips commenting on the saucer's landing were included of major news commentators of the day, including H.V. Kaltenborn (who also appeared in *Mr. Smith)*, Elmer Davis, Drew Pearson, and Gabriel Heater (in radio voice only).

The Washington scenes were shot by a second unit (see below).

Influence: *The Day the Earth Stood Still* was meant as a "serious" science fiction film though its special effects today might seem simplistic and period reviews were not that laudatory (*The New York Times* reviewer called it a "tepid entertainment" and thought Rennie's performance was "likely to cause unguarded yawns"). It has, however, earned praise over the years as one of the seminal science fiction films. In 2008, it was named by the American Film Institute as among the "Top Ten" films (it placed fifth) in the sci-fi category. It also made the American Film Institute's best lists for "100 Heroes" and "100 Years of Film Scores." In 1995 it was placed on the National Film Registry of the Library of Congress.

The phrase that Patricia Neal must deliver to Gort to save Klaatu (Rennie)– "Klaatu barada nikto"–has become one of the most quoted lines from any American film, surfacing often in popular culture references.

DC/Hill Notes: All the location shooting in Washington was done by a second unit (none of the lead actors went to DC), but their material figured prominently in the picture. The unit shot both action sequences and background scenes. For the DC scenes that show Klaatu and Bobby (Gray) touring DC sights, process shots were used which inserted the actors into the setting. Other distant shots used acting doubles.

The striking opening sequence has a flying saucer gently invading Washington, spinning over some major buildings until coming to rest at the President's Park on the Ellipse.

In a sequence where military personnel are seen cruising the streets of DC, one shot is taken on Pennsylvania Avenue, SE, with a Peoples Drugstore (now CVS) on the corner of 7th and Penn. The Sewall-Belmont house on Capitol Hill (2nd Street and Constitution Avenue, NE) is also featured.

Goofs: In the opening sequence cited above, there is one geographical glitch: the saucer enters over the Capitol dome, passes over the Smithsonian's Arts and Industries building, over the Agriculture Department, then, out of sequence, right over the Smithsonian Castle, before passing the Washington Monument on its way to landing on the Ellipse.

When Helen (Neal) and Klaatu are in a cab heading for the professor's house, the army states that their cab is heading northwest on Connecticut Avenue at Columbia Road. The film then shows the cab going under the Dupont Circle underpass on Connecticut Avenue, but that underpass is *south* of Columbia Road, not north.

Postscript: *The Day the Earth Stood Still* was remade in 2008, with Keanu Reeves in the role of Klaatu. This time the setting was not Washington, but New York, and the intergalactic concern was environmental degradation, not nuclear power.

5 WASHINGTON STORY

1952. Metro-Goldwyn-Mayer, 81 minutes, black & white.

Original Screenplay and Direction by Robert Pirosh.

Cameraman: John Alton.

Editing: John Durant.

Music: Conrad Salinger.

Principal Cast :

Van Johnson	Cong. Joseph T. Gresham	Patricia Collinge	Miss Galbreth
Patricia Neal	Alice Kingsley	Moroni Olsen	Speaker of the House
Louis Calhern	Cong. Charles W. Birch	Elizabeth Patterson	Miss Dee
Sidney Blackmer	Phillip Emery	Reinhold Schünzel	Peter Kralik
Phillip Ober	Gilbert Nunnally	Fay Roope	Caswell

Synopsis: The plot starts with the presumption–typically made by both the public and the media–that all of Congress is crooked, and then it turns the tables. Joe Gresham is a hard-working but reticent congressman from Massachusetts. Reporter Alice Kingsley arrives in Washington, DC hired by Gilbert Nunnally, a tabloid columnist and cynic who wants Alice to uncover a ripe political scandal. They choose "No Comment Joe" Gresham as their target, and she begins developing a story on him, telling him it will be a benign "profile."

Gresham is struggling with a genuine legislative dilemma, weighing the funding of a ship building facility which would favor his own district against broader national defense requirements. To get to know him better–and to dig up some appropriate dirt–Alice agrees to travel with Joe to his home district, meets his mother, and observes him in his local context. In time, Gresham's wholesome image appears unfeigned, and Alice becomes torn between her commission to write a "tell-all" story and her growing attraction to Joe. At the finale, the congressman casts the "right" vote, punches out the crass Nunnally, and gets the girl with an embrace on the Capitol steps.

Background: The writer/director of *Washington Story*, Robert Pirosh, had a lengthy career as a screenwriter for movies and television but he directed only a few films in the late 1940's and 1950's. A previous film of his, *Battleground* (1949), had won him an Academy Award for Best Screenplay. After reviewing Pirosh's script for the film (originally titled "Mr. Congressman"), the Architect of the Capitol, David Lynn, said (according to a contemporary report in the *Washington Times-Herald*) that it was the best one ever written about the seat of government. Lynn liked it because it didn't "have any propaganda or sensational occurrences," and it might do a "lot of good" by showing people "just how Congress operates."

Production Notes: With a scenario that promised an honest look at congressional life, Pirosh and company attained considerable access to Capitol Hill in those much less security-minded days. The director remarked that "We are most grateful for the complete cooperation we are receiving from everyone here."

Authentic locations included offices and committee rooms in the Old House Office Building (now the Cannon Building) and the Capitol's underground tunnel (see photo insert) and subway. Most importantly, the production received final approval for shooting inside the Capitol itself from legendary Speaker of the House Sam Rayburn. A version of the House chamber is featured in the film, but, with no access to the floor allowed, the production used the reworked Senate set from *Mr. Smith Goes to Washington* as a substitute.

Most tellingly, the production team was permitted to set scenes within the Capitol Rotunda, something rarely allowed (in a climactic moment, the congressman slugs the evil columnist right under the Capitol dome!). Although the filmmakers agreed to leave the Capitol as they found it–a condition of the shoot–the local *Times-Herald* reporter who observed the filming noted that the production left the typically messy aftermath of location shooting, comparing it to that of August 21, 1814, when the invading British burnt the Capitol.

The reporter bemoaned the corridors littered with electric cords and the junky presence of movie paraphernalia, and then he went into down-and-dirty detail:

> *Against one wall of the Rotunda...were the broken remains of a packing case. Trapped in the irregular wooden pile were bits of torn newspapers and paper cups. Stacked in regular rows beside a doorway leading to the Statuary Hall were empty and half-empty soft drink bottles. And underfoot were partially smoked cigarette butts.*

It was the last time that Congressional authorities allowed filming inside the Rotunda and its flanking chambers.

Comment: *Washington Story* was an earnest attempt to show drama within the Capitol's corridors, graced with two of MGM's most attractive stars of the day. The movie tried to give a genuine feel for congressional activities, showing details of committee work and constituent services, as well as the constant time demands on the member. Perhaps more importantly, it tried to present a genuine political dilemma of the kind often faced by legislators but almost never addressed in commercial films: how to balance the interests of one's own constituents against the broader national need. The film is rare, too, among congressional movies in that it has a significant sequence back in the member's home district.

The fact that it did little business may have been due to the fact that it was too earnest, with not enough punch or dramatic contrast for most moviegoers. Political verisimilitude may have been achieved, but audiences may have found the romance element too muted. Critics found it no blockbuster, one British writer labelled it a "standard flagwaver which takes itself a shade too seriously." The film is one that proves the viewpoint that (even semi-realistic) political films don't draw an audience.

DC/Hill Notes: Besides showing the Senate monorail and the Old House Office Building, the film stands out among Washington, DC movies for its surprising access to the Capitol itself. Sequences inside the Rotunda have been mentioned above, but other sequences show Statuary Hall, the Congressional press room, and some of the Capitol's Brumidi-decorated corridors. The very last sequence is a real time capsule with a 1950's sightseeing bus rolling past the Capitol steps.

Goofs: When Alice makes a visit to the Congressman's office, we see the Capitol dome clearly out the window. However, by the angle of the view—showing clearly the East Front with the House entrance—his office would have to be approximately where the Supreme Court is located.

In the final clinch, the newly-reconciled Alice and Joe meet on the **Senate** steps of the Capitol (we can see East Capitol Street behind them) rather than on the House side where the Congressman would normally have exited.

6 A MAN CALLED PETER

1955. 20th Century Fox, 111 minutes, color.

Direction: Henry Koster.

Screenplay: Eleanore Griffin, from the biography by Catherine Wood Marshall.

Cinematography: Harold Lipstein.

Editing: Robert Simpson.

Original Music: Alfred Newman.

Principal Cast:

Richard Todd........The Rev. Peter Marshall
Jean Peters......... Catherine Wood Marshall
Marjorie Rambeau...... Miss Laura Fowler
Jill Esmond........................... Mrs. Findlay
Les Tremayne ....Sen. Willis Harvey
Robert Burton ....Mr. Peyton
Gladys Hurlbut....................... Mrs. Peyton
Richard Garrick .... Col. Evanston Whiting
Gloria Gordon.............................. Barbara
Billy Chapin....... Peter John Marshall (son)

Synopsis: Scotsman Peter Marshall experiences a strong calling to the ministry from God as a young man, and with 50 dollars in his pocket, travels to New York. He graduates from Columbia Theological Seminary in Georgia and eventually becomes the pastor of the Westminster Presbyterian Church in Atlanta. There he meets Catherine Wood, a student, whom he woos and marries. By the late-1930's Marshall becomes pastor of the New York Avenue Presbyterian Church in Washington, DC, dubbed the "Church of Presidents," where Abraham Lincoln once worshipped. Though his reformist ways and unorthodox sermons alienate older parishioners, he finds backing from people like U.S. Senator Willis Harvey, and his dramatic presence soon attracts a wide following. His faith is tested when his wife contracts tuberculosis, but her disease is overcome and the family finds respite in a house on Cape Cod. Marshall becomes nationally known for his sermons on radio and is asked by a group of senators to become the U.S. Senate Chaplain. At the height of his renown, he suffers a heart attack in the pulpit, and though he survives the first attack, he dies from another just two years later.

Production Notes: *A Man Called Peter* was based on the 1951 biography of the same name written by his wife, Catherine, and she was engaged as a technical advisor on the screenplay. The book was a phenomenal best seller of the time, spurring both a movie and a stage play, as well as a series of Caedmon Records of Marshall's radio sermons. Filming was done in the middle of 1954 and included locations in Scotland and Georgia, as well as Washington (see **DC/Hill Notes** below) and at the studios at 20th Century Fox. The film was a solid success, earning back roughly four times its production costs.

Richard Burton was originally assigned to the role of Marshall but was unavailable. To prepare for the role, Richard Todd studied recordings of Peter Marshall's sermons. He reads, with some potency, the actual words of Marshall's texts in several parts of the film. This was Jean Peters last Hollywood movie; she vanished from public view after marrying the reclusive Howard Hughes.

The film earned an Academy Award nomination for Best Color Photography for Harold Lipstein.

Comment: At a distance of more than 50 years, *A Man Called Peter* could be considered quaint, a period piece of a more innocent, credulous time. It was an era (never repeated since) in the United States when inspirational religious leaders–figures like Norman Vincent Peale, Bishop Fulton J. Sheen, and Billy Graham, as well as Marshall–were prominent in the mainstream media and appealed across the board with their general urgings of faith.

A Man Called Peter plays to this spirit, being full of swooping inspirational music, a rather syrupy over voice (from Jean Peters), and special calls from the Lord and urgent appeals to him. The film may be seen as cornball to many contemporary viewers, but it was inspiring to many in its time.

In fact, however, the film plays its religion pretty straight–little fire and brimstone, more gentle appeals to just be righteous. Todd, as Marshall, mostly avoids the saccharine in his performance because he is both so obviously the jovial Scotsman (though Todd was Irish) with a ripe brogue, and an energetic, forceful presence, one that makes his charisma believable. The film may be Holier Than Thou in some ways, but it aims at honest sentiment. And Washington looks lovely through this camera's color lens.

DC/Hill Notes: The film used numerous locations in the DC area, and they show to luminous effect in the rich color photography of cameraman Lipstein. Exteriors of the actual New York Avenue Presbyterian Church, at the corner of H Street and New York Avenue, NW, are featured in the film, though its interior (much smaller on film) was shot elsewhere. During the film, Marshall also speaks at the actual chapel of the US Naval Academy in Annapolis. There is also a sequence when the starry-eyed Marshalls drive past the front of the Lincoln Memorial.

Without today's security restrictions, there was a good deal of shooting on Capitol Hill for *A Man Called Peter*. The Marshalls, for example, are shown to be living at the building now housing Stewart R. Mott and Associates on the 100 block of Maryland, Avenue, NE, just across the street from the Supreme Court. Once Marshall is made Senate Chaplain, several shots around the Capitol are featured. The minister walks from the south side of the Capitol Plaza to enter the Senate side of the Capitol building. Later, Marshall and his family gaze on the Capitol at dusk at about the level of First Street SE (a process shot of the Library of Congress can be seen in the background).

Since there was no shooting in the Senate chamber, the filmmakers used a Hollywood set, but not a very effective one; it is obviously too small and plain.

7 EARTH VS. THE FLYING SAUCERS

1956. Columbia Pictures, 83 minutes, black & white.

Director: Fred F. Sears.

Written by Bernard Gordon, Curt Siodmak, George Worthing Yates; book by Donald E. Keyhoe.

Cinematography: Fred Jackman, Jr.

Editing: Danny B. Landres.

Music: Mischa Bakaleinikoff.

Principal Cast:

Hugh Marlowe....... Dr. Russell A. Marvin	John Zaremba......................... Prof. Kanter
Joan Taylor........................... Carol Marvin	Thomas Browne Henry ..Vice–Adm. Enright
Donald Curtis...................... Maj. Huglin	Grandon Rhodes................. Gen. Edmunds
Morris Ankrum..... Brig. Gen. John Hanley	Larry J. Blake........... Motorcycle Policeman

Synopsis: It's 1956 and the Department of Defense's secret "Project Skyhook," a US space-exploration program, is disrupted by aliens. A misunderstanding by the Earthlings leads to the aliens being fired upon, and they retaliate by destroying the project site with their flying saucers, abducting a general, and killing everyone except Dr. Russell Marvin, lead scientist of the project, and his wife Carol. The Marvins are rescued and head to Washington to warn of the aliens' intent to take over the planet. The aliens' demands for a worldwide summit of leaders to present their demands is delayed, and they react by launching a global invasion from their saucers. Their invasion leads to a dramatic attack on Washington, DC, and its principal monuments. In the end, however, the aliens are defeated over the skies of Washington by a device using high-power sound coupled with an electric field that disables the saucers' propulsion systems.

Production Notes: The film was a classic B-picture of its time, released as one part of a double feature by Columbia and shown typically at drive-in theaters. Very low budget, it had only about a week to shoot in DC, mainly to get shots of its actors at major sites. Its special effects might now appear quaint, but more than 50 years ago, they were state-of-the-art, the work of the renowned special effects expert Ray Harryhausen. Among his many effects, he used modeling, figure animation, stop motion photography, and double printing.

Harryhausen described his techniques in a DVD audio commentary from 2007, when the film was re-released by the studio in a colorized video version. He noted, for example, that the saucers in the film were small models with moving parts, ranging from three to 12 inches across, and made on a lathe by his father. Some figure animation was used in distance shots to show the aliens emerging from the flying saucers. In showing attacks on monuments, Harryhausen used both breakaway models for some or miniatures mixed with real photos, as when a saucer crashes into the very top of the Capitol.

In his autobiography, *An Animated Life*, Harryhausen addressed how he did much with little.

> *I am often asked how I was able to land a flying saucer on the grounds of the White House. We didn't ask permission to film, but we thought it would have been a place an alien force would land. We couldn't afford detailed miniatures, so we poked the camera through the bars of the fence at the rear of the White House. When the footage came back to me in Hollywood, I simply used it as rear projection and animated the saucer in front of the White House. All very simple, effective, and inexpensive.*

Some stock footage was also used in the film, including shots during the alien invasion that showed batteries of US 90 mm M3 guns and an early rocket launcher. Stock footage of the explosion of the warship HMS Barham during World War II was also used to stand in for a US Navy destroyer that is attacked by a flying saucer.

Renowned voice-over artist Paul Frees (probably best known as the voice of Boris Badenov on "The Rocky and Bullwinkle" cartoon shows) was the voice of the aliens. Frees' recorded voice was manipulated by jiggling the speed control of a reel-to-reel tape recorder so that it continually varied from a slow bass voice to one higher pitched.

DC/Hill Notes:

The climax of this sci-fi movie involves an elaborate set-piece depicting an invasion of flying saucers over Washington, DC, featuring many recognizable landmarks. First, aerial footage of Washington shows the superimposed saucers spinning over the Lincoln Memorial (where the temporary government buildings built during World War II can still be seen), Constitution Avenue, the Smithsonian Castle, Union Station, and the terrace of the Capitol.

The aliens then begin attacking, first the Pentagon, including its front stairway, and one immobilized saucer is seen crashing into the Potomac with the Pentagon in the background. The saucers continue to attack, dropping on to the White House lawn, and zapping military units. They are shown approaching Union Station's Columbus Fountain, and one saucer crashes inside the station. In the spectacular finale, the Washington Monument is cut in two, the Supreme Court is whacked in the front (with the lead actors clinging to its porch), and, as the true capper, a saucer crashes into the House wing of the Capitol, then the dome is sliced off by a second spaceship.

Goofs: A rendezvous Dr. Marvin has with a flying saucer is set for a Chesapeake Bay location, but the site is, in fact, Malibu Beach in North LA.

An alien saucer blows up the top of a tower that looks like the Old Post Office in DC but which is actually Los Angeles City Hall.

After the Washington Monument is hit by a saucer (achieved with a decent "process shot"), the next image of the fallen Monument shows it made out of ludicrously large bricks with obvious interior mortar showing. This is an example of a hilariously bad model, even from Ray Harryhausen, the master.

8 HOUSEBOAT

1958. Paramount Pictures, 109 minutes, color.

Direction: Melville Shavelson.

Screenplay: Shavelson and Jack Rose.

Cinematography: Ray June.

Editing: Frank Bracht.

Music: George Duning.

Principal Cast:

Cary Grant	Tom Winters	Mimi Gibson	Elizabeth Winters
Sophia Loren	Cinzia Zaccardi	Paul Petersen	David Winters
Martha Hyer	Carolyn Gibson	Charles Herbert	Robert Winters
Harry Guardino	Angelo Donatello	Madge Kennedy	Mrs. Farnsworth
Eduardo Ciannelli	Arturo Zaccardi	John Litel	William Farnsworth
Murray Hamilton	Capt. Alan Wilson	Werner Klemperer	Harold Messer

Synopsis: Widower Tom Winters has a hard time with his three disaffected children, David, Elizabeth, and Robert, who come to live with him in Washington, where he works at the State Department. The estranged children resent their father, and, during an outdoor concert at the Watergate, Robert runs away. He is found by Cinzia Zaccardi, the socialite daughter of a Italian conductor. She also wants to get away from her overprotected life and is taken with "Roberto." When she brings him home, Tom offers her a job as a maid, which she accepts. Carolyn, Tom's sister-in-law, suggests that he and the children use her old guest house, but the house is smashed in an accident involving a tow-truck driver, Angelo. Feeling guilty, Angelo sells Tom his decrepit houseboat on the Potomac.

Once moved in, Tom learns that Cinzia cannot perform any domestic chores, but she does win the affection of the children. Meanwhile, Tom spends his evenings with Carolyn, who is secretly in love with him. When Carolyn and some friends offend Cinzia during a visit to the houseboat, Tom asks them to leave. Later, however, he reconciles with Carolyn, even agreeing to marry her, but ultimately, he realizes he loves Cinzia. She, however, learns of his proposal to Carolyn and runs away. Though the children don't want Tom to marry Cinzia, Tom pursues her, and they marry on the houseboat.

Background (of the gossipy kind):

Cary Grant's wife at the time, Betsy Drake, wrote the original script of *Houseboat*, with the idea that the two of them would star in the film. But in the spring of 1956, Grant began filming *The Pride and the Passion* in Spain with the young (22) Sophia Loren as his co-star and fell completely in love with her. Grant then arranged for Loren to take Drake's place in the *Houseboat* project without telling his wife and called for a totally new script for which Drake received no credit. By the time the film was shooting in the summer of 1957, Grant had hoped to make a romantic move on the Italian, but she was accompanied on the set by her intended, producer Carlo Ponti. It was during the shooting of this film, in fact, that Ponti and Loren made a quick trip to Mexico, where Ponti obtained a quickie divorce from his then wife and married Loren. In *Cary Grant: A Biography,* author Marc Eliot provides a neat wrap-up to the Grant-Loren affair. He writes that after the Mexican marriage, Grant welcomed the couple back after a day's shooting:

> *Grant kissed a beautiful Loren on the cheek, shook a giggling Ponti's hand, and wished them both much happiness and health. The next day, in a beautifully fitting tux, Grant "married" a luminous Loren in the film's climactic wedding scene, while Ponti stood just off camera, intently watching every move both of them made.*

Later that evening in his favorite Hollywood bar, Cary lamented that he had lost Sophia forever.

Houseboat received two Oscar nominations, one for Best Original Screenplay (by Shavelson and Rose) and one for Best Original Song ("Almost in Your Arms," sung by Sam Cooke), but neither took home the prize.

DC/Hill Notes:

Coming to his "flat" in DC, Tom (Grant) drives a Jeep down Maryland Avenue in near Southwest (with the Capitol Dome in the background) to turn into his hotel (the Hotel Continental was used).

Tom drives over the Memorial Bridge from the Virginia side, heading for a concert at what was called the Watergate (one can see the 'Gate itself from the bridge shot). The film presents an actual Watergate concert with the steps below the Lincoln Memorial filled, and the orchestra playing on the famous barge (the concerts were earlier featured in *Born Yesterday*, q.v.). Only later, after the infamous 1972 break-in at the Democratic Party Headquarters, did "Watergate" become indelibly associated with the grand building complex north (completed in 1971) of the Kennedy Center.

After hiring Cinzia (Loren), Tom and his brood drive along the Potomac River on the Maryland side to the houseboat of the title. The Potomac location used was the Fort Washington Estates, at the time a new waterfront development.

Goofs: In a walk around the Tidal Basin with his three kids, Tom points out the sights, then says he will take them to the very vague "National Museum."

9 ADVISE AND CONSENT

 1962. Columbia Pictures, 139 minutes, black & white.

Director: Otto Preminger.

Screenplay: Wendell Mayes; Story by Allen Drury, based on his novel.

Cinematography: Sam Leavitt.

Original Music: Jerry Fielding.

Principal Cast:

Walter Pidgeon................. Sen. Bob Munson	Paul Ford .... Sen. Stanley Dana
Henry Fonda .... Robert A. Leffingwell	Burgess Meredith ....Herbert Gelman
Charles Laughton...... Sen. Seabright Cooley	Eddie Hodges................Johnny Leffingwell
Don Murray.......... Sen. Brigham Anderson	Inga Swenson .... Ellen Anderson
Franchot Tone....................... The President	Edward Andrews .... Sen. Orrin Knox
Lew Ayres.... Vice President Harley Hudson	Will Geer................Sen. Warren Strickland
Peter Lawford.................... Sen. Lafe Smith	Paul McGrath................Hardman Fletcher
Gene Tierney .... Dolly Harrison	Betty White ....Sen. Bessie Adam
George Grizzard.. Sen. Fred Van Ackerman	Malcolm Atterbury........... Sen. Tom August

Synopsis: A Senate confirmation battle rages over a controversial nominee for Secretary of State, Robert Leffingwell, a nomination fervently desired by the President and managed for him in the Senate by Majority Leader Senator Munson, aided by Senator Smith, a DC playboy. The President is ailing and wants to assure that his man gets approved to ensure his legacy. Leffingwell, however, is seen as too "egg-headed" for Senate conservatives, led by the crafty Senator Cooley. A bright young light, Senator Anderson, who has his own doubts about the nominee, heads the committee assessing Leffingwell for the post.

Leffingwell's cause is also pressed by Senator Van Ackerman, an aggressive liberal with few scruples who will do anything to get the nomination through, including defaming Senator Anderson for hiding a homosexual past. The right-wing Cooley, meanwhile, roots around in Leffingwell's background to find evidence of youthful communist leanings to tar the nominee. Cooley assures that the committee hears from an old colleague of Leffingwell's, Herbert Gelman, who testifies that the nominee was a member of the Communist Party. Von Ackerman blackmails Anderson by setting up a New York bar liaison with an old male flame, a troubling episode that leads to the Senator's suicide in his own office. The film climaxes on the Senate floor in a tight vote to confirm Leffingwell, during which the President dies of a heart attack with Vice President Hudson presiding.

Production Notes: Based on the best-selling novel by New York Times Capitol Hill correspondent Allan Drury, *Advise and Consent* was the talk of the town when filming; President Kennedy entertained the filmmakers at the White House during the summer of shooting in 1961 (see photo insert). Director Otto Preminger wanted to use as many DC locations as possible, including the Senate chamber, and he eventually got permission to use most of them. Yet despite his considerable lobbying of individual senators, he, too, was denied access to the chamber and had to return to Hollywood to re-use the classic *Mr. Smith* set (it had been used almost ten years before in *Washington Story,* q.v.).

Advise and Consent boasted an all-star cast. Besides Fonda, Laughton, and Murray, the film's key player was Walter Pidgeon as the courtly Senate Majority Leader Bob Munson who presents one of the most well-rounded portraits of a decent, reliable, seeker-of-compromise legislator there is on film. For the younger and smarter set, Peter Lawford played the playboy senator–appropriate for a "Rat Pack" actor who had married into the family of then-President Kennedy.

Laughton's preparation for his role as an oleaginous Southern senator was particularly extensive, according to Preminger, who wrote about the production in his biography. The director reported that Laughton spent weeks in Washington watching Mississippi Senator John Stennis on the Senate floor to study the speech patterns of a lawmaker from the Deep South. He even asked Stennis to read his part into a tape recorder so he could attain a proper accent. It was Laughton's final film role.

Several film veterans of the 1930's and 40's–Gene Tierney, Franchot Tone, and Lew Ayres–were brought out of virtual retirement by Preminger for this picture and came off well. Of the same generation, and memorable in the supporting role of weasely committee witness Herbert Gelman, was Burgess Meredith, who, according to Preminger himself, "gave one of the greatest performances I have ever seen."

Preminger offered Dr. Martin Luther King, Jr. a cameo role as a U.S. Senator from Georgia–although there were no serving African-American Senators at the time. According to Preminger himself, "Dr. King was intrigued but at the last moment declined. He decided that the hostility his presence would create in that role would jeopardize his cause."

Background: The film, and Drury's novel, offered a parlor game for Washington insiders: guessing the real senators behind the fictive ones. Senator Robert Byrd, comparing the novel with Drury's own diary notes as a correspondent, unearthed a number of likely parallels between the two, finding, *inter alia*, Cooley a "dead ringer for Kenneth McKellar of Tennessee," while Van Ackerman is a caricature of Senator McCarthy (though a left-winger), and Anderson "reminds us of Senator Lester Hunt of Wyoming, who took his life in the Russell Building in 1954."

A private Washington premiere of *Advise and Consent* was held at Washington's Trans-Lux Theater (then on 14th Street) in March 1962. Time magazine's reporter on the scene said the full house held 76 Senators, "enough to override a presidential veto," as well as Supreme Court justices and other government heavies. Snatched reviews from members were not particularly positive. Senator B. Everett Jordan said that he didn't "recognize a thing in it." Senator Eugene McCarthy insisted that "we're much more complicated than that," while Senator Strom Thurmond felt the film wasn't "wholesome."

Upon its release, the movie, like *Mr. Smith Goes to Washington*, was criticized by Congress, patriotic groups, and some critics as presenting to the world a perverted and inaccurate picture of American democracy. According to Preminger, Senator Stephen Young of Ohio announced a bill to prevent Columbia Pictures from distributing the film overseas, declaring it would do "irreparable harm" to American prestige abroad. The most influential movie critic of the day, *The New York Times*'s Bosley Crowther, denounced the film as a "deliberate endeavor...to make scandal and deception appear profuse." The outcry was strong enough to force Preminger to publicly defend his film on freedom-of-speech grounds.

Comment: *Advise and Consent* crystallized a new cynicism in Hollywood's treatment of congressional figures–if not also congressional process. It lifted what was considered a "racy" novel into public consciousness and shone what was, for many, an unforgiving light on our political personalities. The picture was made in a changing Hollywood context where filmmakers were trying to compete with ever expanding national television by taking on the "mature" themes that TV could not yet touch. This was also the beginning of a trend where American mainstream movies tried to portray more realistically, and graphically, serious subjects like the Cold War and nuclear showdown (like *Seven Days in May* two years later).

Though the film does achieve a new naturalism in depicting the senior body, it also reveals a world replete with ignoble characters and sordid events, constituting overall a fairly grim picture of Senate politics. For example, Leffingwell's cause is pressed viciously by Senator Van Ackerman, a *rara avis* in congressional movies as a liberal politician who is unrelentingly iniquitous (and who is always surrounded by a set of robotic bodyguards).

The plot turns on two primal fears of the era, the horror of world communism–personified by the "leftist" nominee–and the dread of homosexuality–expressed through the blackmail of Senator Anderson. As in *Mr. Smith*, however, the institution of the Senate proves to be larger than the contesting egos of its members, and the political process finally "works," however clumsily, triumphing over the frailties of its individual members.

DC/Hill Notes: The film is a cornucopia of locale spotting for Washington history buffs. It features on-location scenes in the Capitol, the street tram running on Constitution Avenue, the fabled Senate Caucus Room (site of the filmed committee hearing), and the Senate's old underground monorail, among others. There were also sequences in the Russell Senate Office Building, the lone Senate Office Building at the time (before the Dirksen Building was built). It was the last motion picture where a Hollywood film team had such significant access to the Capitol and Senate buildings.

Other scenes were filmed in the canteen of the US Treasury Building, on the National Mall (see photo insert), at the Washington Monument, at Washington National Airport, and at the Crystal Room of the Sheraton-Carlton Hotel, where the President (Tone) addresses the press. An apartment building which houses two senators is actually the Marriott Wardman Park Hotel on the corner of Connecticut Avenue and Woodley Road, NW.

Preminger's biographer detailed the shooting of a lavish Washington cocktail party which was filmed at the Tregaron Estate, then owned by Ambassador Joseph Davies and now the site of the Washington International School in the Cleveland Park section of Northwest DC. Hundreds of local socialites were invited to play themselves for a "fee" of $25 per head to go to charity, only to discover that the drinks served were strictly non-alcoholic.

Those who know the Capitol Hill neighborhood well will also notice the storied Sewall-Belmont House at 2nd and Constitution, NE, when Leffingwell's son rides his bike up to the house and his dad greets him.

Goofs: Assessing the film in the 1980's, Senator Byrd, a noted parliamentarian, chided the film for its fiddling the rules of the Senate, as when the Vice President asks for the "yeas and nays," which is "a question which is never asked by the chair in the Senate."

After the opening of one Senate session, a cluster of reporters rush to interview Senators on the floor, a no-no for journalists.

Nominee Leffingwell (Fonda) is ex-head of the non-existent "Federal Power Authority."

Sequences inside the Senate chamber always have the Vice President in the chair—highly unlikely, since he rarely presides. Only in the last scene, when the critical nomination is being voted on, does it appear probable.

Vice President Hudson (Ayres) is not shown traveling with Secret Service protection in the film. Even less likely, he is shown traveling alone in coach on a New York to DC flight.

10 SEVEN DAYS IN MAY

1964. Paramount Pictures, 120 minutes, black & white.

Director: John Frankenheimer.

Screenplay: Rod Serling, based on the novel by Fletcher Knebel and Charles W. Bailey, II.

Cameraman: Ellsworth Fredricks.

Editing: Ferris Webster.

Music: Jerry Goldsmith.

Principal Cast:

Burt Lancaster ...... Gen. James Mattoon Scott	John Houseman .... Vice-Admiral Barnswell
Kirk Douglas .... Col. Martin "Jiggs" Casey	Whit Bissell .... Sen. Fred Prentice
Frederic March .... President Jordan Lyman	Hugh Marlowe .... Harold McPherson
Ava Gardner .... Ellie Holbroook	Col. Murdock .... Richard Anderson
Edmond O'Brien .... Sen. Raymond Clark	Andrew Duggan .... Col. "Mutt" Henderson
Martin Balsam. .... Paul Girard	Bart Burns .... Arthur Corwin
George Macready .... Christopher Todd	Lt. Dorsey Grayson .... Jack Mullaney

Synopsis: In the slightly near future, a weakened incumbent President Jordan Lyman and the popular and ambitious four-star General Scott contend for control of the US government. Lyman has negotiated an arms reduction treaty with the Soviet Union, but it is publicly unpopular and particularly offends the right-wing Scott, Chairman of the Joint Chiefs, who sees it as treasonous appeasement and goes public in his opposition. Marine Corps Colonel Jiggs Casey, principal aide to Scott, comes to suspect an elaborate plot to overthrow the government by senior military and political officers led by Scott.

Working with the President and small circle of loyal officials, including Senator Clark, Casey uncovers evidence implicating Scott, and uses both Clark and White House staffer Paul Girard to unearth elements of the plot involving a mysterious project called ECOMCON. As part of his effort to undermine Scott, Casey discovers incriminating love letters from Scott to Ellie Holbrook, which he contemplates using as blackmail in an effort to save the Lyman Administration. Girard dies in a plane crash in Spain—along with evidence from Admiral Barnswell, which unmasks the plot. Clark locates a secret base, "Site Y" in Texas, and is held captive there only to escape, with Col. Henderson's help, back to Washington. A dramatic confrontation occurs in the Oval Office between the President and the General just before the President addresses the nation. Then the Barnswell evidence comes to light, and the coup attempt collapses, leaving the General with no option but to resign.

Background: *Seven Days in May* was based on a best seller of 1962 of the same name. Its authors, Knebel and Bailey, certainly were aware of a renegade general of the Eisenhower era, the virulently anti-communist Gen. Edwin Walker. Walker had been relieved of a command in 1961 by President Kennedy and resigned form the army that same year.

Douglas, who agreed to produce the film with director Frankenheimer, initiated the production. Douglas also consented to star, but he wanted his frequent co-star and friend Lancaster in the film as well. This almost caused Frankenheimer to back out, since he and Lancaster had butted heads on a previous picture *(The Birdman of Alcatraz)*. Only Douglas's assurances that Lancaster would behave kept the director on the project. As it happened, Lancaster and Frankenheimer became close friends during the filming, and they even agreed to work on their next project together. That project was *The Train,* shot in France later the same year. It was while they were in Paris for that latter film that Frankenheimer wrapped up the sequence at the end of the film where a defeated Scott gets into a taxi to head home.

Production Notes: *Seven Days in May*'s interiors were shot at the Paramount studios in Hollywood, and its locations included Paris, Washington, DC, San Diego, Arizona, and in California's Imperial Valley. Some effort was made to have the film appear to take place in the near future, for instance, the use of the then-futuristic technology of video teleconferencing, shown in a sequence in the Oval Office.

The facsimile of that Oval Office at Paramount was the first of many significant Hollywood attempts to recreate that famous space. Writer Fletcher Knebel, reporting on the project for *Look* magazine at the time, said the office "was a painstaking copy of the real thing. The carpeting even had the President's seal–cut into the rug with a pair of barber's clippers."

In was in that Oval Office set that the key scene of the movie takes place: the showdown between the beleaguered but principled president, played by Frederic March, and the nearly unhinged General played by Lancaster. After rehearsal, Frankenheimer got this extended scene shot in one day, adding: "I have never seen two actors more concentrated. Burt had to show March he could do it; March had to show he was king."

Seven Days in May was nominated for two Academy Awards, to Edmond O'Brien for Best Supporting Actor as Senator Clark and for the Best Art/ Set Direction in black and white. Screenwriter Rod Serling, at that time wrapping up his famous *Twilight Zone* TV series, was nominated for an award by the Writer's Guild of America.

DC Notes: The movie contains an example of "guerilla" (or, on-the-fly) film-making. Frankenheimer wanted a shot of Kirk Douglas entering the Pentagon, but he could not get permission because of security considerations. So he rigged a movie camera in a parked station wagon to photograph Douglas walking to the Pentagon's entrance and up the main steps. Frankenheimer recalled: "Three men saluted him. Three other officers saluted him. They really thought he was a colonel." In five minutes, the crew filmed Douglas in entrance and exit shots. "Then we cut the scene out of the movie. We didn't need it," the director said.

Getting permission to tour within and shoot near the White House was easier. Frankenheimer said that Pierre Salinger conveyed to him President Kennedy's wish that the film be made. On the weekend of July 27, 1963, the President was conveniently away on a visit to Hyannis Port. Salinger then arranged for the film's production designer to tour the mansion and sketch, photograph, and "do everything needed to duplicate the set in Hollywood," recalled the director. When the film needed to shoot the rowdy demonstration outside the White House (see photo insert), Knebel offered a lively, first-hand account of the demonstration:

The scene was filmed July 27 (1963), just two days after the nuclear test-ban treaty was initialed in Moscow. Real pickets, bearing placards thanking Kennedy for the treaty, had to be shunted down the sidewalk so that the fictional brawl could take place. The fight...flowered into a beautiful brannigan. Former boxers hired as extras slugged one another to the sidewalk with a vigor any New Frontiersman would have admired.

The film also had two sequences in Dulles Airport, the first time the new, then futuristic, airport had been used in the movies.

Goofs: In an early sequence, General Scott (Lancaster) is testifying in a congressional hearing room (a set) which is way too small, with only two persons giving testimony, one aide, and no back rows for public or press.

In the same scene, there is also a portrait of the sitting president Jordan Lyman displayed above the committee chairman's head, a complete no-no on the Hill (remember separation of powers!).

There is a later sequence showing a car being tailed in what is supposedly DC which was actually shot on Rossmor Avenue in Hollywood. The tailed car ends up driving up to the front of the Dobney Hotel in LA.

In one of the Dulles Airport sequences, when Colonel Casey is shown leaving the airport, the scene shows palm trees–suspiciously like the landscape at Los Angeles Airport.

Low Angle – The Seventies and Eighties

The 1970's produced some of the best films about Washington ever made and in a variety of genres: horror (*The Exorcist*), suspense (*All the President's Men*), comedy (*Being There*), and political drama (*The Seduction of Joe Tynan*). In truth, though, only two of these were box office hits, and there were few other pictures of the decade that featured Washington themes.

The 1980's showed a greater number of DC films, but the decade produced relatively few movies that highlighted Washington's political institutions. It was, after all, the Reagan Era, and the population (and Hollywood, ever reflecting it) was relatively content and benignly ignored political themes. Having had some time to digest the Vietnam War, filmmakers in the late Seventies and Eighties did begin to produce motion pictures about America's Vietnam War experience, but only one–*Gardens of Stone*–had any significant DC content.

Almost no movie output during these two decades looked very seriously at the Congress or the Executive Branch, and only one took on the Supreme Court (*First Monday in October*). One film of the period, *The Godfather II* (1974) might be mentioned because, within its complex structure, it provided one of the best re-creations of a congressional hearing ever on film, as well as adding to the litany of venal legislators in movies, this one a Nevada senator nestled in the pocket of the Corleones.

Only one DC-based movie of this period, Sidney Lumet's *Power* (1986) tried something new in the political arena, concentrating on behind-the-scenes campaign practitioners (led by Richard Gere as Peter St. John, a hot-shot campaign consultant) and their cynical handling of candidates. However, the writing betrayed the intent, the plot was a spongy muddle, and the chilly protagonist attracted no one. The movie-going public stayed away, way away.

Otherwise, the period produced an intriguing miscellany of entertaining and amusing fare, especially in comedy, with highs–*Broadcast News*–and lows–*Three for the Road* (1987).

11 THE EXORCIST

 1973. Warner Brothers, 122 minutes, color.

Director: William Friedkin.

Screenplay: William Peter Blatty, based on his novel of the same name.

Cinematography: Owen Roizman.

Editing: Norman Gay.

Music: Jack Nitzsche.

Principal Cast:

Ellen Burstyn	Chris MacNeil	Jack MacGowran	Burke Dennings
Max von Sydow	Father Lankester Merrin	William O'Malley	Father Joseph Dyer
Jason Miller	Father Damien Karras	Barton Heyman	Dr. Klein
Linda Blair	Regan MacNeil	Pete Masterson	Dr. Barringer
Lee J. Cobb	Lt. William Kinderman	Arthur Storch	Psychiatrist
Mercedes McCambridge	Demon's Voice	Vasiliki Maliaros	Karras' Mother
Kitty Winn	Sharon Spencer	Robert Symond	Dr. Taney

Synopsis: At an archaeological dig in Iraq, archaeologist Father Merrin discovers foreboding icons of another time, while, at Georgetown University in Washington, Father Damien Karras begins to doubt his faith after his mother becomes ill. In Georgetown, actress Chris MacNeil, in town for a film, is shocked by the increasingly strange behavior of her 12-year-old daughter, Regan, who exhibits unnatural powers and spouts vile language in a demonic male voice. Doctors are of no help in helping her, and eventually one of them suggests an exorcism as an outside possibility for a cure. It then appears that Regan is responsible for the death of a housekeeper, a death which draws suspicions from the police. In desperation, Chris consults

Father Karras, who is also a psychiatrist. At first Karras thinks Regan is suffering from psychosis, but he ultimately decides to request permission from the Church to conduct an exorcism.

Father Merrin, an experienced exorcist, is summoned to Washington to assist. He and Karras try to drive the demon from Regan, but he threatens and taunts both men. Merrin then tries the exorcism alone, which results in his suffering a fatal heart attack. Karras attempts to revive him to no avail, then attacks Regan, challenging the demon to leave the girl and enter him. The demon does just that, and the priest sacrifices himself by jumping through the bedroom window to fall down the long staircase outside. At the bottom of the steps, another priest, Father Dyer, administers last rites to Karras as he dies, while Regan is restored to health, unaware of her ordeal.

Production Notes: *The Exorcist* was based on the 1971 blockbuster novel of the same name by William Peter Blatty, who received more than $600,000 for the film rights from Warner Brothers. Blatty wrote the screenplay and was coproducer on the film, actively involved in every aspect. Warners considered a number of name directors for the film, including Arthur Penn, Stanley Kubrick, Peter Bogdanovich, and Mike Nichols, but Blatty insisted on William Friedkin, who had great success with his previous effort, *The French Connection*.

The shoot began in the summer of 1972. Scheduled for 85 days, it took more than seven months. That shoot became famous for the lengths to which director Friedkin went to get authentic reactions from his cast. During different violent sequences, both Burstyn and Blair suffered back injuries from being jerked around in harnesses they wore for movement effects. Friedkin shot a gun on the set to get a surprise reaction from Jason Miller in one scene, and, in another, he slapped Father Dyer (O'Malley) to obtain his desired effect. For another sequence, a bedroom set was filmed inside a freezer so Friedkin could get the actors' actual breath on camera.

The casting also went through sundry changes. Jack Nicholson was tapped for the role of Father Karras, but Stacy Keach was signed by Blatty. Only after Friedkin saw Jason Miller in a New York play was the actor cast, with the studio buying out Keach's contract. This was Miller's first film.

Several Hollywood leading ladies were also approached for the role of Chris, including Shirley MacLaine, Jane Fonda, Anne Bancroft, and Audrey Hepburn, before Bursytn was signed. Casting was especially difficult for the role of Regan, a child who had to literally go through hell. Linda Blair, 14 at the time, had made dozens of commercials as a child actor, but this was only her second film. For Regan's demon dialogue, the singular alto voice of veteran character actor Mercedes McCambridge was used. One actor, Lee J. Cobb as the police lieutenant, was agreed upon from the start. Another cast member, William O'Malley, was a long-time teacher in New York state. It was his only movie role.

Background: *The Exorcist* was a true motion picture and mass entertainment phenomenon, breaking box office records, sparking a trend for exorcist movies, and, for months, eliciting controversy over its powerful shock effects. Movie patrons were said to have fainted or become physically ill during some screenings, and such violent reactions just triggered more interest in the film. Warner Brothers studio would not permit publicity stills or clips showing the fully possessed Regan, adding to the film's buzz—and its ticket sales—since you had to buy a ticket to see how horrifying the film must be.

The Exorcist ranked second in total receipts in 1973 (after *The Sting*) but has gone on to earn more money worldwide than any other horror film in history (over $441 million) with its several re-releases over the years. If its receipts were adjusted for inflation, it would rank as the 9th highest grossing film of all time and the top-grossing R-rated film ever. The film and the hullabaloo about it made the cover of *Time* magazine, and it was argued about vigorously on radio and TV talk shows. The Blatty novel and subsequent screenplay was based on an actual incident in 1949 when a young boy in a Maryland village adjoining Washington, DC, was deemed to be under demonic possession, and his family asked a priest to perform an exorcism.

The film was nominated for ten Academy Awards, including Best Picture, but won only two: for Best Adapted Screenplay (for Blatty) and for Best Sound. Burstyn, Miller and Blair were all nominated for acting awards.

DC Notes: *The Exorcist* became well known for its significant use of Georgetown locations. Most memorably, the house of the MacNeils at 3600 Prospect

Street in Georgetown remains in people's memories (see photo insert), as well as the steps which are adjacent to the house and lead precipitously down (still somewhat spookily) to M Street, NW. The climactic scene when Father Karras throws himself through the bedroom window on to the steps outside required some ingenuity. The actual residence has a large yard between it and the steps, a distance that would have made it impossible for anyone to fly out of the window and actually land on the steps. So, for the movie, the set decorators added a false wing—supposedly holding Regan's bedroom—so the house could extend to the steps (see photo insert).

Georgetown University locales were used, including the Dahlgren Chapel, which was where the film's desecration scene was shot, as well as the Healy Hall steps, where Burstyn's character is first introduced. In the neighborhood, Georgetown's Holy Trinity Church at 3513 N Street, NW, was the site of the church sermon scene. There was also a bridge scene at the C & O canal, and a scene shot at The Tombs, a student hangout which was also featured in *St. Elmo's Fire* (q.v.) and which is across the street from the house. Most of the interiors for the movie were filmed in New York City.

Goofs: Rubber mats can be seen on the steps for the famous fall down the staircase. The ½-inch padding was placed to cushion the fall of the stuntman standing in for Father Karras (it took just two takes to capture the sequence).

Postscript: *The Exorcist* was followed by two sequels: *Exorcist II: The Heretic* (1977) , and *The Exorcist III* (1990). Blatty and Friedkin had nothing to do with the first of these, which was directed by British director John Boorman. It starred Richard Burton as a Father Lamont and a 16-year-old Linda Blair as Regan, still possessed to a degree. Although it uses sequences involving the original Georgetown house, the production had to use a set because permission was not granted to film there. Likewise, DC authorities would not allow film on the famous steps, which had to be re-created. The film, which also had New York and faux African settings, was a box office and critical bomb.

The Exorcist III was both written and directed by William Peter Blatty, adapting his own successful 1983 novel, Legion. This film, starring George C. Scott (taking on the Lee J. Cobb role), Ed Flanders as Father Dyer, and Jason Miller as "Patient X" (i.e. Father Karras resuscitated), again used Georgetown as a central film location in a very different kind of story involving a demonic serial killer. This time, footage was used of Georgetown University, M Street, and, again, The Tombs bar. The film as originally shot did not ever have an exorcism scene (as the novel had not), but the studio, 20th Century Fox, insisted that one be added for popular acceptance and to match the title. Blatty reluctantly agreed and had to do an extensive re-shoot to include it. The film was a modest money-maker but has, since its release, garnered some critical recognition as a competent, efficient horror film.

A mere month after *The Exorcist III* appeared in 1990, Carolco Pictures released a coarse and silly *Exorcist* parody, *Repossessed*, starring Leslie Nielsen as a nutty priest and Linda Blair, reviving her earlier possessed character as an adult.

12 ALL THE PRESIDENT'S MEN

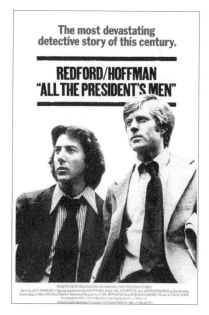

The most devastating
detective story of this century.

REDFORD/HOFFMAN
"ALL THE PRESIDENT'S MEN"

 1976. Warner Brothers Pictures, 138 minutes, color.

Director: Alan J. Pakula.

Screenplay: William Goldman. Based on the book of the same name by Bob Woodward and Carl Bernstein.

Cameraman: Gordon Willis.

Editing: Robert L. Wolfe.

Music: David Shire.

Principal Cast:

Robert Redford	Bob Woodward	Stephen Collins	Hugh Sloan, Jr.
Dustin Hoffman	Carl Bernstein	Meredith Baxter	Debbie Sloan
Jason Robards, Jr.	Ben Bradlee	Robert Walden.	Donald Segreti
Hal Holbrook	"Deep Throat"	Ned Beatty	Martin Dardis
Jack Warden	Harry Rosenfeld	Jess Osuna	FBI Agent Joe
Martin Balsam	Howard Simons	Penny Fuller.	Sally Aiken
Jane Alexander	Bookkeeper	Lindsay Crouse	Kay Eddy

Synopsis: Based on the Pulitzer Prize-winning 1974 book of the same name, the film focuses on the first five months of the Watergate story, starting with a re-enactment of the break-in at the Democratic National Committee headquarters in June 1972 and leading up to *The Washington Post*'s revelations about the Nixon Administration's campaign of sabotage against its political rivals. Beginning with the first coverage by Woodward and Bernstein, obscure writers on the Metro beat, the story chronicles both their dogged reporting work as well as the development of a personal and professional rapport between two very different individuals, each with investigative and journalistic skills of his own.

A parade of Nixon Administration sources are incorporated into the narrative, most notably Hugh Sloan and the bookkeeper, who give the pair crucial information about suspect monies from the "Committee to Re-Elect." Highlighted, too, are details of Woodward's secret meetings with his crucial source "Deep Throat," an administration insider who guided the reporters on their investigation. The tension rises with Woodward and Bernstein under threat and editor Ben Bradlee having to take a chance on his novice reporters. The noose closes in on the White House as the *Post* details its involvement in a cover-up which reaches up to and including the President, whose demise is coolly and efficiently spelled out in clattering teletype.

Background: The production was initiated by the politically-minded Redford, who was fascinated by the Watergate story. He bought the rights to the book in 1974 for $450,000 and got it financed from Warner Brothers with a budget of $5 million. William Goldman's original script pleased no one involved with the project. A second version came out of the blue from Bernstein and his wife at the time, Nora Ephron, but Redford rejected it. Then Redford and his director, Alan Pakula, took a crack at it, booking rooms at the Madison Hotel across from the *Post* offices for a month to finalize the script.

The film had a special DC premiere on April 4, 1976 at the Kennedy Center in Washington before its general release. The director and the principal actors hobnobbed with political leaders and other dignitaries in what was a benefit for the Fund for Investigative Journalism (see photo insert).

Although little of Goldman's script remained at the end, he would go on to win the Academy Award for Best Adapted Screenplay.

Production Notes: *The Washington Post* itself covered the filmmakers' invasion of its premises in a long article written in April 1975, one year before the film's release. It noted that Dustin Hoffman and Redford "hung out in the *Post* offices for months, sitting in on news conferences and conducting research for their roles," with Redford often a distraction to employees when he roamed the floor.

Redford, in a recent biography, stated that "contrary to what's been written," Katherine Graham "did not block us filming at the *Post*. We filmed for two weeks, but it went haywire." The reason, said Redford, was that "the journalists and secretaries went crazy when Hollywood came in their midst. It was all giggling women and people doing their makeup and a general feeling of disorder...we knew we had to get out of there."

Before fleeing the fabled newsroom, however, set designers took measurements of the newspaper's offices and photographed everything. Even boxes of authentic *Post* trash were gathered and transported to sets recreating the newsroom on two soundstages in Warners' Burbank studios at a cost of $200,000. The filmmakers went to great lengths for accuracy and authenticity, including making replicas of phone books that were no longer in existence, the article noted.

According to the film's producer. Walter Coblenz, the shoot in DC was difficult: "They just didn't want us in Washington, so every permission was a stranglehold," he said. "We shot at the Library of Congress, for example, and they just didn't want us. There was anger and denial all around. We were told that the incident portrayed in the book was inaccurate, that the library had never been involved. That drove Woodward mad, because he knew what was true, he was *there*."

Coblenz also reported that the filmmakers thought they had approval from Ron Nessen, President Ford's press secretary, to stage a briefing scene in the White House, and even scripted it in. "Of course, we were naïve," Coblenz added: "There was no way Ford would allow Redford to come to the White House to diss the previous president. We were suddenly told it was all off, the administration didn't approve. It felt hugely ironic."

There was an argument over the film's ending. Director Pakula wanted the iconic footage of Nixon's defiant wave from the Presidential helicopter, but Redford demurred, saying "This isn't about Nixon. It's about journalism. I want to end with the guys just working away." A compromise was reached which closes the film–the clattering image of a teletype announcing Nixon's resignation.

Comments: Rare for a serious political drama, the film proved a considerable financial success, earning Warners over $30 million in the US during its first release. The film was also a great critical success, winning four Oscars (for adapted screenplay, sound, art direction, and Robards' supporting performance) and being nominated for four others, including Best Picture of the Year (it lost to *Rocky*).

The film was universally lauded, *The New York Times'* rave review by critic Vincent Canby being fairly typical:

> *Newspapers and newspapermen have long been favorite subjects for mov-iemakers,...yet not until* All the President's Men, *the riveting screen adaptation of the Watergate book..., has any film come remotely close to being an accurate picture of American journalism at its best.*

DC/Hill Notes: Outside of its singular set for the *Post's* newsroom, *All the President's Men* uses DC locations as fully and consistently as any Washington-based movie ever made by a Hollywood studio. Not only are many locations used, but they are used appropriately, and in a few cases, strikingly. Scenes take place at the Kennedy Center, in Lafayette Park, at the Hoover FBI Building, in an actual District courtroom, at the exterior of *The Washington Post's* building, at the White House's north gate, at the Justice Department (FBI), and, most appropriately, at the Watergate complex and the Howard Johnson Motor Lodge across the street (where the infamous Plumbers had their base). The apartment where Woodward (Redford) lives, and signals Deep Throat (Holbrook) with a potted plant, is located at Webster House at 1718 P Street, NW.

One significant location–the ominous parking garage where Woodward meets Deep Throat–did not use a DC site. Those sequences were shot in the garage of the ABC Entertainment Center building in Century City, Los Angeles.

The filmmakers also provided a neat cameo: the security guard in the film who discovers the Watergate burglars is played by Frank Wills, who was the actual guard on duty on the night of the break-in. The sequence was recreated in the Watergate building itself.

Library of Congress Filming: Perhaps the film's most imaginative use of locales is the sequence when Woodward and Bernstein visit the Jefferson

Building of the Library of Congress to gain access to some White House records (see photo insert). The most effective part of the sequence is shot inside the Library's famed Main Reading Room, where, as the reporter's rifle through library check-out cards, the camera slowly backs up vertically to the very top of the Library's grand dome, with a view down on the now puny protagonists, struggling against the odds. According to one source, the production "devoted three weeks to pulling apparatus up 600 stairs to achieve a dramatic upward pull-away shot."

That dramatic shot almost never happened. According to a contemporary report in a local business journal, the company, after spending two weeks building a platform from which a camera could obtain a bird's eye view of the Reading Room, hit a snag. Then:

Forty-eight hours before the shoot, permission to film was suddenly revoked by an official who was horrified to see the platform hanging from pulleys attached to the Library dome. After hours of desperate telephoning, the producers finally reached...Jack Valenti (head of the MPAA). Valenti put them in touch with Congressman John Brademas, who sits on the Library committee of the House of Representatives. Thanks to Brademas' intercession, the scene was shot.

The Library shoot was also the scene of an unfortunate incident that affected future access to the building. Stuart Neumann, long a DC location manager and a production assistant during this filming, recalled the event in an interview: A member of the rigging crew was running cables up in a false ceiling with acoustical tiles when the ceiling broke and the fellow fell right on an office desk of a Library of Congress employee. The Librarian of Congress was not happy, and the building was considered off limits for a time to commercial filmcrews (see **Location, Location, Location**).

Goofs: There are not many, in fact, for such a complex location shoot.

Bernstein eats out with a contact at an open air "restaurant" overlooking the Jefferson and Lincoln Memorials. It was actually filmed on the top deck of the Kennedy Center to attain that view, yet, while it provides a wonderful vista of Washington, there has never been outdoor service at the eateries on that top floor.

Woodward is shown driving east in front of the White House then is immediately shown in front of the Kennedy Center, which is west of the White House.

Woodward walks on 17th Street to the corner of the Corcoran Gallery at G Street, NW (The Old Executive Office Building is seen in the background) and uses a phantom telephone booth (there has never been one at that corner)

Quote: *Post* editor Ben Bradlee, warning Woodward and Bernstein about their coverage:

> *You know the results of the latest Gallup Poll? Half the country never even heard of the word Watergate. Nobody gives a shit. You guys are probably pretty tired, right? Well, you should be. Go on home, get a nice hot bath. Rest up...15 minutes. Then get your asses back in gear. We're under a lot of pressure, you know, and you put us there. Nothing's riding on this except the, uh, first amendment to the Constitution, freedom of the press, and maybe the future of the country. Not that any of that matters, but if you guys f*** up again, I'm going to get mad. Goodnight.*

BEING THERE

1979. United Artists, 130 minutes, color.

Director: Hal Ashby.

Screenplay: Jerzy Kosinski (from his novella) and Robert C. Jones.

Cameraman: Caleb Deschanel.

Editing: Don Zimmerman.

Music: Johnny Mandel.

Principal Cast:

Peter Sellers	Chauncey Gardiner	Elya Baskin	Karpatov
Shirley McLaine	Eve Rand	Sam Weisman	Colson
Melvyn Douglas	Ben Rand	Richard Venture	Wilson
Jack Warden	The President	David Clennon	Thomas Franklin
Richard A. Dysart	Dr. Robert Allenby	Denise DuBarry	Johanna Franklin
Richard Basehart	Soviet Ambassador	Ruth Attaway	Louise

Synopsis: Chance is a middle-aged, simple-minded gardener who has lived his entire life isolated in the DC townhouse of a wealthy old man who raised him. His whole sense of the world comes from watching television. When the old man dies, lawyers handling the estate force Chance from the house, and he wanders aimlessly about Washington. While wandering, he sees his own image in a TV store window. While watching, he is struck by a car owned by Ben Rand, a wealthy businessman. Rand's wife Eve, concerned about him, invites him to their palatial home to recover. When asked his name, it is misinterpreted as "Chauncey Gardiner" rather than Chance the gardener.

Now residing with the Rands, Chauncey's description of his narrow life is totally misread by Ben, who sees him as a businessman like himself unjustly suffering hard times. Ben also assumes his cryptic remarks (about gardening) reveal deep wisdom, and he introduces him to the President, to whom Rand is an advisor. The President is likewise impressed, and Chauncey becomes a media and social celebrity. Rand, dying of anemia, encourages his Eve to become close to Chauncey. Rand's physician, Dr. Allenby, is skeptical about Chauncey and learns that the man has zero paper trail, but he refrains from revealing his doubts because he sees that Chauncey has given Rand peace of mind. At Rand's funeral, the President offers a long-winded eulogy, while Rand Co. board members whisper about supporting a potential replacement: "Chauncey Gardiner."

Background: Filming the Jerzy Kosinski book *Being There* was a long-time desire for Peter Sellers, who thought the part of Chance was ideal for him and would give his career a boost by portraying an off-beat, semi-serious character—after he'd had a run of tepid comic roles during the 1970's. Sellers expressed his desire for the chance to play Chance soon after the novella came out and even lobbied Kosinski personally for the part. His hunch proved correct, because the role earned him an Academy Award nomination for Best Actor, as well as other accolades.

Sellers was disappointed in not winning the Oscar and just as upset by the credit sequence on the final release print (done by Ashby without his knowledge) which shows outtakes of the actor laughing hysterically as he blows some lines. He saw its inclusion as a travesty, undercutting his "austere and technically controlled performance." Sellers' biographer indicates that it caused him to send an angry telex to Ashby, saying: "It breaks the spell, do you understand? Do you understand, it breaks the spell!...." It was the last Sellers' film to be released before the actor died in 1980.

Sellers' co-star Melvyn Douglas's performance was also recognized at award's season, and he won the Oscar for Best Supporting Actor for playing Ben Rand. It was a good year for Douglas, then 78, who also offered a fine acting turn in another significant DC film, *The Seduction of Joe Tynan* (q.v.), released just four months before.

Comment: The film, though not a box office smash, was a *succès d'estime* for director Hal Ashby and his cast, especially Sellers. Many critics then and now consider it one of the actor's greatest roles, second only to his triumph in *Dr. Strangelove* (1964). Critic Frank Rich of *Time* magazine offered fairly typical praise of Sellers' "meticulously controlled performance, then expanding:

> *He is a master at adapting the surreal characters of modern fiction to the naturalistic demands of movies. His Chance is sexless, affectless, and guileless to a fault. His face shows no emotion except for the beatific, innocent smile of a moron...Sellers' gestures are so specific and consistent that Chance never becomes clownish or arch. He is convincing enough to make the film's fantastic premise credible; yet he manages to get every laugh."*

DC Notes: *Being There* used a mix of both "real" and imaginative locations. After being ejected from the only house he has ever known (the exterior is on the 900 block of Vermont Avenue, NW), an overdressed Chance (Sellers) wanders a section of run-down inner-city Washington. Here he encounters a group of black kids at a store front located at Rhode Island Avenue and 14th St., NW. The store was "Leon's TV World," whose owner, Leon Gibson, said Hollywood came calling because they liked his store's lively yellow exterior.

His wanderings also take him to the front of the White House, on to North Capitol Street (see **Goofs** below), and to a storefront on K Street, NW displaying a wall of TVs (the store was actually a clothing store re-dressed for the film).

Solid Stand-ins: The interiors of the house where Chance lives at the beginning of the picture were shot at the Fenye Mansion on Walnut Street in Pasadena, CA. The Rand mansion in the film, supposedly in the DC suburbs, is actually the Vanderbilt family's palatial Biltmore House and Gardens in Asheville, North Carolina. The film has a good facsimile of a Presidential motorcade, including the presidential limo, arriving at the Rand's "suburban" mansion. The Oval Office re-creation, a set, is also quite convincing.

Goofs: During Chance's wandering about the city, a sequence begins with a shot of the statue of Mexican patriot Benito Juarez, located on Virginia Avenue, NW, just north of the Watergate complex, but the next cut shows him positioned in front of the National Gallery of Art's West Wing–an amazing physical jump of about two miles for the dawdling Chance.

Later in his wanderings, there is a dramatic shot of Chance walking at dusk on the narrow median strip coming up from the underpass on North Capitol Street, with traffic flooding beside him in both directions and the Capitol dome in the background (the mood is heightened by the soundtrack booming an electronic rock version of Richard Strauss' tone poem "Also Sprach Zarathustra"). This is a place where it would be almost impossible for a pedestrian to tread, but it makes for a wonderfully symbolic depiction of a truly lost soul in an unforgiving DC. *(Personal Note: this sequence represents the author's favorite single shot in all Washington movies and can be seen in the photo insert.)*

THE SEDUCTION OF JOE TYNAN

1979. Universal Pictures, 107 minutes, color.

Director: Jerry Schatzberg.

Original Screenplay: Alan Alda.

Cameraman: Adam Holender.

Editing: Evan Lottman.

Music: Bill Conti.

Principal Cast :

Alan Alda	Senator Joe Tynan	Carrie Nye	Aldena Kittner
Barbara Harris	Ellie Tynan	Michael Higgins	Senator Pardew
Meryl Streep	Karen Traynor	Blanche Baker	Janet
Rip Torn	Senator Kittner	Chris Arnold	Jerry
Melvyn Douglas	Senator Birney	Maureen Anderman	Joe's Secretary
Charles Kimbrough	Francis	Robert Christian	Arthur Briggs

Synopsis: Senator Joe Tynan of New Jersey is a rising young liberal Democrat with a warm and understanding family back home. The venerable Senator Birney of Louisiana favors a judge from his home state as a nominee to the Supreme Court, and, realizing that Tynan cannot support a nominee from the South, asks that the popular Tynan at least not oppose the nominee. Tynan agrees but is then subject to the wiles of the attractive labor lawyer Karen Traynor. She represents forces opposed to the judge, who see him as a Southern bigot.

With Ellie and his family back home, where she pursues her work as a doctor, the busy Senator succumbs to an affair with the lobbyist. Through her influence, he eventually compromises his agreement with Senator Birney and becomes the Senate leader contesting the naming of the controversial judge. His turnabout causes particular distress to the aged Birney, who is showing signs of senility. Yet, even as Tynan triumphs in killing the judge's nomination, his marriage begins to show strains and problems arise with his teenage daughter. His new-found celebrity earns him the chance to keynote the party's national convention, but, with a skeptical Elle in attendance, the fate of his marriage appears uncertain.

Background: *The Seduction of Joe Tynan* was an Alan Alda project in that he wrote the script with the aim of starring in the movie. A political activist himself, Alda did his homework, offering ample Hill lore and detail (including some convincing staff meetings) with a feel for smart dialogue and plausible characterizations.

The year 1979 was a breakout year for Meryl Streep, who won several critic's awards for her performances that year, including *Joe Tynan*. One critic compared her, most favorably, to Katherine Hepburn in "her regal beauty and bearing." In 1979, Streep also appeared in Woody Allen's *Manhattan* and Robert Benton's *Kramer vs. Kramer* (for which she won an Oscar).

The picture received mixed reviews but did reasonably well financially, perhaps because of Alda's presence (he was starring in TV's popular *M*A*S*H* at the time).

Comment: In its ambiguous finale, *The Seduction of Joe Tynan* leaves its protagonist at his political peak with his home life shaky; he savors the cheers of a convention crowd (and even a possible spot on the ticket) while looking into his defeated wife's forlorn face. What seduces here–besides the lovely Meryl Streep–is political power, the necessary maintenance of which produces the sundry pressures that color the politician's life. Alda's solid script is better than most at limning those real pressures on our elected representatives.

Further, though Hollywood is usually not very good at depicting bureaucracies, even small ones like congressional offices, *Joe Tynan* presents a plausible portrait of staffers and their importance to a member, something exceedingly rare in US political movies. Particularly effective in this context is the performance of Charles Kimbrough (much better known later as a pompous character on TV's *Murphy Brown*) as Francis, the Senator's chief aide who combines just the right mix of unctuous fealty and ready admonition. Just as rare for political movies are the sequences in the film that show the Senator's actual home life, complicated and believable, back in his own state. Only *Washington Story* (q.v.), 27 years earlier, had given any screen time to that part of a politician's experience.

Terry Christensen, writing in his important study of politics and film entitled

Reel Politics, felt that the picture was an "advance" for films about politics:

> *Joe Tynan...more than most films about politics, ...rings true on the personal costs of political life, its small compromises, and its corruptions. The process is convincingly portrayed without resorting to dirty little secrets...thus keeping the melodrama within the realm of credibility. (Joe Tynan) may sell out, but we understand why because the movie makes sure we continue to like him."*

Film critics, too, were generally positive, with some caveats. Stanley Kauffman, for example, writing in *The New Republic*, thought the film "an odd mixture of freshness and leftovers," but he praised the authenticity of the film's senatorial atmosphere: "It sensitively and effectively deals with the conflict between maintenance of ethics and the moulding of ambition in a realistic, uncyncial fashion."

DC/Hill Notes: A number of DC and Maryland locations were used during filming, with the latter probably providing more screen time. Baltimore, for example, was used for a supposed "Georgetown" scene, and space in an office building in that city served for Senator Tynan's office. Additionally, a "Louisiana" shore scene was shot at Maryland's Eastern Shore, and the Senate chamber shown in the film is actually the Senate chamber in the Maryland State House in Annapolis.

Still, there was a good deal of Washington-area material as well in the film.

The opening credit sequence shows a group of local black kids in a school bus touring Washington; their route takes them via North Capitol Street, then past the White House (going east), by the Washington Monument, past the Lincoln Memorial, before finally heading south down First Street, NE, to enter the Capitol grounds.

The film achieves decent approximations for real Senate locations although the production could not shoot inside the Capitol or the Senate Office Buildings. The director used the Library of Congress and other monumental spaces effectively as stand-ins. Senator Tynan (Alda), for example, is shown in his "hideaway office" in a corner of the Capitol–which was actually shot in the basement of the Library of Congress. There is a shot of Senate staffers walking in the Great Hall of the Library, standing in for one of the Senate Office Buildings. Also, the office of Senator Birney (Douglas) used the interior of the Folger Shakespeare Library at 201 East Capitol Street, SE.

Another location is the restaurant on top of the Hotel Washington on 15th Street, NW (now a "W" hotel), where the Senator and lobbyist Karen Traynor (Streep) have lunch. In another scene, Tynan runs around Dulles Airport looking for Traynor.

FIRST MONDAY IN OCTOBER

1981. Paramount Pictures, 98 minutes, color.

Director: Ronald Neame.

Screenplay: Jerome Lawrence and Robert Edwin Lee, based on their play.

Cinematography: Fred J. Koenkamp

Editing: Peter E. Berger.

Original Music: Ian Fraser.

Principal Cast:

Walter Matthau	*Justice Daniel Snow*	*Wiley Harker*	*Justice Harold Webb*
Jill Clayburgh	*Ruth Loomis*	*F. J. O'Neill*	*Justice Waldo Thompson*
Barnard Hughes	*Chief Justice Crawford*	*Charles Lampkin*	*Justice Josiah Clewes*
Jan Sterling	*Christine Snow*	*Lew Palter*	*Justice Benjamin Halperin*
James Stephens	*Mason Woods*	*Richard McMurray*	*Justice Richard Carey*
Joshua Bryant	*Bill Russell*	*Herb Vigran*	*Justice Ambrose Quincy*

Synopsis: An Associate Justice's death has created a Supreme Court vacancy. The remaining justices speculate about the new nominee, joshing that the President might pick a black man–or even a woman. The pick is, indeed, a woman, Ruth Loomis, a relatively young judge from the Ninth Circuit in California, who is a staunch conservative. Liberal-leaning Associate Justice Daniel Snow is appalled at the appointment, knowing Loomis's views to be diametrical to his own.

In testimony before the Senate, Loomis is questioned particularly about her late husband's business ties but is ultimately confirmed as the first female justice. She and Snow clash intellectually on just about every judicial issue before them. One particularly contentious case involves a pornographic film and testy arguments over freedom of speech. Yet, over time, the two judges develop a mutual respect and even affection for each other while acknowledging their different viewpoints. Snow comes to Loomis's defense when her late husband's reputation is threatened by a scandal, and she is sympathetic when Snow suffers a stroke.

Background: *First Monday in October* (the date that marks the beginning of a Supreme Court session) is the only Hollywood feature that has focused specifically on our high court and its justices as dramatic material. The film was based on the Broadway play of the same name which had a run in 1978 with Henry Fonda and Jane Alexander as the leads. The playwrights, Lawrence and Lee, also wrote the screenplay. Henry Fonda was unavailable to reprise his role in the film, and the producers and the studio, Paramount, rejected Alexander because they wanted a more "bankable" star. Instead, two very hot movie actors of the day were hired for the leads–Matthau and Clayburgh. One of the film's producer's deemed Clayburgh "a better investment." The film, however, was only a modest success, earning about $12 million in box office.

Matthau's biographers described how the actor researched his role as Justice Snow, noting that: "...Matthau read a couple of books by William O. Douglas, the justice his character resembled. He patterned the character's outward manner on Democratic Party power broker Robert Strauss, throwing in bits of Walter Huston and Henry Fonda..."

First Monday in October is one of those instances where life imitates art. The film was originally scheduled for a February 1982 release, but on July 7, 1981, President Reagan appointed Sandra Day O'Connor as the first female Supreme Court justice, which pushed the studio, for publicity reasons, to release the film just a month later in August 1981. As luck would have it, Lawrence and Lee had anticipated other elements of this historic nomination: like the real O'Connor, the Ruth Loomis character was a conservative Republican from the West.

DC/Hill Notes: The production did appropriate location shooting in DC, especially in and around the Supreme Court in near Northeast (see photo insert). In the credit sequence, for example, a mix of clips includes both building details and distance images of the Court, and it ends with a group of visitors coming up the front steps on to the porch. There are other views of the court building later as establishing shots. In another sequence, a car is shown going into the Court's back garage entrance on 2nd Street, NE and later, exiting the garage. Justice Loomis (Clayburgh) is also shown driving past the Court on 1st Street, SE, then heading downtown on Constitution Avenue. Veteran Washington newshounds will note the presence of long-time ABC correspondent Martin Agronsky on the steps of the Supreme Court covering Loomis's presence on the first Monday in October.

To establish the confirmation hearing of Judge Loomis before the Senate Judiciary Committee, a sequence begins with the steps of the Russell Senate Office Building in the foreground and continues with committee attendees entering the building at its southwest corner.

Early in the film, to illustrate the funeral of the deceased justice, scenes were shot at Arlington National Cemetery, including a cortege that leaves the cemetery and the car of Justice Snow (Matthau) looping around the cemetery circle and heading on to the Memorial Bridge. Snow and his wife live in a house on a cobbled street in Georgetown.

In a scene unique in Washington movies, Justices Loomis and Snow drive to the Smithsonian's Arts and Industries Building, parking on the Jefferson Drive side and entering the centennial exhibition "1876" and into the exhibition space itself.

In the scene where Snow is rushed to the hospital, the ambulance peels down Pennsylvania Avenue and ends up at what was then the emergency entrance of George Washington Univesity Hospital located on Washington Circle, NW (this was where President Reagan was treated after being shot by John Hinkley in March 1981, mere months before this film's release).

Though filming inside the Supreme Court was not permitted, the production used a very creditable reproduction of the Court's Chamber, looking especially authentic from an interior "aerial" shot.

Goofs: A minor one: when the two Justices go inside the Smithsonian Arts and Industries Building, there is absolutely no one else around, a practical impossibility when the museum (closed at the time of this writing) was open.

16 D.C. CAB

1983. RKO Pictures/Universal Pictures, 100 minutes, color.

Direction: Joel Schumacher.

Screenplay: Schumacher and Topper Carew.

Cinematography: Dean Cudley.

Editing: David E. Blewitt.

Music: Giorgio Moroder.

Principal Cast:

Adam Baldwin	Albert Hockenberry	Anne de Salvo	Myrna Oswelt
Max Gail	Harold Oswelt	Whitman Mayo	Mr. Rhythm
Mr. T	Samson	Paul Rodriguez	Xavier
Charlie Barnett	Tyrone Brewster	Peter Barbarian	Buddy
Gary Busey	Dell	David Barbarian	Buzzy
Gloria Gifford	Miss Floyd	Jill Schoelen	Claudette
Marsha Warfield	Opehlia	José Pérez	Ernesto Bravo
Bill Maher	Baba	Irene Cara	Herself

Synopsis: Naive young Albert Hockenberry comes to DC to live with and work for his late father's army buddy Harold, owner of D.C. Cab, the sorriest cab company in town. Harold dreams of remaking his company to challenge the popular Emerald Cab outfit, but his disreputable collection of drivers, who all see driving as a dead end job, make it tough. The cabbies include an Elvis fanatic, a wiry black "brotha," a muscle man, a Latin Lothario, among other misfits. The guileless Albert wants nothing more than to run a decent cab company, and his upright example begins to inspire the group to work as a team.

Harold earns a $10,000 reward when a valuable violin is found in one of the cabs, and he aims to invest it in D.C. Cab, but his spiteful wife Myrna absconds with the reward money and kicks Harold and Albert out of the house. Albert saves the day by donating money he has saved to completely overhaul the business and to obtain cab licenses for every driver. When Albert and a diplomat's two children are abducted by kidnappers, the D.C.

Cab team comes together to save them from harm. They are saluted by the city for their heroism.

Background: *D.C. Cab* aimed at being a "funky," profane send-up of DC during the Marion Barry's first term as mayor. It was co-written and directed by Joel Schumacher, his second effort as a director after having been a costume designer and writer on other films. The mixed ensemble of comic actors within a working class environment, the punchy soundtrack, and the urban vibe recall the flavor of an earlier screenplay of Schumacher's, *Car Wash*, a low-budget hit of 1976. This was an early role for Mr. T. (Laurence Tureaud), an ex-bouncer who, shortly after this appearance, had his greatest fame as Sgt. Bosco Baracus in the popular TV series *The A-Team*. It was the film debut for a trio of American comedians: HBO raconteur Bill Maher (he was 27), Mexican-American comic Paul Rodriguez (28), and the foul-mouthed Charlie Barnett (29).

Comments: For fans of DC movies, *D.C. Cab* might rank as a guilty pleasure. There may be more guilt than pleasure in watching it at a distance of almost 30 years. It is, in many ways, just a mess. The acting is alternately crass and wooden, the story line is wandering and incoherent, and many of the gags go on too long. Adam Baldwin's dippy smile turns quickly irritating and then unsettling, while Mr. T. is just ornery loud. Barnett's mugging is a modern variation on Stepen Fetchit, and Busey's gaping leer is barely under control. Then there is poor Irene Cara. Fresh off her debut in *Fame* and with a couple of hit records under her belt, she gets one measly, embarrassing scene in the back of Tyrone's cab—and a song over the end credits.

With skin, dirty jokes, and steady profanity, it earns its solid "R" rating.

DC Notes: *D.C. Cab* did, however, made extensive use of Washington locations, and because it tried to depict a District that was "down and dirty," some of the locations were distinctive. Most specifically, a well-known local eatery, the Florida Avenue Grill (located at Florida Avenue and 11th Street, NW) was an important and repeated location. It was where the movie's cabbies gathered to share meals, chew the fat, and bond. The daughter of the woman who ran the Grill was the lead's love interest, Claudette.

Another distinctive sequence takes place on F Street, NW, at about 14th

Street, once the heart of the city's downtown shopping area. Tyrone (Barnett) is selling tawdry junk at a souvenir stand on what once was a median strip of E Street, and he eventually swipes a cab from Dell (Busey) at the corner where Garfinckel's clothing store once stood.

A significant nighttime sequence has the *D.C. Cab* gang all gathering on a wide street at the base of a large structure, trying to decide how to locate the kidnappers. After some back and forth, Mr. T finally energizes his colleagues and, as he speaks, the camera pulls back to reveal the full-lit Lincoln Memorial (cue the "Battle Hymn of the Republic").

The end-credit sequence of *D.C. Cab* is a celebratory parade of the revivified company, with all its motley drivers sitting atop the cabs as they glide past crowds around the District Building, now the Wilson Building at 1350 Pennsylvania Avenue, NW. The lively parade, led by the Cardozo High School Marching Band, runs past a large sign carrying a hot slogan of the day: "Washington Is a Capital City."

Other locations shown in the movie were: Massachusetts Avenue, NW, by the British and Brazilian Embassies, Dulles Airport (both from afar and at the Arrivals ramp), a night time shoot at Arlington Cemetery, and a view of a cab going north on 16th Street, NW with a view of the White House in the background.

Goofs: The opening credits provide one of those "get-it-all-in" sequences which eschew all sense of geography to get the iconic sights included. Newbie Albert (Baldwin) is seen on Third Street, NW, crossing the Mall (Capitol dome, check), then is seen walking at the corner of 15th Street and Constitution, NW (Washington Monument, check), only to be driven east on Pennsylvania Avenue in front of the White House (check!).

To allow time for all the credits at the end, the cab parade takes several minutes to traverse just one long block of Pennsylvania Avenue.

17 PROTOCOL

1984. Warner Brothers Pictures, 96 minutes, color.

Director: Herbert Ross.

Screenplay: Buck Henry.

Story: Nancy Meyers, Harvey Miller, and Charles Shyer.

Cinematography: William A. Fraker.

Editing: Paul Hirsch.

Original Music: Basil Poledouris.

Principal Cast:

Goldie Hawn	Sunny Davis	Cliff De Young	Hilley
Chris Sarandon	Michael Ransome	Keith Szarabajka	Crowe
Richard Romanus	Emir	James Staley	Vice President Merck
Andre Gregory	Nawaf Al Kabeer	Kenneth Mars	Lou
Gail Strickland	Amb. Marietta St. John	Jean Smart	Ella
Ed Begley, Jr.	Hassler	Kenneth McMillan	Senator Norris

Synopsis: Ditzy Sunny Davis is working as a cocktail waitress in the sleazy Safari Club in DC. By a trick of fate she saves a visiting dignitary, an emir from the Middle East nation of "Ohtar", from an assassination attempt. In the act, she is shot in the tush and becomes a national heroine. The Administration, which wants to curry favor with the Emir's country, then hires Sunny as a protocol officer who can get close to the Emir, who wants her for his harem. Sympathetic Foreign Service Officer Ransome is assigned as Sunny's minder, but the scheming Ambassador St. John, jealous of her, looks to have Sunny shipped off to the Emir in exchange for a military base. Sunny goes to Ohtar only to find she has been used. She resigns, returning home to testify before Congress, then to run for office herself, with the help of her now-boyfriend Ransome.

Background: Produced as a star vehicle for Goldie Hawn, *Protocol*, though it had a name director in Herbert Ross and a script by practiced comedy writer Buck Henry, was not a critical success and did only middling box office (total receipts were $26 million). The principal criticism was centered on its blatant use of the most egregious Arab stereotypes, crude even for the mid-1980's. Hawn was the executive producer, the first time she had taken on that role. Goldie herself had a local connection; she was born in DC in 1945, grew up in Silver Spring, Maryland, and graduated from Montgomery Blair High School there. She first found work as a dancer before getting into television (*Laugh-In*) and film.

DC/Hill Notes: The film was mostly shot at Warner Brothers Studios in Hollywood, though the filmmakers did do some location shooting in Washington.

The rowhouse where Hawn's character lives (with a comedic gay couple) is located on the corner of 9th and A Streets, NE, just north of East Capitol Street. It is shown at the end of the sequence where Sunny has her car towed from downtown by a local Esso service truck.

There is also a sequence shot at the District Building on Pennsylvania Avenue and two elaborate (and utterly confusing) transportation movements around the city (see **Goofs** below).

Goofs: During the film's credit sequence, there is a drive showing an Arab dignitary (the Emir) on his way to the White House but which is essentially a cinematic postcard of DC's monuments. The motorcade circles the Lincoln Memorial, goes past the Jefferson Memorial, doubles back past the Washington Monument, only to end up at the Treasury Building beside the White House. Unless the chauffeur was scouting for cherry blossoms, a more round-about route could hardly be imagined.

Sunny (Hawn) is on her stomach (having been wounded in the rear) at the George Washington University Hospital on 21st, NW, when, on the phone with her mother, she says: "I can see the Capitol from the window!" a clear impossibility.

Michael Ransome (Sarandon) is the Department's "Middle East Desk Chief," a title and position which does not exist.

In one scene a set of State Department and White House officials–together with the Emir–emerge inexplicably from the Wilson Building (formerly the District Building), probably because it looks "official."

There is another baroque vehicular movement later in the movie: a car heading for the Capitol goes south on 17th Street past the Eisenhower Executive Office building, then is abruptly shown coming from Virginia and passing the Jefferson Memorial, then past the Air and Space Museum on Independence, to finally drive south on Third Avenue, then to Pennsylvania Avenue towards the Capitol.

Sunny, giving congressional testimony on her Middle East exploits, announces that she lives at "1442 G Street," with no city quadrant given.

THE MAN WITH ONE RED SHOE

1985. 20ᵗʰ Century Fox, 92 minutes, color.

Director: Stan Dragoti.

Screenplay: by Robert Klane based on an original French
screenplay by Yves Robert and Francis Veber

Cinematography: Richard H. Kline.

Editing: O. Nicholas Brown and Bud Molin.

Music: Thomas Newman.

Principal Cast:

Tom Hanks	Richard Drew	Jim Belushi	Morris
Dabney Coleman	Cooper	Irving Metzman	Virdon
Charles Durning	Ross	Tom Noonan	Reese
Lori Singer	Maddy	Gerrit Graham	Carson
Carrie Fisher	Paula	David L. Lander	Stemple
Edward Herrmann	Brown	David Ogden Stiers	The Conductor

Synopsis: Cooper, deputy director of the CIA, lusts for the job of the director, Ross, and aims to smear him into resigning. Ross learns of the plot against him and feeds Cooper false information: a man will be arriving at a DC airport who might be able to clear Ross of Cooper's false charges. Cooper counters by sending his own man to the airport along with Ross's minion, Brown, to make contact with the mystery man. But Brown is instructed by Ross to identify any random traveler as the mystery man, and he picks the naïve Richard Drew because he stands out: he is wearing obviously mismatched shoes, one of them a red sneaker.

Cooper then learns that Drew is suspicious because he has traveled the world (turns out he is a violinist with the local symphony orchestra) and sets up surveillance on him. He also sends his femme fatale, Maddy, to find out what Drew knows, even to decoding his sheet music. Ross gleefully watches the shenanigans unfold in his favor while the frustrated Cooper orders that Richard be killed, eventually attempting to murder him himself. The violinist at all times remains completely oblivious to the action swirling around him, while Maddy begins to fall for him.

Background: The film is a remake of a 1972 French classic comedy *The Tall Blonde Man with One Black Shoe ("Le Grand Blond avec une chaussure noire")* starring Pierre Richard and Mireille Darc and written by Francis Veber and Yves Robert. Why the American scenario changed the shoe color and didn't cast a tall blonde is unknown, but the changes did them no favors. While the French farce was a major hit in France and worldwide, *The Man with One Red Shoe* grossed less than $10 million, even with the popular Hanks in the title role.

The film offers a look at Tom Hanks in one of his earliest comedies. Not yet 30 at the time of filming, Hanks had personal and financial success with his first two starring roles, in *Splash* and *Bachelor Party,* but this time the project flopped. More than 20 years later, Hanks was at the top of his game in another DC-based film *Charlie Wilson's War* (q.v.).

DC/Hill Notes: The film used locations in Georgetown, where Drew (Hanks) lives, and a few other locations around town. Most of those used, however, are the subject of **Goofs** (see below).

Goofs: The spotting of the man with the red shoe is supposed to happen at a DC airport, but LAX Airport was used as a stand-in.

In one traveling sequence, Richard rides his bike out of Georgetown, then is next seen going east to the Lincoln Memorial, then on to Memorial Bridge and into Arlington to see his dentist–not the most direct way to get there. Once in the vicinity of the dentist's office, he is clearly in another city, with buses clearly not from DC area transit.

The Drew character plays first violin with the "Washington Symphony," which is supposed to be the city's principal symphony. They play in a small hall, however, which looks nothing like the Kennedy Center.

Near the end of the picture there is a confounding chase sequence: Richard and Maddy (Singer) run down into the Dupont Circle Metro stop and end up on the Baltimore subway (the subway train gives it away by being labeled "Special"). They then come up in the middle of the Mall (Smithsonian

Metro stop) and run up the grand southern steps of the National Gallery's West Wing. They are supposed to be running to a Congressional hearing on Capitol Hill, but the Gallery is nowhere near the Congressional office buildings. The director does get what he wants, however: a background shot of the Capitol dome!

19 ST. ELMO'S FIRE

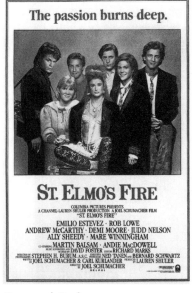

1985. Columbia Pictures, 110 minutes, color.

Director: Joel Schumacher.

Screenplay: by Schumacher and Carl Kurlander.

Cameraman: Stephen H. Burum.

Editing: Richard Marks.

Music: David Foster.

Principal Cast:

Judd Nelson	Alec Newbury	Demi Moore	Jules Van Patten
Ally Sheedy	Leslie Hunter	Mare Winningham	Wendy Beamish
Emilio Estevez	Kirby Keger	Andie MacDowell	Dale Biberman
Andrew McCarthy	Kevin Dolenz	Martin Balsam	Mr. Beamish
Robe Lowe	Billy Hicks	Joyce Van Patten	Mrs. Beamish

Synopsis: Seven close friends—Alec, Billy, Jules, Kevin, Kirby, Leslie and Wendy—are testing adult life and each other after graduating from Georgetown University. Alec, an aspiring politician, switches from Democrat to Republican to obtain a job, while his girl friend Leslie looks to "find herself" before marriage. Kirby is in law school, paying his tuition by working as a waiter at Saint Elmo's Bar in Georgetown, where his buddies congregate. He is enamored of a hospital intern, Dale. Kirby's roommate Kevin is a budding writer who doesn't date, leading his friends to suspect he's gay (though he has a yen for Leslie). Married Billy is the randy, reckless member of the group, reliving his frat days. Unable to hold a job, he plays the saxophone and sleeps around. Jules, a beauty with a wild streak and an addictive personality, lacks the means to sustain her cocaine-filled lifestyle. Innocent Wendy comes from wealth but works at a soup kitchen while her

family supports her financially. She is in love with the irresponsible Billy.

The film traces the variable confrontations and liaisons of the seven as their commitments to each other wax and wane, and their friendships are tested. A major crisis finds them all trying to rescue an agonized Jules, high on drugs and locked in her apartment. The finale sees Billy, having divorced, leaving town to try a new life in New York, and the remaining friends deciding that perhaps they should try a new hang out.

Background: Joel Schumacher, as director and co-writer, was the principal impetus behind *St. Elmo's Fire*. Schumacher had started in Hollywood as a costume designer in the 1970's (making two films with Woody Allen, among others) before moving on to directing in 1978. *St. Elmo's Fire* was his third feature, made after another Washington-themed film, the raucous comedy *D.C. Cab* (q.v.). While making the latter picture in the early 1980's, Schumacher lived in Georgetown.

In the DVD of the film released in 2001, Schumacher remarks on the basis of this movie: "There's a group of people. Everyone had their group and you always think you're going to be best friends forever. But life comes in. So, can you be best friends forever?" Schumacher is perhaps best known for two versions of the *Batman* series he directed in the 1990's.

Production Notes: Understandably, Schumacher wanted to shoot on the Georgetown campus. There was precedent: *The Exorcist* (q.v.) had shot there the decade previously. When he discussed that prospect with university authorities, however, they refused. Having read the script, he said, in his DVD commentary, that the Jesuits "wouldn't allow us to film on the Georgetown campus because there was premarital sex in the film." The University of Maryland stepped in and allowed the production to shoot there (see **Goofs** on next page).

Comment: The cast of the film became well known as some of the core members of "The Brat Pack," a loosely associated group of young actors of the early and mid-1980's. Six months before making *St. Elmo's Fire*, three of the same cast members–Emilio Estevez, Judd Nelson, and Ally Sheedy–had worked on *The Breakfast Club*, another signature "Brat Pack" film. Interestingly, where in the latter film all the actors played teenagers, they all played college grads just six months later (all the actors were in their twenties). *St. Elmo's Fire* became a touchstone for an untold number of young college-aged Americans who identified with the groping, egocentric, yet somehow attractive, lives depicted in the film, and while the picture was not a smash box office hit upon its release, it has long since provided a nostalgic balm for many in that audience.

DC Notes: "St. Elmo's Bar" in the film is based on The Tombs, a popular watering hole with Georgetown University students located on 36th Street, NW, a few blocks away from the university campus. The exterior shots of the bar appear on a full street set built at Universal Studios in Los Angeles. To directly establish the Georgetown vibe, there are occasional establishing shots of scenes at the Key Bridge, on the C & O Canal, and on M Street, NW.

Goofs: The film is supposed to take place in and around Georgetown and its university, however, some characters in the film sport red and white varsity letter jackets, the colors of the University of Maryland (where the campus scenes were actually filmed).

In a phone call, Jules (Moore) says she is stuck with some Arab visitors in the fictional "Van Buren Hotel" in DC.

At one point in the script, a character indicates that Billy (Lowe) works at an Amoco gas station on Michigan Avenue which is "just around the corner." But Michigan Avenue is miles away in NE Washington, nowhere near Georgetown.

20 BROADCAST NEWS

 1987. Warner Brothers Pictures, 133 minutes, color.

Director and Screenplay: James L. Brooks.

Cinematography: Michael Ballhaus.

Editing: Richard Marks.

Original Music: Bill Conti.

Principal Cast:

Holly Hunter	Jane Craig	Peter Hackes	Paul Moore
William Hurt	Tom Grunick	Christian Clemenson	Bobby
Albert Brooks	Aaron Altman	Jack Nicholson	Bill Rorich
Robert Prosky	Ernie Merriman	Ed Wheeler	George Wein
Lois Chiles	Jennifer Mack	Seephen Mendillo	Gerald Grunick
Joan Cusack	Blair Litton	Marc Shaiman	News Theme Writer

Synopsis: In a Washington, DC, TV news station affiliated with a national network (never specifically named), Jane is a driven, ambitious, but ethical news producer who has a news buddy and soul mate in Aaron. He is a bright but needy reporter for the station who has fallen for her, a love which is not requited. Into their lives comes a new anchor for their show, the handsome, if superficial, Tom. Jane is smitten with Tom, but wishes he shared her journalistic principles, while Aaron sees him as an airhead incapable of real depth. Still, to help Tom look good and appease Jane, Aaron intervenes to help Grunick on a key broadcast, while the network's visiting anchor star, Bill Rorich, looks on.

Later on, Aaron is given a chance to prove—to Jane and the station—that he, too, can anchor, but his on-air appearance is ruined by a appalling case of flop sweat. Tom's self-centered superficiality is proven when he tears up during a poignant interview, tears he can turn on at will. The station, given the news that it is under financial pressure, must lay off staff, and while the competent Aaron is let go, the shallow but silky Tom gets a promotion to the network in New York. At the end, Jane must decide whether to follow her lover or her friend—and chooses another path instead.

Background: James L. Brooks wrote *Broadcast News* especially for actress Debra Winger, with whom he had worked very successfully on his previous film, *Terms of Endearment* (1983), but she turned down because she was pregnant. Holly Hunter took it on just days before shooting began. In a nod to real television journalism, Brooks cast Peter Hackes as Paul Moore, a tough network representative. Hackes was a veteran news correspondent for NBC News and was long associated with the long-running *Monitor* weekend radio show. He had retired shortly before filming.

The film features Robert Prosky, a long-time Capitol Hill resident who first appeared with Arena Stage in 1958, became an important part of its repertory company, and ultimately performed in over 100 productions there. He broke into motion pictures in *Thief* (1981), when he was 51 and thereafter had a steady career in Hollywood movies. Prosky also had a significant Broadway roles in dramas such as *Glengarry Glen Ross* and *A Walk in the Woods*. He also starred in several network TV series, most notably in *Hill Street Blues*. Prosky died in Washington in December 2008, just short of his 78th birthday.

Production Notes: Rare for movies shot in Washington, *Broadcast News* generally eschews the familiar DC landmarks and standard setups but instead concentrates more on DC itself as a city. Its one exception to avoiding the overly familiar is a romantic nighttime scene with Hunter and Hurt in front of the Jefferson Memorial. Moreover, director Brooks shot almost the entire film in DC locations. For example, rather than shoot on an LA set, the filmmakers used space at 1001 Pennsylvania Avenue, NW, for the studio and offices of the television station in the film. The building was empty and being renovated at the time, so the production could fill out the space to their requirements.

Released at the very end of 1987, *Broadcast News* was a solid commercial success, earning over $50 million in box office receipts. Besides its positive reviews country-wide, it received seven Academy Award nominations (Best Picture, Best Original Screenplay, Best Cinematography, Best Film Editing, as well as nominations for the three acting leads–Hunter, Hurt and Brooks). In no category did the film take home a trophy, yet earlier it had won four major awards from the New York City Film Critics Circle and had also been honored at the Berlin Film Festival. The film made the American Film Institute's list of America's 100 Funniest Movies.

Comment: *Broadcast News* was a critical favorite, winning some of the best reviews of the year. There was praise for Brooks' handling of the journalistic milieu and for the all-around solid acting. Roger Ebert of the *Chicago Sun Times* found it "as knowledgeable about the TV news-gathering process as any movie ever made, but it also has insights into the more personal matter of how people use high-pressure jobs as a way of avoiding time alone with themselves." Vincent Canby of *The New York Times* felt the three principals "become emotionally involved in ways that would seem heartbreaking to people less ambitious. Here it's the material of high comedy." Richard Corliss of *Time* agreed, saying "all the performers are tops" in "this judicious, irresistible romantic comedy."

DC/Hill Notes: *Broadcast News* used locations all over the city, many of them new and imaginative. One sequence in the film uses a longtime downtown diner, Whitlow's, across the street from the FBI Building, but with another name (Whitlow's has since moved).

The anchor desk and on-air broadcast newsroom scenes were filmed in the backstage area of the Wolftrap Farmpark for the Performing Arts, in nearby Vienna, VA.

Albert Brooks' character Aaron Altman lives in an ample townhouse on the 600 block of East Capitol Street (see photo insert). The exteriors and interiors were used extensively. *(Personal note: my own house on Capitol Hill was scouted by the film's location manager for possible use as Altman's house, but it didn't make the cut: too small.)*

Goofs: Jane (Hunter) gives a cab driver directions to "Capps" bar on "17th and Vermont," but there is no 17th Street and Vermont, NW (the two streets do not intersect).

Jane (again in a cab) orders the cabbie to "take Connecticut over to 15th and then straight down Vermont, and we should bypass Thomas Circle," but Connecticut Avenue and 15th Street, NW, do not intersect and going straight down Vermont takes you right through Thomas Circle, not around it. In fact, Brooks here is cleverly playing with the idea of a DC control freak telling foreign cab drivers where to go in the city.

Tom (Hurt), calling for an address for a news assignment, gets "17204 Colorado," a totally fabricated address.

There is an airport scene which takes place inside the BWI (Baltimore-Washington International Airport) concourse, but Tom goes to the plane in a Dulles mobile lounge.

21 GARDENS OF STONE

1987. TriStar Pictures, 112 minutes, color.

Director: Francis Ford Coppola.

Screenplay by Ronald Bass from the novel of the same name by Nicholas Proffitt.

Cinematography: Jordan Cronenweth.

Editing: Barry Malkin.

Musical Score: Carmine Coppola.

Principal Cast:

James Caan.......	Sgt. 1st Class Clell Hazard	Lonette McKee................	Batty Rae Nelson
Anjelica Houston..............	Samantha Davis	Sam Bottoms.........................	1st Lt. Webber
James Earl Jones ..	Sgt. Maj. "Goody" Nelson	Elias Koteas...................	Spec. Pete Deveber
D.B. Sweeney......	Spec. Jack "Jackie" Willow	Laurence Fishburne..............	Sgt. Flanagan
Dean Stockwell..........	Capt. Homer Thomas	Casey Siemaszko.........	Sgt. Albert Wildman
Mary Stuart Masterson............	Rachel Feld	Peter Masterson	Col. Feld
Dick A. Williams	Sgt. "Slasher" Williams	Carlin Glynn..............................	Mrs. Feld

Synopsis: It is 1968, and Army Sergeant First Class Clell Hazard, a hardened Korean and Vietnam War veteran who wants to train soldiers for combat, is assigned to a job he hates. He is part of the "Old Guard," the ceremonial honor guard based at Fort Myer, Virginia, which guards the Tomb of the Unknown Soldier at Arlington National Cemetery. However, he is heartened when a new soldier, Jackie Willow, the son of an old friend and fellow veteran, joins his platoon. Willow is eager to fight in Vietnam, but Hazard feels the war is being fought ineptly and worries for him. Hazard's girlfriend, Samantha Davis, is a journalist for *The Washington Post* who opposes the War for political reasons. When Willow's father, and Hazard's friend, dies of a heart attack, the sergeant comes to look upon the youngster as his son.

Willow courts and eventually marries a Colonel's daughter, Rachel, who also opposes the Vietnam War and fears for her husband's safety. Willow is promoted to sergeant and, after a recommendation to attend Officer's

Candidate School, he becomes a second lieutenant and is ordered to serve in a combat unit in Vietnam. Hazard then learns that Jack Willow has been killed in action in Vietnam, and he oversees his burial at Arlington National Cemetery while still a member of the "Old Guard."

Background (of the gossipy kind): While the film was being shot, tragedy struck the Coppola family. On May 27, 1986, director Coppola's son, Gian Carlo, was killed in a boating accident on the South River in Maryland. As United Press International reported at the time:

> *The son of movie director Francis Ford Coppola was killed, and actor Ryan O'Neal's son was injured when their motorboat ran under another boat's towline, officials said today. Gian Carlo Coppola, 23, suffered massive head injuries and was pronounced dead on arrival at Anne Arundel County General Hospital at 6:20 p.m. Monday, a hospital spokeswoman said. The Memorial Day accident occurred on the South River, off the shores of Edgewater, a tourist town with numerous marinas. Police said the only other person aboard the boat was Griffin Patrick O'Neal, 23, son of Ryan O'Neal. Griffin O'Neal suffered a minor shoulder injury but refused treatment, police said.*

The report noted that the two young men were visiting the area because Coppola's father was shooting a movie, *Gardens of Stone*, in which Griffin O'Neal was cast in the role of Jackie Willow. Earlier, O'Neal had been arrested in nearby Rosslyn, charged by police with reckless driving and carrying a concealed weapon (a knife). O'Neal was charged with manslaughter in the incident, and D.B. Sweeney was hired in to take on the Willow role.

Perhaps in part because it was snake-bit after the incident, the film received only a limited release in the spring of 1987 and ended with gross revenues well below its production costs ($13 million).

Comment: Beyond its limited release, *Gardens of Stone* did not fair well critically. Many reviewers compared it, fairly or not, with Coppola's other Vietnam film *Apocalypse Now*, and found it wanting. Fairly typical of the critical tone was Vincent Canby's assessment in *The New York Times*:

> *In these moments in which the peace of the present is layered with desolation from the past..., there is an emotional resonance in "Gardens of Stone" that*

is otherwise remarkably absent. Though a seriously conceived film about the American experience in Vietnam, "Gardens of Stone" has somehow wound up having the consistency and the kick of melted vanilla ice cream.

DC Notes: The film uses extensively both Arlington National Cemetery and Fort Myer, where the Old Guard is stationed. The changing of the Guard at the Tomb of the Unknown is shown as well as the amphitheater at that site. Sequences feature the parade ground at Fort Myer and other sectors of the base.

A variety of other locations in Washington were also used, among them:

An apartment building (exterior and lobby) on New Hampshire Avenue, NW where James Caan's sergeant lives.

The Woman's National Democratic Club at 1526 New Hampshire Avenue, NW, where the wedding scene takes **place.**

The interior of the Islamic Center of Washington on Massachusetts Avenue, NW, which stood in for a Persian carpet store.

Independence Avenue, SW, outside the Department of Agriculture, where Willow (Sweeney) uses a phone booth.

Goofs: Rachel (Masterson), talking to her Army sweetheart, says she is staying at "2218 M Street" in Georgetown, which is actually in the West End.

22 NO WAY OUT

 1987. Orion Pictures, 114 minutes, color.

Director: Roger Donaldson.

Screenplay by Robert Garland and Laura Ziskin, screen story by Robert Garland based on the novel *The Big Clock* by Kenneth Fearing.

Cinematography: John Alcott.

Editing: William Hoy and Neil Travis.

Musical Score: Maurice Jarre.

Principal Cast:

Kevin Costner	Lt. Cdr. Tom Farrell	Fred D. Thompson	CIA Dir. Marshall
Gene Hackman	David Brice	Iman	Nina Beka
Will Patton	Scott Pritchard	Leon Russom	Kevin O'Brien
Sean Young	Susan Atwell	Dennis Burkley	Mate
George Dzundza	Sam Hesselman	Marshall Bell	Contra # 1
Howard Duff	Senator Duvall	Chris D.	Contra # 2
Jason Bernhard	Maj. Donovan	David Paymer	Technician David

Synopsis: Navy Lt. Commander Tom Farrell has a torrid affair with Susan Atwell, unaware she is also seeing the Secretary of Defense, David Brice. Farrell, on a deployment, becomes a hero and returns to serve in the Pentagon in Brice's office. Brice then learns that Susan has another lover and, in a jealous rage, accidentally kills her. Brice wants to confess, but his right hand Scott Pritchard (a closeted gay who loves Brice) persuades him to cover the incident and blame it on "Yuri," an invented KGB agent. Brice asks Farrell to head the investigation to find Yuri, placing the commander in the position of tracking down himself.

The only forensic evidence in the case is a damaged Polaroid negative from Susan's apartment, showing her and her mystery lover. It requires elaborate computerized enhancement to be seen. Farrell tries to slow down the processing so he will not be implicated, while he searches a computer printout for evidence of gifts linking Brice to Susan. Farrell obtains the printout before the photo becomes clear and confronts Brice with the evidence. Brice shifts the blame to Pritchard, saying that his loyal assistant was jealous of his relationship with Susan. A devastated Pritchard commits suicide. Though now cleared, Farrell is still taken away for questioning. One of the interrogators is Farrell's landlord, who addresses Farrell in Russian. Farrell answers in Russian; he is, in fact, the real "Yuri," a "mole" for most of his life.

Background: This film's corkscrew plot was used in the 1948 film *The Big Clock,* which was based on a novel by Kenneth Fearing. The earlier film, a murder mystery in *film noir* style, starred Ray Milland and Charles Laughton. This *No Way Out*, with a new story and screenplay by Robert Garland, used the basic plot elements but placed them in a very different context, making it a DC-based suspense film tinged with Cold War politics and sabotage. It confirmed the star status of the then 32 year old Kevin Costner, who had starred earlier in the year in *The Untouchables* as Eliot Ness. Though very well reviewed, the film did not gain any recognition during the 1987 awards season. It did decent box office, earning back more than double its production costs.

Comment: The film had (for the times) a very risque back seat scene between Costner and Young in a limo which became a kind of marker for the time. A pair of commentators gave a sense of the couple's fervor: "The heat from the lovemaking of Costner and Young in a limousine is enough to make the vehicle throw a rod."

DC Notes: The film was a full location shoot during the spring of 1986, with sequences captured in Annapolis, Arlington, Virginia (where Arlington Ridge Road appears), and throughout DC.

Two major downtown hotels–The Hotel Washington and the Omni Shoreham on Connecticut Avenue, NW–figured in the plot, as did a lengthy Georgetown sequence, notorious for an egregious–perhaps the ***most*** egregious–filming goofs ever seen in Washington movies (see **Goofs** below).

The Pentagon was featured prominently in the picture, and extensive filming was done outside, and inside, the building. According to the location manager on the film, Stuart Neumann, both the Department of Defense (DoD) and the General Services Administration (GSA) were helpful on the project. DoD helped with research and gave a tour of the building to the filmmakers to help them prepare, while the GSA, formal owners of the Pentagon (Defense is a lessee) provided its own protective services for the shoot itself. The filming took two or three days, Neumann recalls. It remains the only Hollywood film that has used locations inside the Pentagon.

Goofs: Costner Lt. Cmdr. Ferrell (Costner) leaves a party in a limo from the Omni Shoreham in NW and, in the next scene, the vehicle is coming eastbound on Pennsylvania Avenue near the National Gallery, a mighty abrupt turn.

The Secretary of Defense (Hackman) uses a giant "stretch" limousine as his official car. These behemoths may have been in use by Hollywood celebrities, but they were *not* provided to cabinet members.

During the film, security officials inside the Pentagon are ordered to do a complete "search" of the building, and they do so in about two hours. This is a complete impossibility since the Pentagon is the world's largest office building by floor area and boasts 17.5 miles of corridors in its five rings. It would probably take days for such a search.

Notorious Car and Foot Chase: After driving out of the Pentagon's parking garage, Ferrell chases another car with two hitmen (going after a friend of Susan's) who are heading into town eastbound on the Whitehurst Freeway. Ferrell cuts off the car and crashes into it, then jumps over the Freeway metal barrier down into Georgetown. He is then chased, running first along K Street and then down the C&O Canal path before ducking into a Metro stop. The Metro post is marked "Georgetown," a stop that is famously wrong since it was precisely Georgetown that has never had a subway stop due to local residents' protests against having the system in their neighborhood. Once inside, Ferrell scurries down the escalator and jumps on to Baltimore subway train, only to–after a brisk ride–run up another escalator into the Georgetown Mall (no subway there either) to warn the friend–thus doing a complete loop.

(Personal Note: when I saw this film in the fall of 1987 at a DC cinema and the "Georgetown" Metro stop appeared, the packed audience exploded in laughter and derision, with quite a bit of popcorn thrown at the screen. The goof was the more egregious because Georgetown residents had famously refused to have a Metro stop built in their "tony" neighborhood—and everybody in Washington knew it.)

23 SUSPECT

1987. Tri-Star Pictures, 121 minutes, color.

Director: Peter Yates.

Screenplay: Eric Roth.

Cinematography: Billy Williams.

Editing: Ray Lovejoy.

Music: Michael Kamen.

Principal Cast :

Cher .... Kathleen Riley	Fred Melamed .... Morty Rosenthal
Dennis Quaid .... Eddie Sanger	Lisbeth Bartlett .... Marilyn
Liam Nesson .... Carl Wayne Anderson	Paul D'Amato .... Michael
John Mahoney .... Judge Matthew Helms	Bernie McInerney .... Walter
Joe Mantegna .... Charlie Stella	Thomas Barbour .... Justice Lowell
Philip Bosco .... Paul Gray	Katie O'Hare .... Elizabeth Quinn
E. Katherine Kerr ... Cong. Grace Comiskey	Bill Cobbs .... Judge Franklin

Synopsis: DC public defender Kathleen Riley is assigned to represent Carl Anderson, a homeless deaf-mute accused of murdering a file clerk at the Justice Department whose body is found in the Potomac. Anderson is accused of her murder after he is found with the woman's purse near a K Street parking lot in Georgetown. Slick Eddie Sanger, a dairy lobbyist, is in the jury pool and is approved to serve by Riley. A bit of a hustler, Sanger begins investigating the details of the murder himself, and eventually begins an unethical investigation working together with Riley. Tough trial judge Matthew Helms, with ambitions for a seat on the US Court of Appeals, comes to suspect that Riley may be collaborating with Sanger but has no real proof.

With a key found on the victim's body, Riley and Sanger break into the Justice Department and learn that the key unlocks a file cabinet containing trial transcripts that implicate federal officials in a rigged 1968 case. Further, Riley finds an audiotape in the victim's car with a confession by a Supreme Court justice of his own involvement in the case fixing.

Her findings, however, place her and Sanger–who have become lovers –in jeopardy. Back in the courtroom, there is a flurry of activity during which Kathleen launches a surprise accusation against a participant in the 1968 case who, she claims, had killed the clerk because she had discovered his involvement in it.

Background: The director of *Suspect*, Peter Yates, was an Englishman who established himself in American cinema with *Bullitt* (1968), the film with which he is probably most identified. Later, he would gain renown for his direction of another very American film, *Breaking Away* (1979) He proved a versatile director, handling action pictures, comedies, and character studies equally in his 40 year career (he died in 2011).

Irish actor Liam Neeson, though he plays a deaf-mute in the film and doesn't say a word, first gained notice from his supporting turn in *Suspect* before he went on to leading roles. Cher was at her movie career peak when the film was made. Although this film was not her finest two hours (see **Comment** below), her very next project was *Moonstruck*, where she shone and won an Oscar for her performance.

The film did only mediocre box office, earning just short of $19 million in gross receipts.

Comment: *Suspect* had a competent director at the helm and a solid, veteran cast, as well as an intriguing premise with some decent plot twists and some moments of real suspense. However, it goes wrong with its tortured ethics and a ludicrous "surprise" ending. Cher, as the dogged but morose public defender, has her status as an attorney undercut way too much as she increasingly comes to depend on the clues and leads provided by the avid jury member Quaid, whose motivation–other than boredom–is not too evident. Not to mention that it's hard to sympathize with a character who is so blatantly guilty of jury-tampering.

Cher's final "j'accuse" revelation in the courtroom just cannot be taken seriously–it is almost farcical. This revelation seems like a clumsy attempt by the screenwriter Eric Roth (who went on to pen important screenplays like *The Insider, Munich,* and *Ali*) to quickly wrap up a story of which he had lost control. Roger Ebert's review at the time said Cher's outburst "made me rethink the whole plot, and made it look less like a case of jury-tampering than audience-tampering." Couldn't have said it better myself.

DC/Hill Notes: The bulk of the film was shot in studios in Toronto. The courtroom set itself, dressed in unadorned brown wood panelling, was based on models studied by production designers who toured the DC Superior Court on Indiana Avenue, NW. Both exteriors and interiors of the real Superior Court were used in the film, including the entrances, the lobby, and the third floor (which contains the courtrooms). Director Yates, in commentary for the film's 2006 DVD release, said the production was also able to use the actual holding cells (when lawyer-defendant consultations take place) in the Superior Court building. The streets around the court, on Indiana Avenue, were also featured.

Several major sequences take place in the one-time parking lot on the Georgetown Waterfront off K Street, NW (now a public park), which serves as the film's "crime scene." The principals keep returning to an abandoned car there to seek clues to the murder. The apartment of Riley (Cher) is in a building north of Georgetown. There is a spooky night sequence shot at the site of the Federal Triangle Metro station just off 12th Street, NW. There are also some night shots taken outside the Justice Department on 10th Street, NW (with the Natural History Museum in the background) and around Union Station.

A key scene—and the best choreographed moment of suspense in the picture—has Riley and Sanger (Quaid) in a major "law library" trying to avoid being seen together by Judge Helms (Mahoney). It was shot in the library of the DAR Building off 17th Street, NW. In Yates' somewhat sour DVD commentary on the shoot, the director criticized the DAR, saying, *interalia*, that the organization had refused an additional day of shooting. His vinegary remarks, however, were belied by a letter at the time from the films's location manager, Frawley Becker, telling the DAR that they had "helped enormously in supplying for us the perfect location for an important moment of the film."

On Capitol Hill, Riley is seen driving to work, going west towards the Capitol down Pennsylvania Avenue, SE near—with the local Distads service station in view—when her car is attacked by a gang of kids at roughly the level of 5th Street SE. Her stalled car creates a traffic jam on Pennsylvania at Seward Square, SE.

Goofs: Lobbyist Sanger bounds up to do business on Capitol Hill by passing through the Grant Memorial, more a tourist route than one a lobbyist would use (they would likely use a side entrance to the Capitol). The shot's purpose seems to be to provide yet another view of the Capitol dome.

Sanger refers to himself as a "congressional advisor," a euphemism not used by lobbyists (it sounds too much like a congressional staff position).

In a too-abrupt transition, Riley is seen leaving her office near the court buildings in near Northwest DC only to next appear at the Federal Triangle Metro stop a mile away.

In one scene, a nasty homeless character calls from a non-existent phone booth at the left front of Union Station.

In the film, during the jury selection process, jurors are called and questioned by name, when, in reality, they are always referred to by their juror number.

As the leads scurry through the Justice Department trying to avoid detection, security guards off-screen converse about something on the "14th and 16th floors," when the building has only five stories.

24 CHANCES ARE

1989. Tri-Star Pictures , 108 minutes, color.

Director: Emile Ardolino.

Screenplay: Perry and Randy Howze.

Cinematography: William A. Fraker.

Editing: Harry Keramidas.

Original Music: Maurice Jarre.

Principal Cast:

Cybil Shepherd	Corinne Jeffries	Josef Sommer	Judge Fenwick
Robert Downey, Jr.	Alex Finch	Joe Grifasi	Omar
Ryan O'Neal	Phillip Train	Henderson Forsythe	Ben Bradlee
Mary Stuart Masterson	Miranda Jeffries	Fran Ryan	Mavis Talmadge
Christopher McDonald	Louie Jeffries	Susan Ruttan	Woman in Bookstore

Synopsis: 1964, Washington, DC: promising district attorney Louie Jeffries is killed in an auto accident. However, in heaven he avoids the pearly gates and is "reborn" instantly on earth. More than 20 years later, his widow Corinne still misses him as she raises their daughter Miranda (whom Louie never knew). Family friend Phillip Train (a *Washington Post* reporter) is devoted to Corinne, but she rejects him romantically. When Phillip brings a young man, Alex Finch, to meet the Jeffries, Alex (who is Louie reborn) realizes he is Corinne's dead husband reincarnated.

Alex's memories of his life as Louie reemerge just as Miranda (his own daughter) becomes interested in him. He spurns her advances and, instead, begins courting Corinne. Meanwhile, Phillip's attempts to court Corinne stumble when she comes to realize who Alex really is, and Alex himself senses he must absent himself. Alex's presence also helps resolve a long dormant criminal case Louie was working on at his death and for which he was murdered. A timely bump on Alex's head comes at just the right time, and, while in the hospital, he is administered a special injection he should have received in heaven which wipes out his previous life. Once revived as a "new" Alex, the couples can sort out their lives.

Comment: As one of Hollywood's many Heaven-sent, body-shifting films, *Chances Are* may not be the best, but it exudes some charm in what is an almost dewy Washington context (the city, shot during a benign Washington springtime, looks great). The quartet of stars display a decent rapport, and all–except for Ryan O'Neal–received good notices at the time. Critic Roger Ebert thought Cybil Shepherd was effective because she "never goes for easy laughs but plays her character seriously." He also found Robert Downey, Jr. "convincing and good" and "filled with confidence at the emotional center" of the movie. *The Washington Post*'s Rita Kempley particularly liked Mary Stuart Masterson whom she found "pensively provocative as Miranda, something of a teen-age Kim Novak."

The film, a fairly early 1989 release, was not a box office magnet; it more or less made its money back for Tri-Star Pictures.

DC/Hill Notes: The film did considerable location shooting in Georgetown, on the Mall, and on Capitol Hill. Corinne (Shepherd), for example, lives in Georgetown, on its cobbled street (at house number 3410). Phillip (O'Neal), the journalist, apparently lives on Capitol Hill, since we see Alex (Downey, Jr.), driving to Phillips' house, pulling up and parking on what looks like New Jersey Avenue, SE, below the Capitol.

Also, Corinne works as a curator at the Smithsonian Castle, and you can see her entering and exiting the Enid Haupt Garden on the Castle's south side. She also has the extraordinary luck of having her car parked right outside the Haupt Garden gate on Independence Avenue, SW.

In one sequence, Shepherd and Downey, Jr. spend a bucolic day out at Glen Echo Park (MD), where they observe the park's well known carousel. This is followed by a drive back towards Washington over the Memorial Bridge. There is also a scene of Phillip and Miranda (Masterson) walking alongside the Lincoln Memorial reflecting pool, and one of Downey, Jr. musing at night on the steps of the Jefferson Memorial.

Early in the film, a nefarious deal is made on Roosevelt Island. The film's two courtroom scenes were filmed at the Old Rockville Courthouse in Rockville, Maryland.

Thirteen years after Jason Robards, Jr. won an Oscar for his portrayal of Ben Bradlee in *All the President's Men* (q.v.), the Post editor is portrayed again, this time by Henderson Forsythe. Bradlee himself appeared in the 1993 film version of *Born Yesterday* (q.v.) but as the Secretary of the Navy–not himself.

Goofs: The film indicates that Corinne is working on the premiere of the First Lady's exhibit for the Smithsonian (in 1989), when the exhibit was, in fact, inaugurated many years earlier at the Smithsonian Museum of American History.

Corinne's very swank and large office, supposedly in the Smithsonian Castle, is way beyond the imaginings of any regular Smithsonian employee.

Corinne gets a donation check from Mavis Talmadge made out to the "Smithsonian Institute" (not Institution).

Tracking Shot – The Nineties

Though movies on politics and politicians could hardly claim a track record of boffo box office, Hollywood studios continued to find and develop enough scripts with Washington settings to produce a significant boomlet in such films during the 1990's. During this decade political personages had become more and more familiar to Americans–if not more esteemed–especially through television's greater reach, as multiple channels proliferated to challenge the long-established national networks.

Expanded news networks and coverage and proliferating chat shows (all constantly needing talking heads) exposed many more political actors on the airwaves. Even presidential candidates lowered themselves to late-night gambols (Bill Clinton playing the sax on Arsenio Hall's show). There was also C-SPAN, hardly the sexiest television and never claiming a large audience but supplying an endless succession of clips for other news outlets showing legislators (often not in the most attractive light). Opening to little fanfare in 1979 with House floor coverage, C-SPAN added Senate coverage in 1986.

In a more and more media saturated land, politicians became constant--if still usually bit players–on the national entertainment scene. By the end of the decade, political players and themes were accepted enough that they could form the basis of a mainstream television show, *The West Wing,* created by Aaron Sorkin. Sorkin's long-running drama (1999-2006) on the administration of President Jed Bartlet and his merry band was the only politically-themed program to ever rank in the Top Ten of TV's Nielsen ratings.

Films that treated Congress or congressional actors included (besides the ones covered in this chapter) *Quiz Show* (1994), *Time Cop* (1994), *National Lampoon's Senior Trip* (1995) *The Birdcage* (1996), *Striptease* (1996), *Contact* (1997), *G.I Jane* (1997), and *Bulworth* (1998). There were even more which dealt with presidents or the Presidency (again, avoiding listed films): *JFK* (1991), *Clear and Present Danger* (1994), *Nixon* (1995), *First Kid* (1996), *Independence Day* (1996), *Mars Attacks!* (1996), and *Shadow Conspiracy* (1997) and *Air Force One* (1997).

It need hardly be repeated that the vast majority of politicians in these films, comedies or dramas, are corrupt, inept, or stupid—or some combination of all three. The only exceptions are the very macho president/flyboy (Bill Pullman) who challenges the aliens in *Independence Day* (1996), the kick-ass president (Harrison Ford) in *Air Force One* (1997), and the amenable Michael Douglas as *The American President*.

Besides movies of a political bent during this decade, there was a miscellany of others in the comedy, mystery, and spy genre, and one complete outlier, *Slam*, a unique film in this volume.

25 TRUE COLORS

1991. Paramount Pictures, 111 minutes, color.

Director: Herbert Ross.

Screenplay: Kevin Wade.

Cinematography: Dante Spinotti.

Editing: Robert M. Reitano and Stephen A. Rotter.

Musical Score: Trevor Jones.

Principal Cast:

John Cusack	Peter Burton	Dina Merrill	Joan Stiles
James Spader	Tim Garrity	Paul Guilfoyle	John Laury
Imogen Stubbs	Diana Stiles	Philip Bosco	Sen. Frank Steubens
Richard Widmark	Sen. James Stiles	Brad Sullivan	FBI Agent Abernathy
Mandy Patinkin	John Palmeri	Don McManus	Doug Stubblefield

Synopsis: At the University of Virginia's Law School in 1983, apparently mismatched roommates Tim Garrity and Peter Burton become fast friends. Garrity is a WASP blueblood who plans to dedicate himself to public service, while Burton (nee Burtokski) is a working-class New Englander eager to get ahead in politics at any cost. Garrity's girlfriend is Diana, the sophisticated daughter of the powerful Senator James Stiles of Connecticut, and Tim looks to have a rosy future ahead of him as a Justice Department official. The nakedly ambitious Burton latches on to the smooth Garrity to use him for his own ends, including getting a staff job with the senator.

When Tim and Diana encounter some differences, Peter moves on the vulnerable Diana and beds her, and the two men have it out on a ski trip. Tim basically cedes to his best friend, while Peter wins the prize of Diana and weds her. In his bid to get ahead, Burton gets involved with Palmeri, a Bridgeport racketeer, and he also tries to blackmail Senator Stiles in order to secure a New England House seat for himself in the 1990 elections. Garrity is called upon by the Justice Department to get the goods on his old roomy by working undercover in his campaign.

Background: Some significant Hollywood talent was involved in *True Colors*, but the stars were not aligned for a success this time. It is a fairly honest attempt by director Herbert Ross and screenwriter Kevin Wade to fashion a political film that is more naturalistic than many other Hollywood dramas of the genre. Ross began his performance life as a dancer and a choreographer and was a major director on stage and in film by the mid-1970's with films like *The Sunshine Boys, The Turning Point,* and *The Goodbye Girl.* He had a long association with playwright Neil Simon, several of whose works he transferred to the screen. *True Colors* was made on the downside of his career; after it, he made only two other features (another Ross film, *Protocol,* is also featured in this book). Kevin Wade's most significant success came with his scenario for *Working Girl* (1988), written just before *True Colors.*

Comment: The film highlights the class differences between the WASP Garrity and the prole Burton–a small-time Willie Stark–and Spader and Cusack are well-cast in these contrasting roles. It could be argued, though, that it is highly unlikely that two such characters of such differing intrinsic values would remain "best friends" over almost a decade. Veteran Richard Widmark (in his last film appearance) does his best to bring some dimension to the role of an influential, if flawed, lawmaker who eventually becomes father-in-law to the social-climbing Burton.

Though more realistic than many films about Congress, *True Colors* ultimately displays the thoroughgoing cynicism about politics so prevalent in Hollywood (see **Politics and Film**). Burton's creed is the crass "Don't get caught," and Wade's script highlights one-liners like: "There are only two things that can truly wreck a man's political career–getting caught with a live boy or a dead girl." Such smart cracks are in tune with the prevailing American view that politicians simply cannot be trusted to protect the commonweal. Also, the morale of the film–if taken literally–is that you cannot escape or redeem a deprived upbringing, a particularly harsh and deterministic verdict.

Though it offers a relatively complex take on American politics, *True Colors* was almost invisible as a feature film when it came out in 1991 and since. The picture was barely released in theaters and did less than $500,000 worth of business before it fell off a cliff.

DC Notes: The production did only a couple days shooting in Washington and, according to Stuart Stein, a cameraman on the shoot, the filmmakers "didn't have much of a feel for Washington." Most of the location shooting was in Virginia.

The first Washington scene shows the protagonists in a red convertible tooling west down Pennsylvania Avenue, NW, past the National Archives. Excited by their new DC jobs, Garrity (Spader) beams outside the Justice Department, while Burton (Cusack) eagerly bounds up the steps of the Russell Senate Office Building.

Characters are seen leaving the Georgetown Mall, and moving across the street to a parking garage with a sign announcing: "Reserved for Peking Pavilion and American Cafe customers only."

For the first time in a Hollywood movie a scene is shot in the interior of the Kennedy Center. It shows Tim and Diana (Stubbs) coming out of the Opera House and sitting on the entry steps of the theater, debating their future together.

Goofs: While Peter and Tim ride on a ski lift (in Montana), Peter explains that he has been given a promotion in Senator Stiles' office, having been named "chief administrative aide." The correct Hill term would be "administrative assistant."

Garrity, who is supposedly working ***undercover*** for the Department of Justice, is put up at the very conspicuous Willard Hotel on Pennsylvania Avenue–not very far undercover.

26 THE DISTINGUISHED GENTLEMAN

 1992. Hollywood Pictures, 112 minutes, color.

Director: Jonathan Lynn.

Screenplay: Marty Kaplan and Jonathan Reynolds.

Cinematography: Gabriel Beristain.

Editing: Barry B. Leirer and Tony Lombardo.

Musical Score: Randy Edelman.

Principal Cast:

Eddie Murphy.....	Thomas Jefferson Johnson	Charles S. Dutton...	Cong. Elijah Hawkins
Lane Smith	Cong. Dick Dodge	Victor Rivers	Armando
Sheryl Lee Ralph	Miss Loretta	Chi McBride	Homer
Joe Don Baker	Olaf Andersen	Sonny Jim Gaines	Van Dyke
Victoria Rowell	Celia Kirby	Noble Willingham...................	Zeke Bridges
Grant Shaud	Arthur Reinhardt	Gary Frank	Iowa
Kevin McCarthy..............	Terry Corrigan	James Garner.................	Cong. Jeff Johnson

Synopsis: Con man Thomas Jefferson Johnson hears there are big bucks to be had in Congress and uses the death of a long time Congressman from his Florida district, Jeff Johnson (who has died of a heart attack while having sex), to gain the seat. Shortening his middle name to "Jeff" Johnson, he re-uses the other Johnson's campaign materials. He runs on name recognition alone, and wins the seat as the "name you know."

As a very junior member, he is the lowest of the low, but brings to Washington his own con game brain trust, headed by Miss Loretta, to dip into the capital's "money pot." He also gets to know both the most influential members, like Power and Industry Committee chairman Dick Dodge, and the most bountiful lobbyists, like Terry Corrigan. He thrives for a time, but, as Johnson learns the congressional game, he starts to see how corruption strangles issues such as campaign finance reform and environmental protection. In the latter case, his consciousness is raised by Celia Kirby, a bright young advocate on environmental issues. Further, he comes to suspect that an electric power company may be giving cancer to kids in his district. Ultimately, Jeff finds himself double-crossed by the venal Dodge and gets back at him with what he knows best, a real confidence game.

Comments: *The Distinguished Gentleman* was the first outright congressional comedy film since *The Senator Was Indiscreet* (1947), but this one had a distinct DC setting while the latter took place entirely in a movie-made New York City. The picture is rare among Hollywood efforts in that it really shows something of the inner workings of a congressman's life: actually operating with staff, making deals, sizing up fellow members, working with lobbyists, and fashioning legislation. It is also, of course, a farce whose core joke is that the work of a representative turns on exactly the same kind of hustles in which the dodgy Murphy character already excels. Its rancid vision of the institution meant that it received no cooperation from people on the Hill. This is Congress as Con Game.

The film's easy cynicism also carries a crass '90's sheen, its corruption being much more about money than about power. Its sarcastic spirit is nicely capsulized by the silly (and funny) victory speech that the political novice Johnson gives as his accepts his office before a boisterous crowd. It consists entirely of political cliches:

> *"The issue is change...the people have spoken; ask not what your country can do for you; you have nothing to fear but fear itself; if you can't stand the heat, get out of the kitchen; live free or die; and, in conclusion: Read my lips!"*

The crowd roars.

Like other Eddie Murphy films of the time, however, *The Distinguished Gentleman* banks plenty on the star's toothy charm and clever voice characterizations but without a very incisive script (co-written by Disney Executive Marty Kaplan) to back him up. Frankly, the screenplay is dated, presenting a 1990's House culture which hearkens back more to the earlier days of super-powerful committee chairmen (personified by scenery-chewing Lane

Smith as a House autocrat). The movie is a harmless diversion but punchless, too, and ultimately demeaning towards congressional life. Commentator Tom Rosenstiel found it a sad chapter in the evolution of these films:

> "*These (congressional) films trace an arc, from hope in* Mr. Smith *to madcap fun in* The Senator Was Indiscreet *to a sense of renewed expectations about government in* Advise and Consent *to simple disgust and antipathy in* The Distinguished Gentleman."

DC/Hill Notes: The filmmakers did some work on the Hill and in downtown DC, as well as in Baltimore. Locations include Pennsylvania Avenue, NW, intersecting at 7th Street, NW, where a car wreck scene takes place, the Tidal Basin at night (with a sweet boy-girl stroll), the White House from Pennsylvania Avenue, and Union Station. Also, the car ride across the Memorial Bridge from Arlington towards Washington–so common in DC movies–is again revisited.

One Capitol Hill night sequence takes place at the Ulysses S. Grant Memorial at the foot of the Capitol. Another shows Johnson's car drive east down East Capitol Street, passing the Folger Library on his right. He turns north and parks at the apartment building at 3rd Street and East Capitol, NE, where his girlfriend lives.

Goofs: The impressive congressional office building that Congressman Johnson (Murphy) enters is, in reality, the Hall of Justice in downtown Los Angeles.

The highly desirable committee assignment that Jeff seeks is one on "Power and Industry," a made-up name.

The office of Rep. Dodge (Smith) has an impossible view of the Washington Monument outside the window.

In an era before cell phones, the film uses not one, but two fake phone booths: one on Pennsylvania Avenue, NW across from the Federal Trade Commission and one located at the Grant Memorial.

There is a scene with Dodge being accosted by a senior citizen in the outside gallery of Union Station, which is apparently standing in for a congressional office building.

27 A FEW GOOD MEN

1992. Produced by Castle Rock Entertainment for Columbia Pictures, 138 minutes, color.

Director: Ron Reiner.

Screenplay, adapted from his play: Aaron Sorkin.

Cinematography: Robert Richardson.

Editing: Robert Leighton.

Original Music: Marc Shaiman.

Principal Cast:

Tom Cruise	LTJG Daniel Kaffee	Wolfgang Bodison	Cpl. Howard Dawson
Demi Moore	LCDR JoAnne Galloway	J. A. Preston	Judge Julius Randolph
Jack Nicholson	Col. Nathan R. Jessup	Matt Craven	Lt. Dave Sprading
Kevin Bacon	Capt. Jack Ross	Christopher Guest	Dr. Stone
Kiefer Sutherland	Lt. Jonathan Kendrick	Xander Berkeley	Capt. Whitaker
Kevin Pollak	LTJG Sam Weinberg	Noah Wyle	Cpl. Jeffrey Barnes
J.T. Walsh	Lt. Col. Matthew Markinson	Cuba Gooding, Jr.	Cpl. Carl Hammaker
James Marshall	PFC Louden Downy	John M. Jackson	Capt. West

Synopsis: After an incident at Guantanamo Bay, two junior marines (Dawson and Downey) are charged with assaulting and killing Private William Santiago by stuffing a rag into his mouth, causing respiratory failure. Special JAG Counsel Lt. Commander JoAnne Galloway believes Dawson and Downey "were just following orders," as part of the marine's unofficial "code red" instructions where there is self policing within the ranks, and that there was no intent to murder. Galloway, an investigator with no trial experience, wants to be assigned the case for the defense, but it instead goes to Lt. Daniel Kaffee, a smart but facile lawyer who has a history of cynical plea bargains of behalf of his clients. Eventually, though, Galloway (along with Lt. Sam Weinberg) becomes co-counsel in the case.

After interviews with the principals, including an unsettling visit to Gitmo and a tense exchange with its testy commander, Col. Nathan Jessup, Kaffee rejects the offer of a plea bargain from prosecutor Col. Jack Ross, sensing that higher-ups want the incident buried under one of his plea bargain ploys. The three JAG officers work to find enough evidence to go to trial and get the marines off the murder charge, arguing that they were acting on others' orders. In fashioning their case, they also begin to build a degree of camaraderie. The film climaxes in a lengthy and suspenseful court-martial sequence, where Kaffee slowly proves himself a solid trial presence, one bold enough to confront the martinet Jessup.

Background: The film version of *A Few Good Men* stemmed from the first major play (of the same name) by Aaron Sorkin. The play had its pre-Broadway run at the Kennedy Center in DC before premiering on Broadway in November 1989. Hollywood producer David Brown bought the rights to a film version even before the play was produced, and he hired Rob Reiner to direct it and Sorkin to write the screenplay, his first. Principal photography began in October 1991, most of it done in California locations and Culver City studios. Sorkin has since gone on to specialize in DC-based works, writing the screenplays for *The American President* (q.v.) and *Charlie Wilson's War* (q.v.), as well as creating and writing for the NBC television hit *The West Wing*, which debuted in 1999.

Sorkin got the inspiration for the play after a phone conversation with his sister Deborah, a lawyer who had signed up for a three-year stint with the Navy's JAG corps in the 1980's. She went to the Guantanamo Bay base to help defend a group of marines who had come close to killing a fellow marine in a hazing incident ordered by a superior officer. The Kaffee character was based in part on a composite of lawyers who defended in that case. Sorkin also gets a cameo in the film as a lawyer talking to a woman in a bar scene.

Comment: Tom Cruise, just 30 when the film was released, solidified his meteoric career as defense attorney Kaffee, proving to many observers that he–rather like his character in the film–was fully ready for serious, adult roles. Jack Nicholson's menacing performance as Colonel Jessup was especially lauded by reviewers. He was also nominated for a Best Supporting Actor Academy Award for his role. The film received three other Oscar nominations, for Best Picture, Best Editing, and Best Sound but failed to win any statuettes. Made at a cost of some $40 million, it earned a healthy $237 million in worldwide box office.

The film's line "You can't handle the truth!", memorably delivered by Jack Nicholson as Jessup in the witness box, was ranked at number 29 (out of 100) of the "most memorable movie quotes" by the American Film Institute. In June 2008 AFI also ranked *A Few Good Men* on its list of the 10 greatest films in the genre "Courtroom Drama."

DC Notes: The exteriors of Naval JAG Group headquarters, located at the Navy Yard in DC, were actually shot at St. Elizabeth's Hospital in SE Washington.

Lt. Kaffee (Cruise) is seen hanging out and hitting baseballs at a park north of the Lincoln Memorial and overlooking the Potomac.

The film's defense team meets at the home of Lt. Kaffee, shot in a row house in Georgetown. An autumnal street scene with Cruise and Kevin Pollak and a rain-soaked evening was also shot on Georgetown streets.

When Lt. Col. Martinson (Walsh) comes to Washington, he is clandestinely accommodated by the defense team at the "Downtown Motel" in Northeast, an actual location which features in the film.

The drill team in the opening credits is made up of Texas A & M University's Corps of Cadets Fish Drill Team.

28 DAVE

 1993. Warner Brothers Pictures, 110 minutes, color.

Direction: Ivan Reitman.

Screenplay: Gary Ross.

Cinematography: James Whitaker.

Editing: Dana Glaugerman.

Original Music: James Newton Howard.

Principal Cast:

Kevin Kline ..... Dave Kovic/Pres. Mitchell	Tom Dugan .... Jerry
Sigourney Weaver .... Ellen Mitchell	Faith Prince .... Alice
Frank Langella .... Bob Alexander	Laura Linney .... Randi
Kevin Dunn .... Alan Reed	Bonnie Hunt .... White House Tour Guide
Ving Rhames .... Duane Stevenson	Anna Deavere Smith .... Mrs. Travis
Ben Kingsley ..... Vice President Gary Nance	Charles Hallahan .... Policeman
Charles Grodin .... Murray Blum	Stefan Gierasch ...... House Majority Leader

Synopsis: President Bill Mitchell is a remote, corrupt politician who cheats on his totally estranged wife, Ellen, and is backed by his equally venal Chief of Staff, Bob Alexander, who lusts after the president's job. Dave Kovic is a kind-hearted guy who runs a temp agency in Georgetown and who bears an uncanny likeness to Mitchell. The White House, in fact, uses Kovic as a stand-in to cover events on behalf of the President. On one such occasion where he has a dalliance with a staffer, Mitchell suffers a stroke and goes into a coma. Alexander, fearing that the benign Vice President Nance will take over if the news gets out, convinces Dave to actually impersonate Mitchell full time so he can work out a way to take over the office himself. Even the First Lady–living separately in the White House–doesn't suspect Dave's a double.

Getting into the role, however, Dave begins to reveal his natural good-hearted self and quickly increases the chief executive's credibility, introduces popular legislation, and works out some budget magic with his own accountant, Murray. Eventually, Ellen realizes who Dave really is when she is shown her husband in a coma in a secret White House basement. By now Ellen and Dave have bonded, and they begin to plan a scheme for Dave/Mitchell to leave the office so that Vice President Nance can take over and Dave can return to his normal life.

Background: In creating *Dave*, director Ivan Reitman and his staff went out of their way to recruit prominent Washington political figures and talking heads for the picture. Some dozen legislators, past and present, have cameo appearances in the movie, including luminaries such as Tip O'Neill, and Senators Howard Metzenbaum, Alan Simpson, and Paul Simon, as well as those of more recent vintage, like Senators Chris Dodd and Tom Harkin. Almost the entire chattering class of DC-based media personalities of the time are also featured (mostly in TV clips), with almost 20 journalists and pundits ranging from Fred Barnes to Sandor Vanocur. One of the more amusing sequences has Oliver Stone–conspiracy theorist par excellence–appearing on Larry King's CNN talk show and actually smelling out a real conspiracy (the replacement of a president)!

The film received one Academy Award nomination, to Gary Ross for Best Original Screenplay.

DC/Hill Notes: The opening of the film has President Mitchell (Kline) and the First Lady (Weaver) land by helicopter on the south lawn of the White House, which is a very large and convincing façade of the real thing built on 127 acres at the Los Angeles Arboretum.

The Oval Office is a high-quality replica constructed specifically for this picture on the Warners lot. It was occupied again for Warner's *The Pelican Brief* (q.v.) and Castle Rock Entertainment's *Absolute Power* (q.v.). One source in 1997 said that portions of the *Dave* set "go out all the time" and that sections of it had been used as many as 25 times for additional film and television projects.

In a climactic scene, Dave (as President Mitchell) goes to the Capitol to speak in the House Chamber to a joint session of Congress. Notably smaller in size, this space is actually the House of Delegates Chamber in the Virginia State House in Richmond, Virginia. It was also used for a similar dramatic scene in the 2000 political drama *The Contender* (q.v.).

Goofs: As the presidential helicopter approaches the White House, the American flag is shown flying above the building, but this is a practice used only when the president is in the building, and here he is just arriving.

An event that is staged for the president's double takes place at the invented "Monroe Hotel" in downtown DC.

A White House correspondent–played by Bernie Kalb, ex-CBS newsman– does a stand-up on the South Lawn of the White House, an absolute no-no. Correspondents are confined to very specific spaces on the northwest side of the White House when they file their reports.

The movie uses a lengthy stretch limousine to transport the President, but, while the real President's car is an ample vehicle, it is not a "stretch."

The comatose president is hidden in massive, dungeon-like quarters supposedly below the White House.

Dave, acting as president, and Ellen have a nighttime snack in front of the White House, sitting on a knoll which doesn't exist on the flat Ellipse.

29 IN THE LINE OF FIRE

 1993. Castle Rock Entertainment distributed by Columbia Pictures, 128 minutes, color.

Director: Wolfgang Peterson.

Original Screenplay: Jeff Maguire.

Cameraman: John Bailey.

Editing: Anne V. Coates.

Music: Ennio Morricone.

Principal Cast :

Clint Eastwood	Frank Horrigan	Jim Curley	President of the US
John Malkovich	Mitch Leary	Sally Hughes	First Lady of the US
Rene Russo	Lilly Raines	John Heard	Professor Riger
Dylan McDermott	Al D'Andrea	Clyde Kusatsu	Jack Okura
Gary Cole	Bill Watts	Steve Hytner	Tony Carducci
Fred Dalton Thompson	Harry Sargent	Patrika Darbo	Pam Magnus
John Mahoney	Sam Campagna	Joshua Malina	Agent Chavez
Greg Alan-Williams	Matt Wilder	Tobin Bell	Mendoza

Synopsis: Frank Horrigan is a veteran Secret Service (SS) agent tormented by memories of his inability to stop the Kennedy assassination. Now, a renegade CIA assassin (Leary) is stalking the current President, and, knowing of Horrigan's background, he taunts the agent by telling him openly of his plans to assassinate the President on the verge of an election. Leary aims to get back at the US government that he feels betrayed him. Horrigan makes sure he is given presidential protection duty, working along with fellow agent Lilly Raines. Casually chauvinistic at first with Raines, Horrigan eventually warms to her, and the feeling is mutual.

After testy phone exchanges with Leary, Horrigan and the Service locate his apartment and discover his murderous intentions. Leary prepares an elaborate ruse, using a sympathetic bank staffer in California, to donate money to the President's party and wrangle an invitation to a campaign event in Los Angeles, where he plans to gain access to the President. Horrigan and Leary then play cat-and-mouse games in DC, with chases through Lafayette Park and Capitol Hill, where Leary cruelly dispatches Frank's partner, Al D'Andrea, and is able to escape. The campaign trip to LA is scheduled, even though Horrigan and his boss, Sam Campagna, have doubts about the appearance, sensing Leary's intentions. But White House Chief of Staff Harry Sargent refuses to alter the President's itinerary, feeling the event is crucial to his re-election. Meanwhile, Leary has, in disguise, inveigled himself into the LA hall where the President is to appear, and Horrigan must find a way to stop him and perhaps take a bullet for his protectee.

Production Notes: Jeff Maguire's script for *In the Line of Fire* produced a bidding war among some of Hollywood's elite actors, including Sean Connery and Tom Cruise, but Eastwood won the project by offering $1 million for it. The production rented a White House set from the company that had filmed the comedy *Dave*, released earlier the same year. Another major set recreated the interior of Air Force One (the latter rebuilt at an estimated cost of $250,000).

Some movie magic was used in an historic sequence which shows Eastwood as a young agent with the Kennedys in Dallas. A contemporary report on the production indicated that Eastwood appealed to Warner Brothers to incorporate footage of him from the 1971 Warners movie *Dirty Harry* into the film and then have it retrofitted to the fashion of the previous decade. The report then notes that for the current film, "Eastwood loses the longish hair and sideburns or, as (Jeff Apple) describes it, 'gets the world's first digital haircut.'"

The film was a significant hit for Columbia, earning over $175 million worldwide. It also garnered three Oscar nominations (though no wins): John Malkovich as Best Supporting Actor, Best Editing, and Best Original Screenplay.

This was the last film in which actor Clint Eastwood worked under a director other than himself.

DC/Hill Notes: The production was also able to obtain considerable cooperation and participation from the Secret Service and used a number of exteriors of the Treasury Department to ratify that relationship. In several sequences, Horrigan and other SS agents are shown going up and down the west side steps of the building across from the White House.

Other significant locations are in Adams-Morgan (where agent Horrigan's apartment is located, on Belmont Street), the Lincoln Memorial (two sequences), the National Portrait Gallery, Lafayette Park (site of one lively chase sequence), Pennsylvania Avenue, Dulles Airport, and Capitol Hill.

In the latter case, there is an elaborate chase over rooftops on the Hill which involved shooting over several blocks, with steady views in the distance of the Jefferson and Adams Buildings of the Library of Congress, the Folger Library, the Supreme Court, and the Capitol dome (see photo insert). Shot set-ups were made between the streets bordering East Capitol and Constitution Avenue, NE, and between 3rd and 6th Streets, NE. A full run-down on that sequence, shot in a Northeast neighborhood, is included at the end of this chapter.

A cameraman who worked on *In the Line of Fire*, Stuart Stein, told the author he was impressed how athletic the 60-plus Eastwood was on the shoot. On the roof sequence indicated above, he was, according to Stein, "amazingly efficient for doing rooftops. He was not a youngster, but he was amazingly fast."

In an interview, Quintin Peterson, a veteran of the Metropolitan Police Department's film liaison unit, singled out the film's producers as exemplary in "sticking very closely to the MPD specs on clothing and equipment."

Goofs: Early on in the picture, there is a Presidential motorcade which looks impressive, but whose route—evidently for reasons of efficient location shooting—is circular: it passes the Willard Hotel on Pennsylvania Avenue, NW going west, then turns south on 15th Street to go along the side of the Commerce Department. Next there is a cut to the motorcade going north on 12th Street by the Old Post Office to head right back to Pennsylvania (in this whole sequence, Peterson and his team used digital effects to enhance the size of the crowds lining the streets for the motorcade).

After tracing a call from Leary (Malkovich), Horrigan (Eastwood) runs into Lafayette Park (close to the Treasury) towards a fake pay phone placed just below H Street, NW.

The Secret Service traces a call from Leary to the fictive "St. Francis Hotel" located on Florida Avenue, NE. The "hotel" is, in effect, a standard corner row house with a turret, possibly located in the LeDroit Park neighborhood.

Special Section

This essay is especially directed to my Capitol Hill neighbors, who might enjoy the escapades of Clint running around our neighborhood.

The second chase sequence of *In the Line of Fire*, which begins with that call to the St. Frances Hotel mentioned above, shows Horrigan and his partner D'Andrea (Clint Eastwood and Dylan McDermott) first spotting then running after the villain Leary (John Malkovich). After some pursuit on miscellaneous streets and down two alleys, the Hill sequence proceeds as indicated below (neighbors who were witness to the shoot indicated it took at least two days). This sequence concentrates on the Leary and Horrigan characters; some cutaway shots also show D'Andrea at a few points.

1. Leary, in close up, pops up on the roof of The John Jay apartment building (314 East Capitol Street, NE) with the Capitol behind him. A quick cut shows Leary going north at another angle, with the Adams Building, the Library of Congress, and the Folger Library behind him.

2. Horrigan climbs up on the roof on the same ladder of The John Jay.

3. Leary is shown from the back, running north on the tops of several

Mr. Smith Goes to Washington – Senator Joseph Paine (Claude Raines, left) confronts Senator Jeff Smith (Jimmy Stewart) on the Senate floor in the most iconic Washington movie ever made. In photo inset, director Frank Capra looks over the completed Senate set (1939).

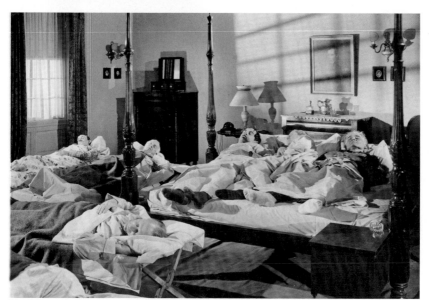

The More the Merrier – In this George Stevens comedy, the plot turned on the World War II housing shortage in Washington. Businessman Benjamin Dingle (Charles Coburn) is the middle man on the crowded four poster (1943).

Born Yesterday – Billie Dawn (Judy Holliday, left) is led down the Capitol steps on the House side by mentor Paul Verrall (William Holden), who is providing her a crash course in democracy in the comedy directed by George Cukor (1950).

Washington Story– Seen walking through the underground passage between the Capitol and a House Office Building are Congressman Joseph Gresham (Van Johnson, left) and journalist Alice Kingsley (Patricia Neal), who is covering the legislator (1952).

Seven Days in May – Stunt police break up a rally by stunt protestors on the White House sidewalk in this tense political thriller directed by John Frankenheimer which tells the story of a planned military coup (1964).

Advise and Consent – Stars Don Murray, Charles Laughton, and Walter Pidgeon, (left to right) all playing senators, walk on the Mall as their director Otto Preminger looks on from his camera (1962).

The Exorcist (1) – (above) Father Merrin (Max Von Sydow) stands in front of the house on Prospect Street in Georgetown, ready to exorcize the demons from the possessed young girl in the shocker directed by William Friedkin.

The Exorcist (2) – (left) A set designer works at the back of the Prospect Street house, adding an extra bedroom on the dwelling to allow the scene where a priest flies out of the room and on to steps leading down to M Street (1973).

All the President's Men – Carl Bernstein (Dustin Hoffman, (above) and Bob Woodward (Robert Redford) leave the Library of Congress after researching information on the Watergate burglars. In photo inset, Redford (center) and Hoffman (center right) at the film's premiere at the Kennedy Center (1976).

First Monday in October – Director Ronald Neame (on lowest step) gets ready to direct a scene on the steps of the US Supreme Court. The film is the only one that has used the highest court as its principal subject matter (1981).

Broadcast News – Journalists Jane Craig (Holly Hunter, left) and Aaron Altman (Albert Brooks) converse on the steps of the townhouse on Capitol Hill in James L. Brooks smart comedy-drama (1986).

In the Line of Fire – The Capitol is backdrop as Secret Service agent Frank Horrigan (Clint Eastwood) pursues a potential presidential assassin across the roof of an apartment building in an intricate chase sequence (1993).

The American President – Michael Douglas (left) as President Andrew Shepard takes direction from director Rob Reiner in a precisely crafted Oval Office set constructed for this film (1995).

Minority Report – This set of nearly identical row houses on the 1700 block of C Street, SE, near Capitol Hill, played a part in a key chase sequence in this science fiction thriller directed by Steven Spielberg (2002).

J. Edgar – Reference librarian of the Library of Congress Sheridan Harvey shows a production crew entries in the Library's card catalog for J. Edgar Hoover (2011).

Being There – The tiny figure of Chance the gardener (Peter Sellers) walks south on the median strip of North Capitol Street, with traffic flying by and the Capitol dome in view. Perhaps the most sublime "Goof" in DC movies (1979).

row houses on 4th Street, NE. The Shrine of the Immaculate Conception can be glimpsed in the distance.

4. Horrigan runs north on the roof of the John Jay in a sequence similar to #1.

5. Leary runs towards the camera between two roof gables; the next shot shows Horrigan repeating the same action.

6. Leary is next shown running past a gray-tiled turret located at the corner of 5th and A Streets, NE.

7. Leary then runs east on the roofs along A Streets, NE, past a row of three rowhouses with white chimneys.

8. Cut to Horrigan on the roofs of 5th Street, turning on to A Street past the same turret (#6).

9. Whoa! Leary runs onto a different roof, where you can see the edge of the Supreme Court, the spire of the Faith Tabernacle Church (on 3rd Street, NE), and a large blue building (since repainted) at 118 4th Street, NE.

10. Leary moves along Constitution Avenue, NE, jumping between two buildings twice.

11. Horrigan repeats the sequence from #8, running past the three white chimneys. He then repeats the same two jumps between buildings.

12. Here D'Andrea–who has been struggling all this time to get up on a fire escape–finally joins the Hill chase, coming up on the ladder of The John Jay building and repeating the sequences in #1 and #4.

13. Next cut shows Leary jumping down to the lower roofs at 417-419 Constitution Avenue, NE (near the corner of 5th and Constitution), with the Library of Congress and the Capitol in distant view. Behind him, Horrigan readies himself to jump.

14. Horrigan is seen jumping and landing on the same roof as indicated in #13, but the shot switches to the opposite angle, showing Horrigan's back with him facing 5th Street, NE, with Constitution Avenue on his left. There is a large red brick wall in the image (part of a large apartment building on the southwest corner of 5th and Constitution).

15. Leary is shown stumbling up a ladder, again on Constitution Avenue between 4th and 5th Streets, NE, with the same backdrop as #9 above.

16. D'Andrea joins the chase and retraces the steps from #8 above.

17. Horrigan is shown in near close up climbing up the same ladder Leary used in #15.

The next scene switches from Capitol Hill locations to a rooftop in another city, evidently not DC. (Within it, however, D'Andrea repeats one last Hill sequence, the one from #9 before he runs off to a totally different area).

In the dramatic wind-up to this chase, Capitol Hill and Washington give way to another location, and eventually, to the studio. In the final, gripping (pardon the pun) sequence, the nasty Malcovich leans over a roof edge, leering and taunting Clint as our hero first dangles on his fingertips then grasps Leary's arm high above an alley, while his partner tries to get a shot at the bad guy.

30 THE PELICAN BRIEF

 1993. Warner Brothers, 141 minutes, color.

Writer/director: Alan J. Pakula.

Cinematography: Stephen Goldblatt.

Editing: Tom Rolf and Trudy Ship.

Music: James Horner.

Principal Cast :

Julia Roberts	Darby Shaw	John Heard	Gavin Verheek
Denzel Washington	Gray Grantham	James B. Sikking	F. Denton Voyles
Sam Shepard	Thomas Callahan	William Atherton	Bob Gminski
John Lithgow	Smith Keen	Anthony Heald	Marty Velmano
Tony Goldwyn	Fletcher Cole	Jake Weber	Curtis Morgan ("Garcia")
Stanley Tucci	Khamel ("Sam")	Hume Cronyn	Justice Rosenberg
Robert Culp	The President	Cynthia Nixon	Alice Stark

Synopsis: In DC, two Supreme Court Justices have been assassinated. In New Orleans, a Tulane law professor who clerked for one of them is shown a brief from one of his students, Darby Shaw (also his mistress), which speculates on who might have motive for the killings. He passes the "pelican brief" on to an FBI friend, and the FBI director also sees it. The president's chief advisor also reads the brief and is concerned that it can be used to undermine the President. Nefarious forces after the brief kill the professor in a car bomb, from which Darby barely escapes. Knowing she, too is in danger, she appeals to the professor's FBI friend, who is also killed by an anonymous hit man, Khamel.

Afraid for her life, Darby escapes first to New York, then to Washington and reaches out to Gray Grantham, an investigative reporter with the *Washington Herald*, who has, in turn, been contacted by a mysterious "Garcia" who says he has information about the assassinations. Darby and Gray meet, and she tells him about her brief which implicates a corporate figure and a friend of the president, Victor Mattiece, who is trying to manipulate the makeup of the Supreme Court to favor his oil business in a court case. Grantham pitches the story to his editor, Keen, who thinks they have no real story and should drop it. But Darby wants him to press on, and the two form a team to expose the conspiracy, but Mattiece's henchmen aim to kill them.

Background: While *The Pelican Brief* was novelist John Grisham's third legal thriller to be published, it was the second to be filmed, and it appeared in theaters just under six months after the first of his filmed novels, *The Firm*, made it onto the screen. Both films, riding on the author's tremendous popularity, were on the top ten list of box office winners for the year 1993.

The rights to *The Pelican Brief* were bought before the book was even finished, based on a sample from the book. Grisham wrote the part of Darby Shaw with Julia Roberts in mind. Roberts read the book once it was finished and agreed to the role without even seeing a script.

The writer/director Alan J. Pakula had won renown years earlier when he directed one of the most memorable of all DC movies, *All the President's Men* (q.v.). Pakula, was also the producer of the film, and it was his last credit as producer (he died in 1998).

Comment: *The Pelican Brief* is a reasonably taut, if claustrophobic, thriller which transfers much of the novel's suspense to the screen. What it especially offers is the two attractive leads at possibly the height of their looks and starpower. Roberts, after a two-year hiatus from film, comes back strongly as the vulnerable but smart heroine Darby, and Washington exudes both charm and integrity as the crusading journalist Grantham. The roles could be seen as corny, but the two actors are still convincing in them. The movie also offered a titillation for some fans: will this handsome interracial couple become a romantic duo at fadeout (as is implied in the book)? Perhaps as many filmgoers were satisfied with the film's chaste ending as those who found it wanting.

Film Critic Roger Ebert of the *Chicago Sun-Times* used his review of *The Pelican Brief* to make a point about movies made from popular fiction:

> *It's an old law of the movies that ordinary novels are easier to film than great ones, because the director doesn't have to worry about the writer's message and style, if any. The Pelican Brief is a good illustration of that principle. By casting attractive stars in the leads, by finding the right visual look, by underlining the action with brooding, ominously sad music, a good director can create the illusion of meaning even when nothing's there.*

DC/Hill Notes: *The Pelican Brief* was very much a on-site shoot, with significant location shooting in both New Orleans and in and around DC. The Washington locations included:

Capitol Hill, where reporter Grantham (Washington) is seen jogging around a corner and entering a Hill row house, his home.

The south entrance of the National Cathedral, where the President (Culp) is seen leaving a service and getting into his motorcade.

The triangular park at the intersection of Pennsylvania Avenue, NW, Indiana Avenue, and 7th Street, where Grantham is scouting for source "Garcia" and spots him in the park (where the Temperance Statue is) and chases him down a walkway between the buildings on Pennsylvania and Indiana Avenues.

Both the Georgetown Law library and Law Center (McDonough Hall) appeared in the film. In the library, the main reading room and one of its study rooms was used. Scenes at the Registrar's Office and in the Career Services Office were shot in McDonough.

The Washington Monument, where a collection of nefarious types are seen hanging around the base of the Monument.

Riggs National Bank, at its downtown main office across from the Treasury Building, is seen in both indoor and outdoor shots.

With an ample DC shooting schedule, the filmmakers hired on a significant number of local actors for parts in *The Pelican Brief*. For those familiar with Washington area stage performers of that time–especially those who attended Arena Stage or Folger Theater shows–they will have fun spotting the following:

Stanley Anderson: one of the shadowy henchmen out to get those involved with *The Pelican Brief:*

Terrence Currier, as a nonspeaking bit as a caregiver (shot dead) to a Supreme Court judge;

Ralph Cosham, another non-speaking role, as one of the murdered Supremes, unceremoniously strangled while attending a porn house movie;

Helen Carey, interacting with Darby Shaw (Roberts) as a law clerk in New Orleans;

Richard Bauer, as the managing editor of *The Washington Herald;* and Franchelle Stewart Dorn, interacting with Grantham as a clerk at the Georgetown University Law Center.

Goofs: The opening of the film features a puzzling, all-purpose, protest demonstration in front of the Supreme Court, including a welter of placards, such as: "Handgun Control," "Save Our Cities," "Keep Dolphins," "Honor Mother Earth," "Support the Inner City," "Fur is Death," "Silence=Death," "AIDS Cure Now," "Lesbian Rights," and "Death to Rosenberg," one of the Supreme Court justices.

The President gets into has an enormous stretch limo coming out of the service at the Cathedral, a kind of car never used by the White House.

The Grantham character stays in Washington at the non-existent "Marbury Hotel," which is really the Omni-Shoreham off Connecticut Avenue, NW.

There is a most disjointed chase sequence late in the film. Grantham grabs a cab at the Omni-Shoreham Hotel and tells the cabbie to take him to Georgetown University Law School, but the next shot has the vehicle coming down Pennsylvania Avenue and turning right on 4th Street, NW (in from of the National Gallery's East Wing), then, all of the sudden, the cab is entering Pennsylvania Avenue in front of the White House, where there is another (this time, a highly unlikely pro-gun) demonstration, into which Grantham disappears.

Prior to going to Riggs Bank main office (see above), Grantham and Shaw walk out of the "Grant Square" parking garage, but there is no Grant Square here.

31 TRUE LIES

 1994. Lightstorm Entertainment, distributed by 20th Century Fox, 141 minutes, color.

Director: James Cameron.

Screenplay: by James Cameron from a story Cameron and Randall Frakes.

Cinematography: Russell Carpenter.

Editing: Conrad Buff, Mark Goldblatt, and Richard A. Harris.

Music: Brad Fiedel.

Principal Cast:

Arnold Schwarzenegger	Harry Tasker	Grant Heslov	Faisil
Jamie Lee Curtis	Helen Tasker	Charlton Heston	Spencer Trilby
Tom Arnold	Albert "Gib" Gibson	Art Malik	Salim Abu Aziz
Bill Paxton	Simon	Eliza Dushku	Dana Tasker
Tia Carrere	Juno Skinner	Marshall Manesh	Jamal Khaled

Synopsis: Harry Tasker is happily married to Helen, a legal secretary, and lives in the DC suburbs with their teenaged daughter Dana. Helen thinks her husband is a boring computer salesman who travels too much, unaware that he is a top-level secret agent working within the counter-terrorist "Omega Sector." Harry's current case involves a Middle Eastern terrorist organization known as "Crimson Jihad," which is threatening the US with nuclear weapons. His attempt to capture the group's leader, Aziz, results in an elaborate chase through downtown Washington, but the terrorist escapes.

Meanwhile, Harry finds evidence that Helen is seeing a used car salesman named Simon, who is trying to seduce her with his tales of a glamorous– but fake–life as a spy. Harry forces his sidekick Gib to use the resources of their agency to trail Simon and Helen, and, to teach her a lesson, they abduct her (while keeping their identities secret) with the aim of assigning her a pseudo-mission. However, Aziz and his group are able to kidnap both Helen and Harry and take them to a private hideout in the Florida Keys. There, Helen finally learns the truth about Harry, and they both are part of an elaborate chase which involves both stopping the terrorists from nuclear blackmail and rescuing their daughter, who has been taken as a hostage.

Background: James Cameron wrote and directed the movie (which was based on the 1991 French film *La totale!*, directed by Claude Zidi). At the time, *True Lies* was the most expensive movie ever made, estimated to cost between $100 and $120 million. In that sense, it could be seen as a warm-up for Cameron's next mega-hit, *Titanic* (1997). *True Lies* was a major domestic and international hit, ending up with a worldwide box office take of over $378 million, most of it from overseas markets. Even though it was rated "R," it was the third highest-grossing picture for 1994. The film was nominated for an Academy Award for Best Visual Effects, and Jamie Curtis won a Golden Globe for her comedic portrayal of Helen Tasker.

True Lies was the first Lightstorm Entertainment project to be distributed under Cameron's multi-million dollar production deal with 20th Century Fox, as well as the first major production for the visual effects company Digital Domain (co-founded by Cameron).

Upon its release, a number of groups, including the American-Arab Anti-Discrimination Committee, condemned *True Lies* for its "depiction of Middle Easterners as homicidal, religious zealots." The Committee was one of several groups that held a protest against the film at a Washington, DC, theater. There was also a demand for a boycott of the movie, as well as a ban of its distribution in Arab and Muslim countries.

DC Notes: *True Lies* did use a number of locations in DC but with some fanciful results (see **Goofs** on next page). The filmmakers did sequences in Georgetown Park, on Indiana Avenue, NW (the National Archives can be seen in the background), in Chinatown (where Helen secretly goes to meet Simon for lunch), at the West Wing of the National Gallery, and on K Street, NW under Key Bridge.

One lengthy sequence was shot at "Jimmy's Auto" at 418 New York Avenue, NW (which is still in business), where Simon the car dealer works. Simon (Paxton) takes Agent Harry Tasker (Schwarzenegger) for a test drive in a Corvette sports car around various indistinguishable neighborhoods that appear to be in near Northwest.

Goofs: In one elaborate chase sequence, Harry is in Georgetown Park where he mounts a police horse to chase the bad guy Aziz (Malik), who is on a motorbike. In no time, Harry is at 13th Street and Pennsylvania Avenue, while the villain, on the bike, drives right in front of a "Marriott Hotel." This hotel, however–with glass elevators and more than 20 stories– is really the Westin Bonaventure Hotel in downtown LA, where the rest of the chase, including a rooftop finale, takes place. *(Note: the film's writers originally had intended that this sequence on horseback splash through the Lincoln Memorial's reflecting pool but access to it was denied by the National Park Service.)*

In the chase sequence described above, Harry commandeers his horse from a mounted policeman of the city's Metropolitan Police Department (MPD), but, according to a knowledgeable police source, DC's police did not have mounted units at the time (1994) and only reinstated them in 2000.

In one driving sequence, there is a reference to a fictional "Franklin Street" in the city.

In another driving sequence, Simon (Paxton) is driving southbound across the Key Bridge, and the Capitol is seen clearly in the background. But there is no point on the Key Bridge which has a view of the Capitol.

32 THE AMERICAN PRESIDENT

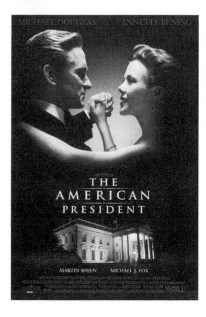

1995. Castle Rock Entertainment distributed by Columbia Pictures, 114 minutes, color.

Director: Rob Reiner.

Original Screenplay: Aaron Sorkin.

Cameraman: John Seale.

Editing: Robert Leighton.

Music: Marc Shaiman.

Principal Cast :

Michael Douglas.....Pres. Andrew Shepherd
Annette Bening.............Sydney Ellen Wade
Martin Sheen....................A.J. MacInerney
Michael J. Fox.................Lewis Rothschild
Anna Deveare Smith...........Robin McCall
Samantha Mathis....................Jane Basdin
David Paymer.........................Leon Kodak
Anne Haney...........................Mrs. Chapil
Shawna Waldron.................Lucy Shepherd
Richard Dreyfuss............Sen. Bob Rumson
Nina Siemaszko.........................Beth Wade
Wendie Malick........................Susan Sloan
Beau Billingslea.......Special Agency Cooper
Gail Strickland.............Esther MacInerney
John Mahoney.........................Leo Solomon
Joshua Malina...................................David

Synopsis: President Andrew Shepherd, a widower, is a Democrat from Wisconsin riding high in the polls when he encounters passionate environmental lobbyist Sydney Ellen Wade, pushing hard on a bill on which the president is soft. Intrigued with Wade (and buoyed by good numbers), Shepherd sends Wade flowers, invites her to a state dinner, and eventually asks her to a White House sleepover. But as the romance blossoms, his popularity plummets as both political nemesis Senator Rumson, wondering out loud "Is she the First Mistress?," and the niggling Washington press corps, questioning the affair, raise the inevitable "character issue."

Shepherd's crack White House staff, led by chief of staff A.J. MacInerney, domestic policy advisor Lewis Rothschild, press secretary Robin McCall, and pollster Leon Kodak, try to keep him in line, attempt to keep his eye on the legislative ball (his concern with a crime bill as well as her environmental legislation are crucial), and urge him to speak out and act presidential. There are waverings, wafflings, and misunderstandings between the couple, one which causes Wade to lose her job at the lobby firm. But just as the romance seems over, President Shepherd steps to the mike in the White House Press Office to deliver a credo that cements his popularity anew. The question of whether a President can balance his personal and public goals is answered with a resounding "yes."

Production Notes: This is romantic comedy, not farce, and director Reiner and screenwriter Aaron Sorkin (the two worked together previously on another Washington-based movie, *A Few Good Men*, q.v) apparently worked hard to make it credible as a story of contemporary Washington. Reiner and Sorkin had several visits to the White House, including two days Reiner spent trailing President Clinton. The lead actors were given private tours to get the feel of the place (see photo insert). The production and design teams were given special access to the mansion and were allowed to take measurements of the rooms to recreate sets and to duplicate art works from White House Museum sources. For the convincing set of the Oval Office, the filmmakers spruced up a set created two years earlier for the film *Dave* (q.v.). As he did also in *A Few Good Men*, Sorkin gave himself a cameo role as a guy in a bar scene.

The production design is most accomplished. Though Hollywood sets, the White House rooms and settings are as convincing as any Washington movie ever made. Convincing, and geographically accurate: the design team made reproductions of the Cabinet Room, the East Wing entrance, the Situation Room, the Press Briefing Room, the Roosevelt Room, and the China Room. California settings were used for some scenes, like those that take place at Camp David.

The film received generally positive reviews and did decent business: its total global box office take was $107 million. Its composer, Marc Shaiman, earned the film's only Academy Award nomination for Best Music, Original Score.

Postscript: Sorkin later adapted a number of elements from *The American President* to his landmark NBC television series *The West Wing* which began airing in 1999. Left-over plot elements from the movie became material for the pilot and early episodes of the TV series. Several actors from the film were prominent in *The West Wing*, first among them Martin Sheen as President Josiah Barlett. Also cast were Anna Deveare Smith, Joshua Malina, and Nina Siemaszko (this time as the president's daughter).

Comments: Adding to the film's believability are the performances, led by Annette Bening, a radiant Sydney whose intelligence and charm make it easy to understand why the President falls for her. She is utterly natural in conveying both the whip-smart lobbyist and the nervous object of presidential affection, cowed as anyone would be by "The Presence." Michael Douglas's Shepherd is a bit stolid but not damagingly so. He gets some good lines and gets to show some tender moments with his 12-year-old daughter, played by Shawna Waldron with artless appeal.

The secondary roles are of a high standard, both sharp and entertaining. Martin Sheen as A.J. personifies the decent, old-shoe sounding board for Shepherd, the perfect behind-the-scenes, number two man. Anna Deavere Smith convinces as the alert press secretary, insisting on the straight story to both feed and foil the press. David Paymer does nicely as a Supernerd, full of pollster paranoia. Michael J. Fox, when first reading the script for his character, said he thought of Lewis Rothschild as Jiminy Cricket, "always in the President's ear." The parallel is apt: he is ever the chirrupy voice of conscience literally bugging his boss.

Sorkin's script is solid. The dialogue of the president's aides seems especially right: jangly, quick, smart, and nervy all at once–constantly balancing deference for the President with getting in his face–and also trying to get a life. The pollster, for example, at a holiday party, chides a colleague: "'It's Christmas; didn't you get the memo?" Or the hyper Rothschild (Fox), dreading a future policy prospect, notes that "It's always a guy in my position who ends up doing 18 months in Danbury minimum security prison."

DC/Hill Notes: The film boasts that excellent reproduction of the Oval Office (also used two years later for Oliver Stone's *Nixon*). The president's "girlfriend" (Bening) moves into No. 310 East Capitol Street (The Colcord building) on Capitol Hill. The last sequence, which shows President Shepherd entering the House Chamber for his State of the Union address, was produced on a Hollywood sound stage with the backdrop created digitally.

Goofs: At one point, Rothschild (Fox), phoning from the White House Situation Room, hurls obscenities at a congressman–highly unlikely behavior for White House staffers who are typically deferential to Congress.

One repeated concern of lobbyist Wade (Bening) is a geographic absurdity: twice she complains about having trouble getting from her Capitol Hill home to the White House "because of traffic on Dupont Circle," a route that would be totally out of her way.

At his climactic press statement, the President introduces "White House Resolution 455," when it is only Congress that can issue resolutions.

33 ABSOLUTE POWER

1997. Castle Rock Entertainment distributed by Columbia Pictures
121 minutes, color.

Screenplay: William Goldman, from David Baldacci's novel.

Direction: Clint Eastwood.

Cinematography: Jack N. Green.

Editing: Joel Cox.

Original Music: Lennie Niehaus.

Principal Cast:

Clint Eastwood	Luther Whitney	Judy Davis	Gloria Russell
Gene Hackman	Pres. Alan Richmond	E.G. Marshall	Walter Sullivan
Ed Harris	Det. Seth Frank	Melora Hardin	Christy Sullivan
Laura Linney	Kate Whitney	Kenneth Walsh	Sandy Lord
Scott Glenn	Agent Bill Burton	Penny Johnson	Laura Simon
Dennis Haysbert	Agent Tim Collin	Richard Jenkins	Michael McCarhy

Synopsis: Jewel thief Luther Whitney is robbing the luxurious mansion of billionaire Walter Sullivan when he witnesses (behind a one-way mirror) the President, Alan Richmond, in a tryst with Sullivan's young wife Christy. When the sexual encounter turns rough, he sees two Secret Service agents kill her, then watches as Richmond's chief of staff Gloria Russell covers up the crime with the help of agents Burton and Collin. Later, Luther escapes with some valuables and an incriminating knife. DC Detective Seth Frank investigates the crime, and Luther becomes the prime suspect in the burglary. When Richmond announces he will find the murderer, Luther decides he will bring Richmond to justice. Kate, Luther's estranged daughter, is a prosecutor who suspects her father of the burglary and helps Frank with his investigation. Luther eventually contacts Kate to explain what he witnessed.

Suspecting that Kate knows the truth, Richmond orders Collin and Burton to kill her, but their attempt fails and she is hospitalized. Collin attempts to kill her in the hospital by injection but is thwarted by Luther, who kills the agent. In remorse over his murder attempt of Kate, Burton commits suicide, but leaves evidence for Frank that implicates Russell. On the television news, Sullivan claims that the President committed suicide by stabbing himself to death, while Luther watches Kate in her hospital room.

Background: *Absolute Power*, based on David Baldacci's best-seller, was Clint Eastwood's second DC-based picture in four years after *In the Line of Fire* (q.v.), this time directing. Screenwriter William Goldman made one very dramatic change from the Baldacci novel. The main character in the book is a young lawyer named Jack Graham, a friend of Whitney's and the ex-boyfriend of his daughter Kate. Goldman's screenplay eliminates Graham entirely, telling the story from the thief's point-of-view. The film had a big budget ($50 million) and a starry cast, but it was not a hit with either audiences or critics and barely made its costs back.

Comment: The film was not one of Eastwood's most successful efforts, perhaps for a couple of reasons. One, there was hardly anyone in the picture to root for, especially given the den of vipers among the White House characterizations. The President as a philanderer, abuser, and liar is bad enough, but, in addition, we have the Secret Service, which has had a generally positive reputation, shown here as a bunch of cowed lackeys and cold killers—worlds away from the stalwarts shown in Eastwood's earlier *In the Line of Fire*. Clint himself portrays a rather sour, unlikable fellow, and even the daughter figure is vinegary and distant. Perhaps only the DC detective can be warmed to—slightly. Second, and this may be more Baldacci's fault than the movie's, the storyline is over-the-top, full of holes, and often utterly implausible. A fair example is when Hackman and Davis, in an overlong, clumsy dance sequence during a White House reception, grimace, through excruciatingly pasted grins, as they fence over the provenance of a gift necklace.

DC Notes: This production was mainly shot in Baltimore, but did use DC for some establishing and landmark shots, such as the front entrance of the Watergate Hotel on Virginia Avenue, NW, and the façade of the Corcoran Gallery of Art on 17th Street, NW. Late in the picture, Luther (Eastwood) drives Sullivan into the city and eventually parks on Madison Place on the east side of Lafayette Park across the street from the White House. The Sullivan mansion in the film was shot at the striking Wickliffe Castle, which is the centerpiece of the campus of the Maryvale Preparatory School, a Catholic all girls' college preparatory school outside Baltimore. One sequence done in studio depicts the inside of the White House where Luther (Eastwood) takes a tour—and leaves an envelope surreptitiously. The production also used an Oval Office set.

Goofs: An early scene supposedly takes place in an art gallery in Washington where Luther has gone to sketch, but it was shot in the Walters Art Museum in Baltimore. There he sketches El Greco's painting of "St. Francis Receiving the Stigmata" which is in the museum's collection. Later on, he returns to the same site, but its façade shows the Corcoran Gallery of Art. Inexplicably, President Richmond (Hackman) apparently has only two men in his Secret Service detail throughout this movie (the easier to cloak a conspiracy, I guess), when, of course, the President almost always has a bevy of agents when he travels out of the White House.

President Richmond conducts a press conference at a court house, but it is not in DC, but in Baltimore.

The imposing headquarters of DC's Metropolitan Police Department has a tall, arcaded front—nothing like their real building in Washington. All the MPD police cars have blue license plates (as they did in California at the time).

On a dizzying night ride in Washington, Luther drives Sullivan (Marshall) from his mansion somewhere outside the city, then, all of the sudden he is motoring on the north side of the National Gallery's West Wing going east, only to find himself later passing the White House going west.

Insider's Note: According to Quintin Peterson, long time Motion Picture & Television Liaison Officer for DC's Metropolitan Police Department (MPD), actress Penny Johnson (Laura Simon) changed the scope of her role simply by changing her wardrobe. Johnson, playing an evidence technician, learned that the wardrobe master wanted to use that unit's shapeless uniform. She consulted Peterson to ask whether MPD evidence technicians must wear uniforms and learned that some technicians asked that uniforms be optional. Consequently, the actress got her wardrobe changed into civilian clothes, which had the effect of making her look like a detective.

34 MURDER AT 1600

1997. Warner Brothers, 107 minutes, color.

Director: Dwight Little.

Screenplay: Wayne Beach and David Hodgin, based on the book *Murder in the White House* by Margaret Truman.

Cameraman: Steven Bernstein.

Editing: Leslie Jones and Billy Weber.

Music: Christopher Young.

Principal Cast :

Wesley Snipes	Harlan Regis	Diane Baker	First Lady Kitty Neil
Diane Lane	Agent Nina Chance	Dennis Miller	Detective Stengel
Daniel Benzali	Agent Nick Spikings	Tate Donovan	Kyle Neil
Alan Alda	Alvin Jordan	Harris Yulin	Gen. Clark Tully
Ronny Cox	President Jack Neil	Tom Wright	Agent Cooper

Synopsis: The dead body of secretary Carla Town is found in a White House bathroom. DC homicide detective Harlan Regis is called in to investigate the murder only to discover that the Secret Service, represented by senior SS Agent Spikings, objects to his presence and claims all the evidence. A frustrated Regis becomes suspicious of a cover-up after preliminary investigations suggest that the Town murder may have been a sex crime and, Kyle, the son of President Jack Neil, has a history of such acts. He gets a break when he convinces SS Agent Nina Chance to assist him with his probe within the agency, which places her in danger.

At the same time, North Korea has taken US soldiers hostage, a crisis which could bring down the President, who is hesitant about sending troops on a rescue mission. Under threat from mysterious nemeses, Regis and Chance band together to solve the murder, which leads them to the president's own involvement with the secretary, to a conspiracy orchestrated by National Security Advisor Alvin Jordan, a chase through secret White House tunnels, and a final confrontation with Neil and Jordan.

Production Notes: This is another one of those "DC films" mostly made in Canada, which offered significant financial advantages at the time. The production's most ambitious element was a set of replicas of White House offices placed on 30,000 sq. ft. of soundstages in Toronto by production designer Nelson Coates. Coates made several visits to the real White House (where filming is not permitted) and studied a series of books on the subject to attain a reasonable accurate duplicate of a "working" presidential mansion. The film's screenplay was very loosely based on Margaret Truman's 1980 crime thriller *Murder at the White House*, which was the first of her more than 20 "capital" murder novels which take place in Washington settings.

DC/Hill Notes: Though filmed essentially in Toronto, *Murder at 1600* uses a good mix of Washington locales. It opens, for example, with a scene of a potential suicide in the intersection of 6th Street and Indiana Avenue, NW (the DC court buildings can be glimpsed on the right in one shot) where the resourceful Regis (Snipe) frustrates a would-be suicide. Another sequence has Regis driving past the National Gallery's West Wing and heading northwest down Pennsylvania Avenue, NW then later turning off Pennsylvania to go south on 15th Street.

There is a protest scene in front of the White House, where four television reporters are describing the scene. One of them is the popular TV anchor Maureen Bunyan, long known for her work at local stations WUSA and, most recently, WJLA. A rather lengthy scene shows Regis and Jordan (Alda) jogging around the rim of the Tidal Basin, allowing the filmmakers to work in iconic backdrops of the Washington Monument and the Jefferson Memorial.

Later in the film, Regis and Chance secretly meet in their respective cars on the Potomac Parkway below the Lincoln Memorial on a rainy night. There is also a scene at Meridian Hill Park in NW, where Regis meets Kyle (Donovan). Agent Chance (Lane) is shown going up the actual front steps of the Treasury Building. The film also incorporates standard Washington footage, especially the aerial views.

Goofs: Regis claims that the Interstate Commerce Commission (ICC) is evicting him from his home to develop a parking garage. The film, however, made in 1997, takes place two years after the ICC was abolished in 1995. To compound the Commission goof, the president tells Regis at the end of the picture that the head of the agency is the "Secretary"–rather than the ruling Commissioners.

In the jogging scene mentioned above, the only extras shown on a bright, sunny day are other joggers; there is not one standard pedestrian tourist, highly unlikely.

Sitting in a university class, Kyle is passed a note asking him to meet at "Meridian Hill," but the place is always called by its full name, Meridian Hill Park.

In escaping from other SS agents, Chance slips out of the Treasury Building to a clanky back fire escape, into a scuzzy alley, and eventually to a busy city street, none of which looks anything like the neighborhood around Treasury (it is definitely Toronto).

Regis and Chance chase through an elaborate–and entirely fictitious–White House "tunnel" system which begins from an equally fictitious mystery steam grate right on the grounds of the Washington Monument.

35 WAG THE DOG

1997. New Line Pictures, 97 minutes, color.

Director: Barry Levinson.

Written by: Hilary Henkin and David Mamet from the novel *American Hero* by Larry Beinhart.

Cinematography: Robert Richardson.

Editing: Stu Linder.

Music: Mark Knopfler.

Principal Cast:

Dustin Hoffman	Stanley Motss	William H. Macy	CIA Agent Young
Robert De Niro	Conrad Brean	John Michael Higgins	John Levy
Anne Heche	Winifred Ames	Woody Harrelson	Sgt. "Shoe" Schumann
Denis Leary	Fad King	Suzie Plakson	Grace
Willie Nelson	Johnny Dean	Suzanne Cryer	Amy Cain
Andrea Martin	Liz Butsky	David Koechner	he Director
Kirsten Dunst	Tracy Lime	Craig T. Nelson	Sen. John Neal

Synopsis: In this pitch-black comedy, the President (unnamed) is accused of fondling an underage "Firefly Girl" in the Oval Office weeks before his re-election. His aides, led by Ames, call in noted spin doctor Conrad Brean to confect a counter-story to divert attention from the scandal. Brean hires veteran Hollywood producer Stanley Motss to create a "made-for-TV" war with Albania to distract the benighted American public from the President's peccadillo. Motss brings in his crack team to "produce" the fabricated war in the basement of the White House by fashioning a scenario, creating artificial footage, and hiring a young "orphan" for sympathy interest.

Motss and Co. also create their own war hero, the criminally insane ex-Army Sgt. Schumann, chosen because his last name serves as a nickname for the war's theme song "Good Old Shoe," an old tune by country singer Johnny Dean. The President wins his election, but the media gives credit to a worn campaign slogan rather than to Motss' show biz efforts. The producer–desperate to receive final credit for something–threatens to tell the media about his enterprise, but such bravado comes with a cost. Brean has Motss killed and sets up his death to look like he suffered a heart attack beside his Hollywood pool.

Background: *Wag the Dog* was a picture made almost on the fly. Director Barry Levinson, who was in the throes of making a big budget science fiction thriller, *Sphere*, found, at the beginning of 1997, that he had a window to direct this political farce. Both films had Dustin Hoffman as their leads. Sphere's budget eventually cost five times that of *Wag the Dog*, but the latter movie did much better box office. The shoot took a little over a month. In the life imitating art category, it should be noted that *Wag the Dog* came out at the turn of the year 1997-98, just when a real White House scandal involving the president and a certain young female intern was breaking.

The credit for the film's script was the subject of some controversy, which was ultimately resolved by the Writer's Guild of America crediting the first draft writer, Hilary Henkin, as well as the writer Levinson brought in later, famed playwright David Mamet. Both were then nominated for an Academy Award for Best Screenplay Adaptation.

Some commentators noted that Hoffman's character was based directly upon the flamboyant and controversial Hollywood producer Robert Evans, copying both his mannerisms and clothing styles. In a *Newsweek* article which appeared at the time of the film's release, the real Evans even joked, "I'm magnificent in this film." Hoffman himself, speaking on the movie's DVD commentary, said that much of his characterization of Motss' was based on his own father, Harry Hoffman, a former prop supervisor for Columbia Pictures. For this role, Hoffman was nominated as Best Actor of the year by the Motion Picture Academy (his seventh nomination), the Golden Globe Awards, and the Screen Actors' Guild.

Comment: *Wag the Dog* offers a sharp, cynical satire on both White House shenanigans and Tinseltown hubris, casting a bitter eye on those twin outposts of our politics and entertainment. The film's temper feels rough-and-ready and somewhat scruffy, which seems perfectly appropriate for a project done in a hurry which describes a campaign (likewise) done in a hurry. This film, even now, at a distance of about 15 years, perhaps comes closer than any other to personify that convergence between Washington and Hollywood which I mentioned in **Politics in Film** at the beginning of the book.

The film offers a string of lively over-the-top efforts, like Anne Heche's railing Winifred, both Andrea Martin and Denis Leary as crazy consultants, Craig T. Nelson as an obtuse senator, and Woody Harrelson as a deranged psycho. Contrasted with them is the underplayed, rumpled Conrad Brean of De Niro, the cool customer who keeps all the circus balls in the air, always intoning "I'm working on it." De Niro's relative restraint, in fact, provides a lovely foil to the standout performance from Dustin Hoffman as a "producer" of a war confected by and for the White House. With his constant mantra of "This is nothing!," his Stan Motss crystallizes beautifully the attitude of the can-do-at-any-cost producer who just "don't get no respect." You feel his pain of self-inflicted injury.

Tagline: "Why does a dog wag its tail?" the unflappable Brean asks at one point. "Because the dog is smarter than the tail. If the tail was smarter, it would wag the dog." (Such as the role of a Hollywood producer.)

DC/Hill Notes: In the commentary on the DVD version of the film, director Levinson notes that there was filming in DC only one day, including a night scene with fixer Brean (DeNiro) and producer Motss (Hoffman) hanging up old tennis shoes (standing in for the ersatz hero "Shoe" that they have created) on East Capitol Street, with a young black kid joining in. *(Personal note: this shoot happened at the end of my block on Capitol Hill on a fairly cold winter night well after 1 a.m. Among a clot of quite a few onlookers, no one had a clue about what was happening.)*

In other DC shots, there is an exit from the west gate of the White House out on to Pennsylvania Avenue, a sequence at the Hay-Adams Hotel on 16th Street, NW, and a night scene with a limo driving away from the Capitol.

36 ENEMY OF THE STATE

1998. Produced by Jerry Bruckheimer Films, distributed by Touchstone Pictures and Universal Pictures, 131 minutes, color.

Director: Tony Scott.

Screenplay: David Marconi and Aaron Sorkin (uncredited).

Cinematography: Daniel Mindel.

Editing: Chris Lebenzon.

Music: Harry Gregson-Williams and Trevor Rabin.

Principal Cast:

Will Smith	Robert C. Dean	Jake Busey	Krug
Gene Hackman	Edward "Brill" Lyle	Scott Caan	Jones
Jon Voight	Thomas Reynolds	Jack Black	Fiedler
Barry Pepper	David Pratt	Jamie Kennedy	Jamie Williams
Regina King	Carla Dean	Jason Lee	Daniel Zavitz
Ian Hart	John Bingham	Gabriel Byrne	The Fake Brill
Lisa Bonet	Rachel Banks	Stuart Wilson	Cong. Sam Albert
Jascha Washington	Eric Dean	Jason Robards	Cong. Phil Hammersley
James LeGros	Jerry Miller	Tom Sizemore	Boss Paulie Pintero

Synopsis: Congressman Phil Hammersley, opposing legislation that would vastly expand the surveillance powers of government, is killed on the orders of National Security Agency official Thomas Reynolds. The murder is caught on video by wildlife researcher Zavitz who is pursued by NSA agents who will do anything to acquire his disc. Zavitz plants the disc on his old college buddy, Robert Dean, without the latter's knowledge. Dean is a successful labor lawyer in Washington, DC who lives in Georgetown with a wife and son. The NSA then goes after Dean, and, within a day, he loses his job, his assets, and his wife.

Dean is then framed for the murder of a former girlfriend, Rachel. Help finally arrives from a man named Brill who tells him he is being sought by NSA agents using sophisticated surveillance technology. Dean and the real Brill, a former communications expert with the Agency, devise a plan to get Dean's life back and turn the tables on Reynolds. They blackmail another congressman and bug Reynolds' home and manipulate his finances. Ultimately, Dean and Brill are able to arrange a deadly showdown between Reynolds and his NSA team and a mafia boss Pintero (whom Dean was pursuing as a lawyer) which resolves the situation in their favor.

Background: With *Enemy of the State*, box office stud Will Smith was just getting warmed up for what became an amazing string of blockbuster successes. Though he started modestly in a dramatic role in his first picture, *Six Degrees of Separation* (based on a stage play), he quickly moved into lucrative action pictures with *Bad Boys* (1995), *Independence Day* (1996), and *Men in Black* (1997)–all international smashes–before taking on the role of Robert Dean. *Enemy of the State* did excellent box office (about $250 million worldwide), even if it did not quite measure up to the success of his two previous films. It was Smith's biggest payday up to that time.

DC Notes: Though set in DC, a number of sequences use Baltimore as a location as well as a surrogate for DC (see **Goofs** below). Some actual Washington locations include Georgetown (where the Dean character lives), near Northwest, and downtown DC. The film incorporates a couple of interesting building stand-ins. One is the "Ruby" lingerie store, which is actually the revamped store front of "Lambda Rising," once a well-known gay/lesbian bookstore on Connecticut Avenue. A second is 601 Pennsylvania Avenue, NW, which houses the Credit Union National Association, the Capital Grille Restaurant, and several offices but which, in the film, serves as a hotel where Dean (Smith) attempts to find a room.

Goofs: One of the mixed up Baltimore-for-Washington scenes takes place during a fire in a supposedly DC hotel (and a subsequent ambulance ride). The responding unit is, in reality, from Baltimore, and one paramedic is seen wearing a Maryland Paramedic patch.

A chase sequence has a character heading for "Mount Vernon Square" in Washington, but the site used is Mount Vernon Square in Baltimore, with that city's own Washington Monument on Charles Street plainly visible.

There are a number of different scenes, supposedly taking place in Baltimore, where the NSA miscreants request satellite surveillance in areas which, given the coordinates they cite, are nowhere near Baltimore.

In another geographical goof, the opening scene is supposedly set in "Occuquan Park, Maryland", but the real Occoquan Park (different spelling) is in Virginia, not Maryland.

The FBI is identified with a shot of the Department of Transportation in Southwest DC not the real J. Edgar Hoover building on Pennsylvania Avenue, NW.

37 SLAM

1998. Distributed by Trimark Pictures, 100 minutes, color.

Director: Marc Levin. Story by Marc Levin and Richard Stratton;

Screenplay: Levin, Stratton, Bonz Malone, Saul Williams, and Sonja Sohn.

Cameraman: Mark Benjamin.

Editing: Emir Lewis.

Original Music: DJ Spooky.

Principal Cast:

Saul Williams	Ray Joshua	Momolu Stewart	Bay (Jail Rapper)
Sonja Sohn	Lauren Bell	Ron Jones	Do Wop Cop
Bonz Malone	Hopha	Reamer Shedrick	Do Wop Cop
Lawrence Wilson	Big Mike	Allan E. Lucas	Chief C.O.
Beau Sia	Jimmy Huang	Richard Stratton	Prosecutor
Andre Taylor	China	Marion Barry, Jr.	Judge

Synopsis: Raymond Joshua is a drifting African-American from Southeast DC who is into both small time drug hustling and hip-hop versifying, or slammin.' Ray works with Big Mike, a big shot in a tough section of DC called "Dodge City." When Mike is shot, undercover cops arrest Ray, who—though not the shooter—is arrested for marijuana possession. Ray's grim options are a plea resulting in two years in prison or a trial where the verdict could result in more time. At the DC jail, Ray finds release in language, and one of his raps is witnessed by Lauren Bell, a teacher there who wants him to join her poetry class but has to cancel the class due to lack of funding.

Ray learns that others think he set up Big Mike, but he finds protection from tough inmate Hopha. With Hopha's help, Ray makes bail and looks up Lauren. The two come to share their poetry and more, but Ray still must face his charges, and his dilemma about admitting his crime –and doing time. Ray revisits Dodge City in the role of a peacemaker for the beleaguered community, and, with Lauren's help, he carries off a triumphant slam riff at a club on Connecticut Avenue. The question remains whether

Ray will do what Lauren wishes him to do–take his jail time–or try to run away from life. The film ends ambiguously, with Ray approaching a ghostly Washington Monument.

Background: Director Marc Levin came to his first feature after a decade working in documentaries with a political and social slant, many treating troubled youth or prison life. Ex-cons he knew contributed to *Slam*. Bonz Malone, who co-wrote the film and plays Hopha, was a 17-year-old graffiti artist serving time at Rikers Island prison when Levin first met him. Richard Stratton, a writer and convicted marijuana smuggler, co-wrote the story with Levin and collaborated on the screenplay.

Levin said the film's genesis stems from the question posed to him in 1993 by a young kid who observed him preparing a documentary on gang wars and asked him: "Are you ever going to make a real movie?" It was a question that stayed with the director.

It was while working in DC that Levin had gotten to know people at the city's Department of Corrections. He asked if he could film DC jail and found, "they were open to it." Levin, in an interview suggested: "It was a seam in time, I call it, where the US Congress under Gingrich had stripped DC of home rule and condemned their whole corrections system. You had a city and a system that felt nobody cared about them. We were the only people interested, so it was a once in a lifetime opportunity." Permission was thus granted to shoot in the city jail, the only time it has been shown in a feature film.

A key element of the story came from Levin's witnessing Saul Williams in a competitive slam performance in Greenwich Village. After casting Williams and co-star Sonja Sohn, the director and his cast did story workshops to prepare for filming, and Levin used an improvisational approach to various scenes.

Slam was the unanimous winner of the 1998 Grand Jury Prize at the Sundance Film Festival, and it was also crowned with the "Prix du Public" (audience award) at the 1998 Cannes Film Festival. Though it offered an intriguing look at a forgotten side of Washington, *Slam* did little business. Released in the fall of 1998, its initial box office run never made back its approximately $1 million cost. It has been very little seen by Washingtonians.

Comments: The film, while modest in production values, offers several re-wards, especially to a DC film fan. Levin and his cinematographer, Mark Benjamin, capture much of the edge and bite of the city in a documentary style. And it's not all grit, either: one handsome, extended shot simply holds on a pensive Ray silhouetted against a blazing, orange-dappled Anacostia River. The photography and direction can signal meaning also, as when Ray leaves jail to walk up the street to the Congressional Cemetery, then leaps the wall to walk among the graves: a short but symbolic journey for a young black man—between incarceration and death.

The film effectively showcases its two leads, both slam poets who can spin extended hip-hop rhymes to transfix a crowd. Williams, a trained actor/performer may not seem very "street" and his acting wavers in tone, but he exhibits easy likability and considerable vulnerability. He is powerful delivering his high-flying, incantatory slams, all of which he wrote for the film. He meets his match in Sohn, a winning actress who can also slam-bam with the best of them (she is probably best remembered for her role as Detective Kima Greggs in the renowned HBO series *The Wire*).

DC/Hill Notes: *Slam* is a singular film in this chronology: a feature film that was shot exclusively in locations in the city—with no studio work. In that, it especially offers a view of Southeast DC that few filmgoers have seen on screen. For locals, the film presents a wealth of recognizable loca-tions, including areas around RFK Stadium, the Congressional Cemetery, Anacostia housing developments, the District Courthouse, the Washington Monument, and, of course, the D.C. Jail itself.

There is a pleasant sequence set at Eastern Market on Capitol Hill, where Lauren and Ray (Sohn and Williams) roam, hand in hand. It plays like an urban dream, which is how many Hillites think about the Market anyway, so it's sweet to see it recognized for once on film. Uniquely at the time among films made in Washington, Slam includes a sequence shot *inside* a Metro station, that of Cleveland Park. This sequence may have been made surreptitiously, since Metro authorities banned filming inside the system at this time.

Among all the local sights, it's a special kick to see Mayor Marion Barry (then in his fourth term) playing a District judge, swathed in a purple robe, and dutifully admonishing Ray's actions by intoning "these drugs are killing our community," years after Barry was arrested on drug charges (in 1990).

Goofs: The film gets DC fundamentally right. Just one quibble (surely done for reasons of convenience): In the Metro sequence mentioned above, the Cleveland Park station ends up serving double duty since protagonist Ray both boards and disembarks there.

38 RANDOM HEARTS

1999. Columbia Pictures, 133 minutes, color.

Director: Sydney Pollack.

Screenplay: by Kurt Luedtke, adaptation by Darryl Ponicsan from a novel of the same name by Warren Adler.

Cinematography: Phillippe Rousselot.

Editing: William Steinkamp.

Original Music: Dave Grusin.

Principal Cast:

Harrison Ford	"Dutch" Van Den Broeck	Susanna Thompson	Mrs. Van Den Broeck
Kristin Scott Thomas	Kay Chandler	Peter Coyote	Cullen Chandler
Charles S. Dutton	Alcee	Kate Mara	Jessica Chandler
Bonnie Hunt	Wendy Judd	Susan Floyd	Molly Roll
Dennis Haysbert	Det. George Beaufort	Dylan Baker	Richard Judd
Sydney Pollack	Carl Broman	Lynne Thigpen	Phyllis Bonaparte
Richard Jenkins	Truman Trainor	Edie Falco	Janice
Paul Guilfoyle	Dick Montoya	Bill Cobb	Marvin

Synopsis: Sergeant Dutch Van Den Broek is a DC cop and Kay Chandler is a first-term Republican congresswomen from New Hampshire. Dutch's wife and Kay's husband are lovers who, headed for a tryst in Miami, die together in a plane crash. Dutch's marriage had become routine, and he is completely focused on work, while Kay is consumed with a tough re-election campaign. In investigating her death, Dutch learns that his wife had lied to him. He pieces together the affair and tells Kay. Revengeful, he wants to find out the whole truth about the affair; Kay, much cooler, just wants to move on and protect her teen-aged daughter Jessica from its sordid reality.

Dutch later goes to Miami to try to learn more about what brought their ex's to Miami, where Kay joins him. The two slowly grow closer and spend a romantic interlude at a secluded cabin on the Chesapeake Bay. Pursuing a tough case involving a crooked cop, Dutch is wounded by a gun shot and ends up in the hospital, while Kay loses her election and prepares to leave

Washington. Their future together remains open.

Production Notes: The film's script generally follows the story of the Warren Adler novel but alters the characters significantly. The picture was in "development hell"–ticketed to be made into a movie which never happened for some years–with Kevin Costner once attached to the project in the early 1990's. Writer Darryl Ponicsan developed a script during that time which was never picked up, but director Sydney Pollack eventually signed on and got journalist Kurt Luedtke to do a new scenario.

Pollack gave himself a decent role in the film as Carl Broman, a political operator who comes to work for the Congresswoman on her campaign. Pollack said it was easier to cast himself as Broman rather than hire someone who had to appear in a series of disparate scenes over the life of the shoot. The film was not a critical success and also proved tepid at the box office. Budgeted at $64 million, *Random Hearts* made less than half that amount in US domestic rentals.

DC Notes: The film did some exteriors in New York and almost all of its interiors, but there were still sundry sequences shot in and around DC. One elaborate scene shot at the Patuxent River Naval Air Station, shows the downed airplane (just a tail piece was used) in the Chesapeake Bay with naval and police personnel swarming the site. The crash idea, used originally by novelist Adler, came from the notorious crash of Air Florida Flight 90 in the Potomac River on January 13, 1982.

There are three scenes filmed at Reagan National Airport just outside Washington, two different ones in a parking lot and the concluding scene of the film in one of the airport terminals. A key scene happens on the National Mall where Dutch (Ford) confronts a jogging Kay (Scott Thomas), and they have a crucial conversation. Another lengthy sequence was shot in the Saks Fifth Avenue store in Friendship Heights, NW, where Dutch receives the first intimations of his wife's affair from store workers. Other scenes feature a car crash shot on Rhode Island Avenue, NE, an ambulance roaring down Independence Avenue, NW (after Dutch is shot), and a Christmas-adorned Union Station.

Goofs: Dutch drives into what purports to be an MPD headquarters but is actually an archway entrance of the Federal Triangle.

In some scenes the Washington Monument is shown with scaffolding surrounding it and in others it is in its normal state (the monument was undergoing a major restoration during that time).

Kay is shown driving back from Chesapeake Bay to DC, going over a bridge that is definitely not in the Washington area.

Dutch and Kay exit the Washington National Airport (now Reagan National) upon their return from Miami, and Dutch says that he lives in Northwest (meaning Northwest DC). Yet the Lincoln Memorial is behind them as they drive across Memorial Bridge, which means they are going into Virginia and away from DC–the wrong way.

When Kay is ready to leave her congressional office after her electoral defeat, she finds that a new staff aide is already in the same office (highly unlikely). She is then shown exiting by walking down the snow-laden East Front steps of the (real) Capitol, an impossibility because she is a junior representative who would have an individual office in one of three House office buildings, but never in the Capitol itself.

39 DICK

1999. Columbia Pictures, 94 minutes, color.

Director: Andrew Fleming.

Screenplay by: Fleming and Sheryl Longin.

Cinematography: Alexander Gruszynski.

Editing: Mia Goldman.

Original Music: John Debney.

Principal Cast:

Kirsten Dunst	Betsy Jobs	Jim Breuer	John Dean
Michelle William	Arlene Lorenzo	Harry Shearer	G. Gordon Liddy
Dan Hedaya	President Nixon	Ana Gasteyer	Rose Mary Woods
Saul Rubinek	Henry Kissinger	Ryan Reynolds	Chip
Will Ferrell	Bob Woodward	Ted McGinley	Roderick
Bruce McCulloch	Carl Bernstein	Karl Pruner	Frank Jobs
Teri Garr	Helen Lorenzo	Devon Gummersall	Larry Jobs
Dave Foley	Bob Haldeman	G.D. Spradlin	Ben Bradlee

Synopsis: It's 1972 in DC: Betsy Jobs and Arlene Lorenzo, two sweet but ditzy 15-year-olds, are best friends: Betsy lives in Georgetown, while Arlene lives in the Watergate complex. One night, they accidentally cause the Watergate break-in to be discovered and happen upon G. Gordon Liddy. The next day, while on a White House tour, they come across Liddy again, who becomes suspicious of the girls. On the same visit, they encounter President Nixon who, in order to keep their silence on what they know, appoints them his "Official Dog Walkers" for Checkers.

On various White House visits, now as "Secret Youth Advisors" to the President, they accidentally influence major events such as the Vietnam peace process and the Nixon-Brezhnev accord and inadvertently learn the major secrets of the Watergate scandal. Arlene becomes infatuated with the president but rejects him when she hears his profane voice on tape just after taping her own 18½-minute profession of love into his recorder. The girls decide to reveal everything to *Washington Post* reporters Woodward and Bernstein. They thus become the secret "Deep Throat," threatening and eventually ending Nixon's political career.

Comment: This giddy lampoon of the Watergate scandal turned out to be, in part, a reunion of sketch-comedy players. From the Canadian group "The Kids in the Hall" came McCulloch and Foley. *Saturday Night Live* was represented by Ferrell, Shearer, Breuer, and Ana Gasteyer, a DC native who grew up on Capitol Hill. Among the principal players, Dan Hedaya's Nixon is fairly effective–if on the overly boobish side, and Saul Rubinek as Kissinger, with a guttural German accent, is amusing. Still, as farce, the representations of a number of the actual White House personnel were, at best, approximate. For example, Dave Foley's lone concession to impersonating the ever-stern Bob Haldeman was a clunky crewcut, and Jim Breuer looks nothing like the bland, balding John Dean. Similarly, Bruce McCulloch's pixie face is not even close to the earnest, pained look of Carl Bernstein.

DC/Hill Notes: Yet another "Washington" movie with major elements shot in Canada, in this case, Toronto, where a decent reproduction of the Oval Office was constructed. There are establishing shots of the White House, the Watergate complex, and the Washington Monument. There is also a sequence with the girls running through Georgetown which shows the C & O canal. Among actual DC locations shown are the Ellipse and the reflecting pool of the Lincoln Memorial.

For multiple shots of the exterior of the White House, a model was used. When the girls wait in line outside for the White House tour, the shooting was actually done at the zoo in Toronto.

Goofs: Nixon's dog in the movie is Checkers (made famous in his 1952 speech as a vice presidential candidate), but Checkers died in 1964, well before Nixon became president.

At one point, Betsy (Dunst) runs from her Georgetown home to Arlene's (Williams) apartment at the Watergate, a dash of probably more than a dozen blocks which takes about three seconds.

Quick Cuts – The Last Decade

Into the millennium and beyond, Washington, DC continues to be a desired location for Hollywood filmmakers. If anything, the variety of films treating our capital has increased and expanded as screenwriters keep finding new stories to tell.

Congress and the Presidency remain on the front burner, of course. Some of those, besides those treated fully in this section, include *Head of State* (2003), *The Manchurian Candidate* (2005), *Rendition* (2007), and *Lions for Lambs* (2007). Other DC-related pictures in a variety of genres can be cited: mystery (*Hannibal* - 2002), spy tales (*The Recruit* - 2003, *The Good Shepherd* – 2006), action films (*XXX-State of the Union* – 2005, *Live Free or Die Hard* – 2007, *Salt* – 2010), science fiction (*The Invasion* - 2007), romance (*Chasing Liberty* – 2003), and comedies (*Wedding Crashers* - 2005, *Man of the Year* – 2006, *Evan Almighty* – 2007, *Get Smart* – 2008). All continue to be made. And, of course, the market still hungers for the facile, blow-em-up-real-good products–like *Transformers: Dark of the Moon* (2011).

Finally, too, a new DC genre may be emerging with films featuring lobbyists, like *Thank You For Smoking* and *Casino Jack* described in this section. Even pieces of the city's history are being treated–witness the recent *J. Edgar.*

40 THE CONTENDER

Sometimes you can assassinate a leader without firing a shot.

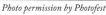

Photo permission by Photofest

2000. DreamWorks and Icon Entertainment, distributed by Paramount Pictures, 126 minutes, color.

Director and screenplay: Rod Lurie.

Cinematography: Denis Maloney.

Editing: Michael Jablow.

Original Music: Larry Groupé.

Principal Cast:

Joan Allen..................... Sen. Laine Hanson	Philip Baker Hall .... Oscar Billings
Jeff Bridges ....President Jackson Evans	Mike Binder...........................Lewis Hollis
Gary Oldman............ Cong. Shelly Runyon	Robin Thomas.................. William Hanson
William Petersen .... Gov. Jack Hathaway	Mariel Hemingway................ Cynthia Lee
Sam Elliott......................Kermit Newman	Kathryn Morris....... FBI Agent Willomina
Christian Slater.... Cong. Reginald Webster	Kristen Shaw ....Fiona Hathaway
Saul Rubinek........................ Jerry Tolliver	Douglas Urbanski...................Makerowitz

Synopsis: President Evans, nearing the end of his term, must fill the vacancy created by the death of his vice-president. Governor Hathaway of Virginia is a logical choice since he is a national hero after rescuing a young woman who crashed her car into a river where the governor had been fishing. But the President is interested in leaving a legacy by placing a woman in high office and names a rising Democratic (ex-Republican) female senator, Laine Hanson. She is, however, doggedly opposed by Republican Congressman Runyon, who is chairing her confirmation hearings for the House Judiciary Committee. The Congressman seeks dirt on Hanson and finds it when he learns of an alleged sexual escapade from her college days which could derail her chances.

Hanson vacillates about whether to continue to fight on against Runyon and the general political odds, but ultimately she challenges the Congressman, refusing to answer the scandal charges because they are beneath her dignity and amount to a sexist attack. Runyon, meanwhile pushes Hathaway for the post. The President then discovers that Hathaway's heroic act was staged and confronts the governor and Runyon with this knowledge, which leads up to a spirited finale. While the ever-calm Hanson is doing her routine jogging, the President calls for a special session of Congress, strides into the House chamber, upbraids the glum Runyon, and orders a roll call to confirm his nominee.

Background: Writer/director Rod Lurie is a filmmaker who specializes in political themes. Born in Israel, he grew up in the US and graduated from West Point in 1984. After military service, he became an entertainment and film critic in print and on the air. He moved into filmmaking in the late 1990's, and his first feature *Deterrence* (1999), concerns a stranded president who must confront a military crisis in the Middle East. *The Contender*, released in 2000, was his breakthrough film as a writer/director. His two leads, Allen and Bridges, were nominated for Academy Awards as Best Actress and Supporting Actor for their performances.

In 2005, Lurie created and executive-produced the ABC television drama *Commander in Chief*, a follow-up to *The Contender*. Though he approached Joan Allen about the lead role, Geena Davis was eventually cast as the first female president of the US. In the series, the characters of the President and Vice President were named after the leads in *The Contender*: Teddy Bridges, named for Jeff Bridges (who played President Evans), and MacKenzie Allen, named for Joan Allen (Laine Hanson). The program lasted just one season.

In 2008, Lurie wrote and directed another politically-themed drama, the journalistic thriller *Nothing But the Truth*. The picture, which fictionalized the case of Judith Miller of *The New York Times* and the outed CIA operative Valerie Plame, starred Kate Beckinsale and Vera Farmiga. When it was ready to open, the film's distributor filed for Chapter 11, and it never received a theatrical release.

DC/Hill Notes: The film was mostly shot in Virginia, partly in Richmond and partly in Petersburg, VA (where some studio work was also done). In one local Virginia reference, Hanson (Allen) is seen jogging past the Iwo Jima Memorial. In one party scene, a number of real senators–Orrin Hatch, et.al.–appear. There are numerous White House "interiors," including an Oval Office set.

The climatic finale in the Congress could not use actual locations, so the filmmakers adapted. President Evans (Bridges) goes to a House chamber that is actually the Virginia State House, and which was used for a similar final scene in the political comedy *Dave* (q.v.). This scene is intercut with Sen. Hanson jogging in what is meant to be Arlington Cemetery, but which is actually an open field filled with styrofoam headstones (see **Goofs** below).

Goofs: Driving to the White House from Capitol Hill, Hanson is shown going over Memorial Bridge, with the Lincoln Memorial at her back (wrong direction) then crossing the Mall with the Capitol in the background before arriving.

In Runyon's office, the congressman (Oldman) refers to *The Washington Post*'s "afternoon edition," which does not exist.

Hanson is seen jogging in Arlington National Cemetery, but jogging is not permitted in the cemetery, not even for a senator.

Egregious Ending: Sadly, the final congressional scene is rife with errors. In the film, the President (Bridges) calls for a joint session of Congress, which only the Congress can do. He arrives in a House chamber about the size of a DC grade school auditorium, with some 7-8 rows of seats and open windows on three sides. Then, before the he begins to speak, the President turns to look over his right shoulder to address "Mr. Speaker," but the Speaker would always be seated over his left shoulder during a joint session (the Vice President would be in the other chair) .

Finally, to cap it off, President Evans calls for a "live roll call" of the assembled to confirm his vice-presidential candidate on the spot, an unheard of–and utterly unconstitutional–procedure. For this whole sequence, the writer/director could have brushed up on a little Civics 101.

41 THIRTEEN DAYS

 2000. Beacon Pictures, distributed by New Line Cinema, 145 minutes, color and black & white.

Director: Roger Donaldson.

Writer: David Self.

Director of Photography: Andrzej Bartkowiak.

Editing: Conrad Buff.

Music: Trevor Jones.

Principal Cast:

Bruce Greenwood	John F. Kennedy	Tim Kelleher	Ted Sorensen
Steven Culp	Robert F. Kennedy	Len Cariou	Dean Acheson
Kevin Costner	Kenneth O'Donnell	Michael Fairman	Adlai Stevenson
Dylan Baker	Robert McNamara	Ed Lauter	Lt. Gen. Marshall Carter
Kevin Conway	Gen. Curtis LeMay	Oleg Krupa	Andrei Gromyko
Frank Wood	McGeorge Bundy	Lucinda Jenney	Helen O'Donnell
Henry Strozier	Dean Rusk	Stephanie Romanov	Jacqueline Kennedy

Synopsis: It is late October 1962, and US Air Force U-2 spy planes have confirmed the impending installation of Soviet surface-to-surface missiles in Castro's Cuba. While there is agreement that the missiles must go, there is little agreement within the NSC's ExComm (Executive Committee) as to how. The Chiefs of Staff fear attacks on the population and air bases that would cripple the US and favor destruction of the missiles with an invasion of the island to follow. President Kennedy feels such actions could lead to Soviet moves on West Berlin and to a wider, catastrophic war.

The missiles are not yet operational, however, leaving JFK and his national security team time to figure out a solution–whether by diplomatic means or by force. He pushes his staff and cabinet, coordinated by his brother Bobby, to come up with some other, mutually face-saving, solution. Secretary of Defense McNamara proposes a naval blockade of Cuba, which would stop new missiles from reaching Cuba. Over 13 days, there is a gradual escalation of threat and counter threat, feint and counter feint, up to the final exchanges when the nuclear superpowers were, in Secretary of State Dean Rusk's pungent phrase, "...eyeball to eyeball, and I think the other fellow just blinked."

Background: Robert F. Kennedy (RFK) wrote a posthumous account of the crisis in his 1969 book *Thirteen Days: A Memoir of the Cuban Missile Crisis*. The book was used as the basis for a 1974 television docudrama *The Missiles of October* (with William Devane and Martin Sheen as the Kennedy brothers). *Thirteen Days* used the same title, but the film was based on an entirely different book: *The Kennedy Tapes: Inside the White House During the Cuban Missile Crisis* (by Ernest May and Philip Zelikow).

Kevin Costner was a producer on the film and his box office clout helped realize the project, but, as the star, he gave his character, Special Assistant Kenny O'Donnell, a role out of all proportion to that of the real O'Donnell. Producers of the film saw the O'Donnell character as a necessary "tour guide" for the crisis event, an observer figure who could stand in as a representative for the audience. This is very evident in the numerous committee scenes with internal cuts showing a silent O'Donnell earnestly listening but not contributing to the conversation.

Secretary of Defense Robert McNamara criticized the film's depiction of O'Donnell in a *PBS NewsHour* interview in March 2001, saying: "For God's sakes, Kenny O'Donnell didn't have any role whatsoever in the missile crisis; he was a political appointment secretary to the President; that's absurd." McNamara felt that Ted Sorenson essentially performed the role that O'Donnell is given in the drama. However, in the same interview, McNamara lauded the overall film (as a dramatization) as "an absolutely fascinating...and very constructive and responsible portrayal of a very, very serious crisis..."

Production Notes: The film, on a number of occasions, begins a sequence with black-and-white footage which gradually turns into color. In commenting on the film (on DVD), director Roger Donaldson said this technique was used to mimic a series of famous *LIFE* magazine photos taken at the time of the crisis and, thus, to evoke a documentary feel of the period. The filmmakers invented a scene where O'Donnell spars lightly with Jackie Kennedy upstairs in the White House, a scene aimed at confirming the closeness of O'Donnell to the family.

Thirteen Days was an expensive effort for New Line Cinema ($80 million), but–while critically well received–the movie's receipts came nowhere near its production costs.

Comments: Some viewers will enjoy comparing the performances with real-life figures. Bruce Greenwood is a lean and sincere JFK, with good hair, an under-played Boston accent and a slightly blank visage that fits his character–because he thus hides his views from his older advisors. Steven Culp is an appropriately callow, edgy Bobby, acting tough while looking vulnerable. The two play off each other well as international novices under inordinate pressure from skeptical political veterans. Donaldson felt the two actors turned out to be "the right guys" to play the brothers.

Filmgoers–especially the politically-minded ones–should have fun picking out the players in the crisis. Most of the veteran character actors credibly embody the historical characters they play. For long-time Washington theatergoers, for example, it's fun to see one-time Arena Stage veteran Henry Strozier as the avuncular Dean Rusk. The military advisors (especially Kevin Conway as a barely contained Gen. Curtis LeMay) appear a bit over the top, but only one characterization seems clearly off-base. Michael Fairman, playing Adlai Stevenson (shown reenacting his United Nations challenge of the Soviets), badly misses the qualities of the Illinois governor in both look and tone.

DC Notes: *Thirteen Days* is a hermetic movie, with many tight scenes of earnest men in dark suits in the Oval Office or in the Cabinet Room (made on Hollywood sets). As a movie of mostly interiors, it used relatively little location shooting in Washington, though there was a second unit which contributed some footage. There are some standard scene-setters of the White House, Lafayette Park, the Pentagon, the Justice Department, and, unique to DC movies, the Pan American Union building on 17th Street, NW.

One interesting use of documentary material was the incorporation of actual newsreel footage of a demonstration in front of the White House during October 1962. In order for it to match the film's look, Donaldson said the newsreel was colorized frame-by-frame and then matched up with some contemporary shots outside the building.

Goofs: In a late sequence, O'Donnell is driving RFK to the Russian Embassy (then on 16th Street, NW) but their car is shown motoring east down Pennsylvania Avenue, NW with the Capitol in the background, a direction completely turned around if you are heading from the White House to the Embassy—mere blocks away.

42 ALONG CAME A SPIDER

 2001. Paramount Pictures, 103 minutes, color.

Screenplay: Marc Moss, based on the novel by James Patterson.

Direction: Lee Tamahori.

Cinematography: Matthew F. Leonetti.

Editing: Neil Travis and Nicolas de Toth.

Original Music: Jerry Goldsmith.

Principal Cast:

Morgan Freeman	Det. Alex Cross	Penelope Ann Miller	Elizabeth Rose
Monica Potter	Jezzie Flannigan	Billy Burke	Ben Devine
Michael Wincott	Gary Soneji	Anton Yelchin	Dmiitri Starodubov
Dylan Baker	Ollie McArthur	Jay O. Sanders	Kyle Craig
Mika Boorem	Megan Rose	Anna Maria Horsford	Vickie
Michael Moriarty	Sen. Hank Rose	Kim Hawthorne	Agenct Hickley

Synopsis: Megan Rose, the young daughter of a US senator, is kidnapped by a teacher at her posh private school in Washington. The kidnapper calls Metropolitan Police detective Alex Cross, a forensic expert whose skill the kidnapper, Soneji, aims to test. Cross senses Soneji doesn't want ransom but rather fame through imitating the 1932 Lindberg kidnapping. Cross then takes on as his partner the Secret Service agent Jezzie Flannigan, who was part of the girl's protection detail. Soneji keeps Megan hidden on a boat, but, when he tries to undertake an even higher profile kidnapping of the son of the Russian president, he finds his hostage has been taken–meaning someone else is involved in her capture.

The new kidnapper, this time demanding a ransom of diamonds, sends Cross on a wild goose chase in Washington to test his skills even further, and the detective delivers the goods. But when Soneji ultimately tracks down Cross and Flannigan at the latter's home, Alex learns that he knows nothing of the ransom demand and kills him. A search of Flannigan's computer leads Cross to learn of the true kidnappers and the rescue of Megan.

Production Notes: The screenplay by Marc Moss was liberally adapted from the 1993 novel of the same title by prolific mystery writer James Patterson, with much of the plot elements transmogrified. *Along Came a Spider* was the first book in Patterson's Alex Cross series, although the second one to be filmed, following *Kiss the Girls* in 1997, also with Morgan Freeman. Though hardly a critical success, the film was a box office winner, costing $28 million to make and earning over $105 million worldwide.

DC Notes: For a number of years, Hollywood studios have looked to save production costs by using Canadian locations because of excellent technical personnel and studio facilities available at a lower cost (see **Location, Location, Location**). *Along Came a Spider* was shot in and around Vancouver, British Columbia. The principal DC location shooting was done in the core of the city to describe the elaborate cat-and-mouse chase the kidnappers' foist on Alex Cross (Freeman) when he is trying to deliver a ransom (see **Goofs** below for full description).

Goofs: There are many. To begin with, young Megan (Boorem) goes to the "Cathedral School" in NW Washington, presumably the "National Cathedral School" at the Washington National Cathedral. This building looks nothing like the actual DC school. Further, National Cathedral School is a girls-only school, not a co-ed school as indicated in the film.

The film shows SS Agent Flannigan (Potter) and other agents protecting Megan, but the US Secret Service does not protect Senators and their families. As a branch of the Treasury Department, it protects only Presidents, former Presidents, presidential candidates, and visiting heads of state.

A standard driving goof: heading for the girl's school, Cross (Freeman) heads west into Virginia on Memorial Bridge, the opposite direction of the school.

When Cross and Flannigan arrive at a site on Chesapeake Bay to investigate the scene of a fisherman murdered by Soneji (Wincott), mountains are visible in the background—a real shock to anyone living on the Bay.

Cross carries an officer's badge, not a detective's, and does not carry the Glock 19, the standard issue sidearm for MPD detectives (according to retired MPD officer Quintin Peterson).

One Wild Goof Chase: A kidnapper phones Cross, carrying a thermos full of diamonds as a ransom, and gives him 20 minutes to drive to "The Watergate," where he arrives at the Watergate Hotel on Virginia Avenue, NW, and sprints into the hotel lobby. On the phone again, he is told he must go only on foot to other sites, beginning with instructions to run in "14 minutes" to "Pennsylvania and 6th," to the (National Gallery) Fountain. This distance, 2.1 miles, could hardly be managed by the 60-plus year old Freeman! At the fountain, Cross answers the phone (at a non-existent phone booth) and is told that he must go, "in 12 minutes" to "12th and Madison" in the middle of the Mall at the level of the Smithsonian Butterfly Garden. Again, there is a phantom phone booth, and he is told he has four minutes to run to "Union Station—Main Entrance." To reach Union Station—a distance of 1.5 miles—Cross would have to be a superhuman runner.

At the Station, Cross locates a ringing cell phone in a trash can. There, he is ordered to go to the "Metro, Platform A" (Metro does not list platforms), where he boards a–voila!–Baltimore subway car. Cross and Flannigan both get on the "Metro," but the train they board is an Amtrak car, which allows movement between cars, an action forbidden on the real Metro. Their train, shown coming out of a tunnel, has a red-and-blue "MTA" logo on the front, the logo of the Maryland Transportation Authority. While speeding on the train, Cross dumps the thermos of diamonds on the track to be picked up by a shadowy figure. End of sequence–whew!

43 MINORITY REPORT

2002. Amblin Entertainment; distributed by DreamWorks Pictures and 20th Century Fox, 145 minutes, color.

Director: Stephen Spielberg.

Screenplay by Scott Frank and Jon Cohen, based on the short story *The Minority Report* by Philip K. Dick.

Cinematography: Janusz Kaminski.

Editing: Michael Kahn.

Musical Score: John Williams.

Principal Cast

Tom Cruise	Capt. John Anderton	Jessica Capshaw	Evanna
Max von Sydow	Lamar Burgess	Lois Smith	Dr. Iris Hineman
Colin Farrell	Danny Witwer	Kathryn Morris	Lara Anderton
Samantha Morton	Agatha (lead "precog")	Peter Stormare	Eddie Solomon
Steve Harris	Jad	Mike Binder	Leo Crow
Neal McDonough	Gordon Fletcher	Tim Blake Nelson	Gideon
Patrick Kilpatrick	Knott	Joel Gretsch	Donald Durbin

Synopsis: In Washington, DC in 2054, murder has been eliminated for the last six years. Future crimes are seen and the potential perpetrators apprehended before the crime has ever been committed. The visions are seen by the "pre-cogs," three psychic beings held in liquid suspension who see future murders within a complex in the city's elite PreCrime Unit, headed by Chief John Anderton. As head of the unit, Anderton is the first to see the images as they flow from the pre-cogs dreams. Damaged by the disappearance of his son and the alienation of his wife, Lara, Anderton throws all of his passion into a system that could potentially be used nationwide, the dream of its director, Lamar Burgess. Department of Justice official Danny Witwer comes to audit the system and is skeptical of its effectiveness. Anderton is surprisingly identified by the pre-cogs as a killer himself who will murder a man named Leo Crow in 36 hours. Anderton must somehow go below the radar of this totally automated city, where everyone is monitored, and he must both change his identity and uncover the truth of what the pre-cogs have said of him. It leads him to both drastic measures (he must change his eyeball code) and drastic actions (he kidnaps the purest of the pre-cogs, Agatha, to find the truth). He eventually confronts Crow, who informs Anderton that he has been set up, and then proves himself to Witwer, but he still must find the person responsible in the PreCrime organization and bring him to justice.

Background: Philip Dick's short story (written in 1956) was first optioned for filming as early as 1992, with novelist Jon Cohen hired in 1997 to adapt it. Simultaneously, Tom Cruise and Stephen Spielberg had been trying for years to find a suitable project to work on together, and in 1998, they announced they would develop the Cohen script as a joint venture. However, production was delayed for a few years, and, in the meantime, Spielberg brought in screenwriter Scott Frank to rework Cohen's screenplay. The film was delayed a bit further so Spielberg could finish another science fiction effort, *A.I.*

Minority Report takes place in a near future (2054), and in a newly imagined, technically advanced Washington, yet the filmmakers were careful to create a still believable DC (the original story was set in New York City). Thus, major landmarks, like the Capitol and the Washington Monument, were incorporated to represent the traditional city in the film, while a section of ultra-modern facilities were confected across the Potomac in a newfangled Rosslyn, Virginia. The aim, in all design elements, was to show a place that was modern, but not too modern.

Thus gritty real locations were combined with plenty of elaborate digital effects. The film required massive uses of green-screen technologies, computer-generated effects, animation work (the robot "spyders" that can perform retinal scans), and holographic projections—the latter in dramatic evidence in the "PreCrime" scenes. The film also has a distinct, grey-blue esthetic, giving off a metallic sheen. This look was achieved by a process called "bleach-bypassing" which desaturated the picture's colors to the point that it often approaches a black-and-white movie.

Comment: Critical reception of *Minority Report* ranged from the glowing to the tepid, though almost all reviewers were impressed with Spielberg's daring and striking vision. Mike LaSalle of the *San Francisco Chronicle* raved: "Creative energy and intelligence inform every frame. This is the kind of pure entertainment that, in its fullness and generosity, feels almost classic." Lisa Schwarzbaum, writing in *Entertainment Weekly,* felt that "*Minority Report* becomes an alluring postcard from the edge." J. Hoberman of *The Village Voice* offered the sourer note: "*Minority Report* is a movie of haunting images and mindless thrills."

In general, the film impressed more for its technical dimensions than for its story or characterizations. Its true fans, then and now, were techno-nerds, folks impressed with its cool technologies and gee-whiz futurism. Long after its release, news sources continued to note that many of the future technologies depicted in the film were prescient, for example, a June 2010 report from *The Guardian* entitled "Why *Minority Report* Was Spot On."

The film did solid box office in the United States–over \$132 million–but really cleaned up overseas, bagging more than \$226 worldwide, almost doubling its US take. It was nominated for a single Academy Award, for Best Sound Editing, but did not win.

DC/Hill Notes: Filming took place in the spring and summer of 2001 in Washington, DC, Virginia, and Los Angeles. Film locations included the Ronald Reagan Building (as PreCrime headquarters), a Gap store on Wisconsin Avenue, and in Georgetown. The skyline of Rosslyn, Virginia, is visible when Anderton and his team fly out to a crime scene. A climactic night scene takes place on a computer-generated set of a roof that looks like the top of the Old Executive Office Building with a view of a gleaming Washington Monument in the distance.

The film opens dramatically with an elaborate pre-crime sequence which features the 1700 block of C Street, SE. This sequence, some 12 minutes long, was noted by many commentators as the action highlight of this action thriller. A set of near identical row houses was needed for the sequence, in which Captain Anderton (Cruise) and his team must chase down a potential killer. The sequence is detailed below in the **"Special Section."**

Goofs: In the scene mentioned above, the PreCrime SWAT team's flying squad car is shown heading south directly over the Tidal Basin, then in the next cut, flying straight west towards the Lincoln Memorial, an impossible right turn.

Special Section

The brilliant opening chase sequence follows Captain Anderton (Cruise) going after a potential killer in what is actually a Washington, DC rowhouse.

The first shots are dreamlike images of an affair and a disaffected husband killing his wife and her lover with a scissors...these are the "pre-cognitive" visions of a psychic who sees future scenes of murder. Her "pre-visualization" triggers the system to identify both the victims of the crime and its perpetrator, Howard Marks. It sends Anderton and his team to locate the site and stop the crime, scheduled for 8:04 AM, in less than 15 minutes.

Anderton first brings in live images of two witnesses to confirm the pre-cog vision and to "validate" police action. Then, on a large curved screen, the policeman examines the action to come for clues (as Schubert's "Unfinished" Symphony wells up on the track).

The scene then shifts to Marks leaving a row house on Capitol Hill to pick up his newspaper, when he notices a man in the park across the street, a fact he mentions to his distracted wife.

Back at PreCrime, the police are sorting out the eight Howard Marks who live in the District, identifying them on their screens by driver's license photos. Marks' address is identified, but it turns out that he is no longer there (he's been in a new house for two weeks). 13 minutes to go.

To find Marks, Anderton starts "scrubbing the image," looking for indicators of where in the city he lives, such as the fact that the "brick is being repointed" at his house, as Anderton brings it into close-up.

There are also images of policemen on horseback, which an assistant Jad (Harris) speculates may mean that the site "is near the Capitol." Anderton demurs, however, and suggests Georgetown instead (whoops!). Jad then recognizes that the buildings are by "Dwight Kingsley, the 18th C. architect who did two dozen buildings in DC."

Next Anderton, using his magic screen, cleverly deduces that the lover in wait–seen in real time–is in front of a merry-go-round and, thus, in a park. Jad quickly notes that the merry-go-round they have visualized is one of only a few old ones that remain "in Georgetown, in Barnaby Woods, and in Woodley." "It's gotta be Barnaby Woods," replies Anderton, and he and his SWAT team saddle up in their flying squad car and head for the site of the park. Six minutes to murder.

We switch back to see the paramour entering the house, and Marks, across the street in the park, following him in, leaving the door ajar as he does. He sneaks up to the bedroom to await the lovers.

Once at the scene, the PreCrme team encounters another big problem: a row of houses which look exactly alike! (See photo insert.) Anderton utters an excremental expletive and rightly asks: "Which one it it?" Only by having Jad check back in time (on the magic screen again), can the intrepid policeman identify the single house with its door open and run like hell–30 seconds left!–into the house to disarm the weeping Marks.

According to veteran location manager Peggy Pridemore, who worked on the film, it took her six months to 1) find an appropriate site to match the script (a set of essentially matching houses facing a park) and 2) gain permissions from the homeowners there. It took another six weeks to prep the site and assure that the houses looked truly identical and had similar landscaping. After the location shooting was done, the production threw a big barbecue /block party for the neighborhood and placed new playground equipment in the park. Ever since the filming, the space has been called by neighbors "Spielberg Park."

44 LEGALLY BLONDE 2: RED WHITE & BLONDE

2003. MGM, 95 minutes, color.

Director: Charles Herman-Wurmfeld.

Screenplay: Dennis Drake, from a novel by Amanda Brown.

Cinematography: Elliott Davis.

Editing: Peter Teschner.

Original Music: Rolfe Kent.

Principal Cast:

Reese Witherspoon	Elle Woods	Luke Wilson	Emmett Richmond
Sally Field	Rep. Victoria Rudd	Mary Lynn Rajskub	Reena Giuliani
Regina King	Grace Rossiter	Jessica Cauffiel	Margot
Jennifer Coolidge	Paulette Parcelle	Alanna Ubach	Serena McGuire
Bruce McGill	Rep. Stanford Marks	Stanley Anderson	Michael Blaine
Dana Ivey	Rep. Libby Hauser	Jack McGee	Detective Finchley
Bob Newhart	Sid Post	Bruce Thomas	UPS Guy

Synopsis: Harvard-educated Elle Woods wants her Chihuahua, Bruiser, reunited with its mother, who is being used by a cosmetics company for testing. Elle leaves her home in Boston for Washington to work on legislation to outlaw animal testing. While working for Congresswoman Victoria Rudd, she meets an amiable doorman, Sidney, who shows her how things work on the Hill. She meets obstacles to her legislation—called "Bruiser's Bill"—and begins to lose her faith in politics. She discovers that Bruiser is gay and is close to the dog of another congressman crucial to her bill. She also wins the support of another legislator, a sorority sister. Elle then learns that Rudd has been working against her, backing a major campaign donor who supports animal testing, but Rudd eventually backs the bill when it is discovered, by another staffer, that she lied to Elle. With the help of fashion friends and sorority sisters, she launches a "Million Dog March" on Washington, her discharge petition is successful, and Bruiser's Bill is brought to the floor of the House.

Production Notes: *Legally Blonde 2* was a sequel to Reese Witherspoon's smash success as Elle Woods in *Legally Blonde* (2001), which earned over $140 million worldwide, making it a major sleeper hit for its studio. The sequel, riding on Witherspoon's box office clout at its peak, did reasonably well, but was thoroughly panned by critics and quickly forgotten by filmgoers. Once again, it could be said that the Washington angle didn't help a film property.

Comment: As silly as *Legally Blonde 2* is, it contains plenty of congressional context. Very rare in congressional cinema, the lead is a congressional aide who comes to challenge the typically compromised congressperson (Field), who defensively invokes–yet again–the hoary: "to get along, you have to go along." The challenge comes, surprisingly, in the form of a discharge petition, a rarely used device to dislodge bottled-up legislation. The discharge petition is certainly arcane stuff for the movies, especially for a fluffy comedy, but there is nothing subtle about the way Elle (Witherspoon) tries to promote her bill–with elaborate hairdos and pink accessories. She is, of course, yet another outsider who comes in and shakes up the place, only to move on when her job is done. As she puts it at one point: "trades, deals, and secrets–that's not what people want."

The film is, in many ways, a shameless re-working of *Mr. Smith Goes to Washington* (q.v.). Indeed, at one point, Elle watches the 1939 film on the tube then later winds up questioning her political future at the Lincoln Memorial, communing with Lincoln's statue, just as Jimmy Stewart did. And just as in the earlier picture, the heroine rounds up a country-wide group of political novices to press her point, although, instead of Mr. Smith's Boy Rangers, it's Elle's legions of ditzy sorority sisters.

DC/Hill Notes: Even though the movie supposedly takes place in Washington, the movie was filmed everywhere but. Even the supposed "aerial views" of DC buildings were scale models. Much of the filming was done in Utah, where the Delta Center was used, as well as the Utah State Capitol in Salt Lake City. The Illinois State Capitol in Springfield, Illinois, also appeared.

Goofs: When she first alights in DC, Elle checks into non-existent "Wellington Hotel."

In a sequence inside the House office building, there are way too many staffers running around to give a sense of activity, and they are all dressed (rather stereotypically) in almost identical dark suits.

She has lunch out at a restaurant at "12th and Constitution Avenue," rather tricky since that location marks the corners of the Interstate Commerce Commission and the IRS in the Federal Triangle.

The look of the House Chamber is all wrong: it is way too small, and each member has an individual desk, which is only the case in the Senate (scenes were filmed in the Utah State Capitol's House).

45 SHATTERED GLASS

2003. Distributed by Lionsgate Pictures, 94 minutes, color.

Writing and Direction: Billy Ray.

Cinematography: Mandy Walker.

Editing: Jeffrey Ford.

Music: Mychael Danna.

Principal Cast:

Hayden Christensen.............. Stephen Glass
Peter Sarsgaard...... Charles ("Chuck") Lane
Chloe Sevigny........................ Caitlin Avey
Hank Azaria........................ Michael Kelly
Steve Zahn...................... Adam Penenberg
Rosario Dawson.......................... Andy Fox
Melanie Lynskey....................... Amy Brand
Ted Kotcheff........................... Marty Peretz
Mark Blum .... Lewis Estridge
Cas Anvar...................... Kambiz Foroohar

Synopsis: It's 1998, and young Stephen Glass is the hottest reporter at *The New Republic*, an important Washington political weekly. He spins out clever narratives he has dug up by himself, great stories like "Hack Heaven", which features a kid computer hacker flummoxing major tech companies. Glass is so sharp, so good at getting the dirt, so admired by the other kids in the office—and he's so nice besides. After editor Michael Kelly is fired by the magazine's publisher, Marty Peretz, because he wants a different tone to the magazine, staff writer Chuck Lane gets the job. Lane, a much cooler personality than Kelly and a less witty writer, is suspected by the disgruntled *Republic* staff of having precipitated Kelly's demise.

Then the much-admired Glass piece on the computer hacker is checked out by a New York on-line publication *Forbes Digital Tool*. Staffer Adam

Penenberg, chided by his editor because he missed this major story, starts investigating Glass's report and, with his colleague Andy Fox, discovers some flaws in it. *Forbes Digital Tool* calls Lane with their doubts, and the rest of the picture traces how the phlegmatic Lane unmasks the increasingly frantic Glass, who–ever inventive if not honest–connives to create back stories to support his fabrications. The truth trickles out, until Lane and his magazine learn that the protean Glass has fabricated dozens of his "special" features over the years.

Background: Billy Ray based his *Shattered Glass* screenplay on an article by H.G. "Buzz" Bissinger of the same title that appeared in a 1998 issue of *Vanity Fair.* "This is a cautionary tale," he said, "a story about the difference between being a good reporter and being a hot one." Ray helped his cause considerably by consulting the protagonists in the story (although Glass did not cooperate) and by interviewing *The New Republic* staffers and others involved in the affair.

At the time of Glass's tenure, *The New Republic* prided itself as being the "in-flight magazine of Air Force One." Led by feisty editor Michael Kelly (a Capitol Hill native) and publisher Martin Peretz, the small circulation (80,000) journal was then a must read for the political elite in the capital. Its aspiring editorial staff of bright young things averaged just 26 years of age (Glass was only 24), before Glass almost brought the house down. After leaving the magazine, Glass eventually wrote a 2003 novel, "The Fabulist," which centers–not surprisingly–on a young journalist's unmasking and disgrace.

The film was recognized by critics at the time as a telling and suspenseful docudrama, the more so because its somewhat specialized material did not exactly lend itself to surefire entertainment. Audiences, however, basically stayed away, perhaps because that same material was too "inside baseball," too confined to only the DC cognoscenti. Made for a modest $6 million, the film on first release did not even make back half of its costs.

Comment: Washington is often seen as a navel-gazing town, one full of self-important people full of blind ambition and fervent hustle, gauging others by their proximity to power and whether they are on "in" or "out" lists. "Inside the Beltway," even for folks who have no idea what the Beltway is, has become the standard phrase for our city's picking at its figurative umbilical cord. Such a view ignores—as so many of us who merely live here know—all the real people with real lives who reside here. But *Shattered Glass* takes an inside peek at that very self-conscious, self-referential Washington world and subjects it to a dogged scrutiny, offering a convincing microcosm of what overweening ambition can do to someone wholly caught up in the DC whirl.

Hayden Christensen is spot on as the earnest, sly, ever-ingratiating Glass. He gives off the right mix of rank callowness and grinning cynicism, a forbidding combination. The actor's winning smile charms you just as Glass's must have beguiled his co-workers, and during his demise, his excuses expose him as the petty adolescent he really is. Even better, to my mind, is Sarsgaard's performance. His Lane at first does seem a humorless, sleepy-eyed wonk, miles removed from the personable Glass. But he gradually comes across as serious, and, after he is surprisingly named the magazine's editor, he becomes a bastion of integrity who does what he can to save his journal. An unassuming, but very legitimate hero. Also, in his first outing as a director, Billy Ray achieves a verisimilitude that is both convincing and compelling.

DC Notes: *Shattered Glass,* though a thoroughly DC story, was mostly shot in Montreal (a few standard Washington exteriors grace the film's credit sequence). It essentially takes place in standard office space, flitting around offices, conference rooms, and cubicles. The film's look and feel readily recalls *All the President's Men* (q.v.). It's claustrophobic, and rightly so, as the lies—if not the literal walls—close in on the garrulous Glass.

The closest thing the film has to an "action" sequence is its turning point. Hoping to corroborate the "Hack Heaven" piece, Lane drives Glass out to the real Bethesda to scout the site of the hacker's convention and see where Glass had dinner with conventioneers. The two look around a building lobby, an outdoor eatery, a streetfront restaurant, all the while Lane questioning Glass about the details of his story. The actual restaurant where Glass supposedly had "dinner" is shown in the film, the national franchise "The Original Pancake House" which—as it turns out —has no dinner service.

2004. Jerry Bruckheimer Films, distributed by Walt Disney Pictures, 131 minutes, color.

Director: Jon Turtletaub.

Screenplay: Jim Kouf, Marianne Wibberly and Cormac Wibberly

Story: Kouf, Oren Aviv and Charles Spear.

Cinematography: Caleb Deschanel.

Editing: William Goldenberg.

Music: Trevor Rabin.

Principal Cast:

Nicholas Cage	Benjamin Gates	David Dayan Fisher	Shaw
Justin Bartha	Riley Poole	Stewart Finlay-McLennan	Powell
Diane Kruger	Abigail Chase	Oleg Taktarov	Shippen
Harvey Keitel	FBI Agent Peter Sadusky	Stephen A. Pope	Phil
Jon Voight	Patrick Gates	Annie Parisse	Agent Dawes
Sean Bean	Ian Howe	Don McManus	Dr. Stan Herbert
Christopher Plummer	John Gates	Hunter Gomez	Young Ben Gates
Jason Earles	Thomas Gates	Yves Michel-Beneche	Museum kid

Synopsis: Benjamin Franklin Gates comes from a family of treasure-seekers who have long sought a treasure buried by America's Founding Fathers. His grandfather, John Gates, believes that the forefathers placed clues to the treasure in highly secret locations with cryptic directions. Ben thinks that a key clue resides on the back of the original Declaration of Independence in the National Archives, but one of his previous associates, Ian Howe, aims to pilfer the Declaration, so Ben resolves to steal the document in order to protect it.

Under the cover of a gala event at the Archives, Ben, with the help of his tech-savvy buddy Riley, pulls off the caper but must, in the process, involve Abigail Chase, curator at the Archives. FBI Agent Sadusky takes on the case and aims to get the Declaration back. Ben's team then consults with his father, Patrick, before heading off to Philadelphia and Independence Hall, where the next clue resides. In pursuit are Howe and his men, as well as the FBI. The chase then leads them on to historic Trinity Church in New York City and deep into its bowels to find the long-lost cache.

Background: *National Treasure* aimed at the Indiana Jones market, trying to marry action adventure with a mildly intellectual enterprise and a patina of historic overlay. It offered, as in the Spielberg films, a hero who was a professorial type able to exhibit both grit and chutzpah. It achieved its basic commercial aims by spawning a sequel (see **Postscript)**. The film was a major investment for Bruckheimer Films and Disney, a special effects bonanza which cost approximately $100 million. It also turned out to be a round box office success, grossing over $173 million domestically and a similar amount overseas for a total of over $347 million worldwide. Critically, it was given little respect and deemed only a standard action flick best aimed at young teens.

DC/Hill Notes: Location shooting in Washington included the J. Edgar Hoover FBI building, the National Archives and the Archives Metro stop, an aerial of the Watergate complex, the Lincoln Memorial, and at the DAR headquarters. For a period shot at the latter site, the filmmakers adapted the portico (facing 17th Street, NW) of the building's Memorial Continental Hall to stand in for the White House, circa 1800, bringing in horse-drawn carriages and even laying gravel on the circular drive for authenticity.

The film also uses the Library of Congress by including a lengthy expository scene between Benjamin (Cage) and Riley (Bartha) in the Library's Main Reading Room,with a nice pan from the dome down to the two principals in the circular reading area.

One of the movie's major chase sequence begins on Pennsylvania Avenue, outside the Archives, where Gates (Cage) and his van, chased by the villains in a truck, speed down the Avenue towards the Capitol, turn right at 7th Street, NW, and head south across the Mall. At the end of the chase sequence, the van ends up coming up the Virginia Avenue underpass going east with the Washington Monument in view.

The production used a very believable, almost-to-scale replica of the National Archives' rotunda, where the "charters of freedom," including the Declaration of Independence, are displayed. The dimensions are close to accurate, the large murals are convincing copies and the display cases lined up correctly. Not everything was in perfect synch, however (see **Goofs** below).

Goofs: The movie's depiction of the Archives' rotunda is not accurate in every detail. Some of the vagaries are:

The lighting is definitely Hollywood lighting: much too bright for a room with lights kept dim to preserve the fragile documents.

Guards normally stand on either side of the founding documents, not roaming the hall.

The absence of two captions for the murals on the upper walls.

Beyond the Archives' quirks, the chase sequence described above has a flaw: the vehicles head, not into Southwest as they should after crossing the Mall, but into a random set of urban streets clearly not in DC.

Postscript: The film's success produced a sequel in 2007: *National Treasure: Book of Secrets.* Again with Cage, Bartha, Kruger, Voight, and Keitel in the cast, this version added Helen Mirren, (as Patrick Gates' ex-wife) and Ed Harris to the mix. The puzzle this time involves missing pages from a diary of John Wilkes Booth, fragments of which implicate Ben Gates' great-great-grandfather in the Lincoln assassination. Clues about the diary lead the treasure-seekers to London, Paris, and Washington, by now chasing a "book of secrets" known only to the President of the US.

Washington-area locations used this time include exteriors of the FBI Building, Lafayette Park and 16th Street, NW (to get backdrops of the White House), the Grant Memorial, and an exterior of the Eisenhower Executive Office Building (oddly labeled the "White House Press Office"). Also featured again is the Library of Congress, where the team (Cage,

Kruger, and Bartha) continues its search for the "book" in the actual upper levels of the Library's Main Reading Room.

There is also a night scene at Mount Vernon, where Gates crashes a party for the President, kidnaps him into a secret tunnel, and quizzes him about the book of secrets (the President is played by Bruce Greenwood, who eight years earlier had played President Kennedy in *Thirteen Days* (q.v.). An extra on the film, Nancy Leroy, described this Mount Vernon location shoot, commenting on the length and expense to which Hollywood productions go for what seems, in filmic terms, to be very modest outcomes. She noted:

> *Two overnight shoots with all kinds of extra pay for SAG (Screen Actors' Guild) extras. Tempura at 3 a.m. for dinner, (then) fireworks, tents, an orchestra, flowers, and overhead helicopters delivering the "president." For about 30 seconds of screen time.*

47 THE SENTINEL

2006. Regency Enterprises, distributed by 20th Century Fox, 108 minutes, color.

Director: Clark Johnson.

Screenplay: George Nolfi from a novel by Gerald Petievich.

Cameraman: Gabriel Bernstein.

Editing: Cindy Molo.

Music: Christophe Beck.

Principal Cast:

Michael Douglas .... Pete Garrison
Kiefer Sutherland .... David Breckinridge
Eva Longoria .... Jill Marin
Kim Basinger.. First Lady Sarah Ballentine
Martin Donovan .... William Montrose
Ritchie Coster .... The Handler
David Rasche .... President Ballentine
Blair Brown .... National Security Advisor
Kristin Lehman .... Cindy Breckinridge
Raynor Scheine .... Walter Xavier
Chuck Shamata ....Director Overbrook
Paul Calderon .... Dep. Director Cortes
Clark Johnson .... Charlie Merriweather
Gloria Reuben .... Mrs. Merriweather

Synopsis: Secret Service agent Pete Garrison is a legend in the Service and is responsible for the personal security of the First Lady, Sarah Ballentine, with whom he is having an affair. After the murder of one of the Service's veteran agents, Merriweather, Garrison tries to learn the motive from his regular informer, Walter, who tells him that there is a mole in the Service who is part of a plot to assassinate the president. Placed in charge of investigating the plot is Garrison's former protégé, David Breckinridge, now estranged from Garrison because he believes Pete had an affair with his wife.

All agents are submitted to a polygraph test, and, given his affair with the First Lady, Garrison's answers are compromised. Further, the mole is able to frame Garrison, and he becomes the prime suspect of aiding the plot against the president. Now being sought by his own Service, Garrison escapes and conducts a parallel investigation of the plot, during which he kills one of the conspirators and discovers that his informant is dead. He also learns that the assassins are planning to kill the president at a G8 summit in Toronto. He reconciles with Breckenridge, and the two race to the summit to uncover the mole and thwart the assassination plot.

Background: Director Clark Johnson–who gives himself a cameo as the murdered Merriweather–is well known as an actor to area TV fans for his memorable appearances in Baltimore dramas. He played Detective Meldrick Lewis for six years on NBC's *Homicide,* and he also had a role as a journalist in the last season (2008) of the acclaimed HBO series, *The Wire.* Novelist Gerald Petievich, who wrote the book on which the film was based, had been a Secret Service agent himself.

The film, even with several major stars, got little box office traction. It's total domestic take was just over $36 million, well under its production costs.

Comments: The film at first may make one hark back to that other major Secret Service film, *In the Line of Fire* (q.v.), particularly the parallel theme of a superior, veteran agent Clint Eastwood in the latter film–whose own worthiness is being tested by the threat of an assassination plot on the president. However, *The Sentinel* does not measure up in plausibility or in style to that earlier effort. Though both films have 60-year-old actors running around (improbable for the Secret Service), Douglas somehow seems even less likely than Eastwood to be capable of the work at that age.

Somehow, too, a lower (or more ill-used) budget seems evident in *The Sentinel,* as well as the less convincing locations. While *In the Line of Fire* used many effective DC sites, including Capitol Hill, The Sentinel falls back more on its Toronto locations, giving off a less-than-authentic vibe. Its critical reception was unenthusiastic, with some very faint praise of it as an easy-to-swallow entertainment. Most caustic was the review from *The Village Voice*'s Bill Gallo, who said, in his April 2006 review, that the film "has more holes than Bush's war plan and employs less fluent English."

DC/Hill Notes: According to director Johnson (commenting in the DVD commentary), most of film was shot in sets and locations in Toronto, in-cluding sequences at the Secret Service offices, the Oval Office and White House interiors, a South Lawn helicopter shot, and a Camp David stand-in.

Still, there were plenty of genuine DC locations used. They included the pedestrian Pennsylvania Avenue strip behind the White House, including Lafayette Park, where the film begins and ends. Also used are downtown Pennsylvania Avenue, the Mayflower on Connecticut Avenue, the Grant Memorial (where Garrison meets his informant), and a chase inside Union Station, including its parking garage. The Eye Street Grill (on I Street off 16th Street) stands in for "Las Palmas" coffee shop in the movie. There is also an elaborate night scene featuring a Park Police helicopter which ends up whirling above Georgetown and the C & O Canal (this segment took over four hours to shoot).

The filming had a nice capper, according to the film's location manager Peggy Pridemore, who witnessed it. The final scene shot for the movie, which has Michael Douglas running out into M Street traffic in Georgetown, was shot in the middle of the night. When the last take was done and the film was officially a "wrap," Catherine Zeta-Jones surprised Douglas by running out into the middle of the street with champagne and glasses to salute her husband as the crew cheered.

Goofs: A sequence begins with a presidential motorcade going down Pennsylvania Avenue past the National Archives, but it ends up at the fictitious "Sutton Avenue," which has its street sign erroneously painted black on white instead of DC's white on green signage.

When Garrison (Douglas) takes another phone call outside the Mayflower Hotel, the caller tells him to go to Massachusetts Avenue, NW then walk to 12th Street. He goes the wrong way, heading south for L Street, instead of north towards Massachusetts Avenue. The sequence continues on Connecticut Avenue, NW, with Garrison being pursued on foot by FBI agents but then cuts abruptly to Union Station, several miles away.

Agent Garrison is at Camp David when a phone caller (the suspected mole) orders him to meet him in **20 minutes** at the invented "Allenwood Mall Food Court" in DC, and, miraculously, he makes it there in time by car!

Garrison phones in the address of the conspirators' apartment as "1265 Leslie, NW," but there is no Leslie Street in DC but rather one in Montgomery County.

48 THANK YOU FOR SMOKING

2006. Fox Searchlight Pictures, 92 minutes, color.

Screenplay (adapted from Christopher Buckley's novel) and Direction: Jason Reitman.

Cinematography: James Whitaker.

Editing: Dana Glaugerman. Original Music: Rolfe Kent.

Principal Cast:

Aaron Eckhart .... *Nick Naylor*
Cameron Bright .... *Joey Naylor*
Maria Bello .... *Polly Bailey*
David Koechner .... *Bobby Jay Bliss*
Katie Holmes .... *Heather Holloway*
William H. Macy.... *Sen. Ortolan Finistirre*
Robert Duvall .... *The Captain*
J.K. Simmons.......................................*BR*
Sam Elliott............................. *Lorne Lutch*
Kim Dickens .... *Jill Naylor*
Rob Lowe .... *Jeff Megall*
Adam Brody...*Jack*

Synopsis: Nick Naylor is chief spokesman and vice president of the DC-based Academy of Tobacco Studies, whose own son knows him as "The Sultan of Spin." He forcefully defends the rights of smokers and cigarette makers against health zealots out to ban tobacco and, especially, the moralistic Senator Finisterre who wants to brand cigarette packs with blatant "Poison" symbols. Ever under pressure, he can only relax with his drinking buddies, Polly and Bobby Jay, two other skilled cynics who work for the alcohol industry and the firearms lobby, respectively (they call each other "The MoD Squad," for "Merchants of Death.")

Nick's PR skill attracts the attention of the venerable Captain, founder of the Academy and the eminence gris of the tobacco industry, who encourages Nick to use Hollywood super-agent Jeff Megall to get a top-line movie made which features "cool" smoking, just like the old days. Nick is convinced and comfortable in his role, except for the lingering remorse he feels about his divorce from ex-wife, Jill, and the increasing doubts he feels about his work in the eyes of his devoted son Joey. His opportunistic involvement with an ambitious young newspaperwoman, Heather Holloway (who writes a tell-all article about him), his encounter with the original alienated Marlboro Man, Lorne Lutch (who accepts a bribe from him), and a near-death experience with nicotine patches—all eventually lead to Nick having to gamble his future in hearings before the crusading senator.

Background: The movie rights to Christopher Buckley's 1994 satiric novel were originally purchased by Icon Productions and Mel Gibson, who saw himself as starring as Nick Naylor. Writer/director Jason Reitman independently wrote a draft screenplay from the novel that was accepted by Icon executives, but the company failed to get financing for the project and Gibson dropped out. The project was dormant for some years until David O. Sacks (founder of PayPal) became interested and it found some traction. Sacks acquired the rights, kept most of Reitman's script, and bankrolled most of the film's budget.

Thank You for Smoking was Jason Reitman's first feature-length film as a director, and his script received an Oscar nomination for Best Adapted Screenplay. Reitman (the son of film director Ivan Reitman, who made the DC movie *Dave*, q.v.) made the conscious decision to have none of his cast members smoke during the film (the only people seen smoking are in scenes from old movies). However, Reitman littered the sardonic sound track with a number of songs featuring smoking, beginning with the 1940's novelty number "Smoke, Smoke, Smoke, (that Cigarette)."

Comment: This smart comedy should appeal to any Washingtonian who follows the capital's political life. The targets are many—K Street sharks, corrupt corporations, fanatic do-gooders, smarmy journalists, Hollywood con-men—and the film offers an equal opportunity slam on all of them. The targets are not always depicted with subtlety, but most of the laughs made at the expense of hustlers are well earned. Super slick Rob Lowe is just right as a smarmy, cynical agent—rhapsodizing in a Japanese robe before his twinkling pool. Mr. Cowpoke, Sam Elliott, is spot on as the disaffected Marlboro Man bristling with anger but willing to consider a serious payoff. Functioning nicely as a snappy Greek chorus to Nick are Maria Bello and David Koechner as sarcastic lobbyists.

The movie makes particularly good use of Aaron Eckhart as Nick. In *Thank You For Smoking,* he had his best role to that time, combining contradictory elements of oleaginous charmer and earnest human being (he could be both at once). Eckhart makes believable, too, another strain of his character: the genuine libertarian impulse (representing the author, Buckley) that contends that people have to be left to their own choices, even those that are societally damaging. That element of the Buckley book and the Reitman screenplay allows the film to avoid the predictable, politically correct ending. Nick, who does what he does "to pay the mortgage," also honestly confesses to his son what he does for a living: "I talk–it's my job." Like a lot of other Washingtonians.

DC Notes: Location shooting in Washington was modest for the film and concentrated in the near NW and SW quadrants.

The "Academy of Tobacco Studies," where Nick Naylor (Eckhart) works, is the Department of Energy (the Forrestal Building) located on Independence Avenue, SW. The Academy's sign is superimposed over the Department's sign.

An early street scene has a car heading east on Independence Avenue going past the Voice of America building in SW.

The book's author Christopher Buckley gets a cameo when he is shown, along with a montage of other people, reading a newspaper at the Cleveland Park Metro station.

The kidnap sequence in the film is shot in front of the Capitol Grille Restaurant on Pennsylvania Avenue and 6th Street, NW (the West Wing of the National Gallery can be seen in the background).

Goofs: Building stand-in: When Nick is shown speaking at a press conference outside an official building in DC, the building is not in Washington but is rather the Masonic Lodge in Pasadena, CA. During the press conference, he addresses Heather's article about him, and we see Heather

(Holmes) observing him from a skyscraper window—not possible because of DC building height restrictions. The same Masonic Lodge's interior was used for the Senate hearing room where Naylor testifies.

49 BREACH

 2007. Distributed by Universal Pictures, 110 minutes, color.

Director: Billy Ray.

Screenplay by Billy Ray, Adam Mazer, and William Rotko.

Cinematography: Tak Fujimoto.

Editing: Jeffrey Ford.

Music: Mychael Danna.

Principal Cast:

Chris Cooper	Robert Hanssen	Gary Cole	Rich Garces
Ryan Phillippe	Eric O'Neill	Kathleen Quinlan	Bonnie Hanssen
Laura Linney	Kate Burroughs	Bruce Davison	John O'Neill
Caroline Dhavernas	Juliana O'Neill	Tom Barnett	Jim Olsen
Dennis Haysbert	Dean Plesac	Jonathan Watton	Geddes

Synopsis: Based on a true story, the plot follows Eric O'Neill, a young lawyer and FBI agent-in-training assigned to work undercover as a clerk to Robert Hanssen, a senior agent suspected of sexual deviance. Hanssen has been recalled to FBI headquarters ostensibly to head up a new division. At first Hanssen is distant with O'Neill, but he warms to the young man, taking a personal interest in him and his East-German born wife Juliana. Over time, however, O'Neill finds no evidence of Hanssen's sexual deviance and grows to respect the prickly veteran. He questions his superior on the case, Kate Burroughs, who finally informs him that Hanssen is also suspected of having spied for the USSR for years, leading to the deaths of US agents. The Bureau wants to catch Hanssen in an act of espionage and plants bugs in his car to obtain evidence against him. The tracking devices cause interference with Hansen's car radio, making him think he is the target of Soviet agents. The FBI intercepts a message he sends to his Russian handlers saying he will not provide any more information, but O'Neill convinces Hanssen that he is not being tailed. Hanssen then makes one last dead drop of classified information at his usual spot, and Bureau agents catch him in the act. Discouraged with the undercover life, O'Neill decides to leave the FBI.

Background: This was the second directorial effort of screenwriter Billy Ray, his first being *Shattered Glass* (q.v.), which shares several parallels with *Breach*. Both are contemporary thrillers set in Washington, DC, though both were mostly shot in Canada. Both stories involve real people and trace—with the usual dramatic license—real events. Both also are narratives about protagonists with dramatic secrets who are forced to reveal them. Finally, both take place in undramatic, even mundane locations (stark, bureaucratic hallways and non-descript newsmagazine offices).

Both *Breach* and *Shattered Glass* were also hits with many critics, who appreciated the films' smart scripts and attention to detail within an atmosphere of tension, but neither was a major box office success (though *Breach* more than earned its money back). Ray also wrote another DC-based film, *State of Play* (q.v.) released in 2009.

Comments: The film is dominated by Ray's smart, delicately paranoid script and by the superb incarnation of Hanssen by Chris Cooper. The actor gives weight and shape, mostly through gesture, tone of voice, and body language, to a man who was weirdly hermetic and difficult to read. He nicely alternates hardness and geniality in the man; his intelligence yet his menace. It is a tough balance to pull off, but he achieves it. In Cooper's wake, the callow O'Neill of Ryan Phillippe is little more than a sounding board, a moderate fellow who has to react to the uncanny one. About the only thing that is effective is his brooding lower lip.

DC Notes: As indicated above with *Shattered Glass, Breach* was mostly filmed in Canada, this time in Toronto, where most of the interiors were done. Several sequences use DC scene-setting shots, though, including the FBI building. The FBI allowed shooting at one of the entrances to the building and also had two principals (Phillippe and Linney) in a scene on the second floor colonnade. Phillippe and Linney also have a crucial late-night rendezvous at the Woodrow Wilson Plaza, where massive lighting was used to highlight the Ronald Reagan and Ariel Rios Buildings as backdrops.

The film does acknowledge real events in its capture sequence. Hanssen (Cooper) performs a drop in Foxstone Park in Fairfax County near Tysons Corner (a real site which the spy frequented), and then he is apprehended on a suburban Virginia street where the actual Hanssen capture was made.

The location manager on the film, Peggy Pridemore, provided an interesting anecdote about this sequence shot in Vienna, Virginia. Planning to film on the actual street where Hanssen was captured, the production team knocked on the door of a home seeking permission to shoot the outside of their house. No one answered the door, and the team left. They came back some time later, however, and this time they found a woman at home. An elderly woman answered, saying it was her husband–who had since died–who did not want to grant permission to film. She, however, was most willing, allowed the filming, and even welcomed the crew into her house during breaks.

Goofs: Hanssen exits a "Catholic church" (actually the Treasury Building on 15th Street, NW) but walks out onto a Toronto street.

A sequence begins with a character exiting a Metro station marked "Archives" (written erroneously in black-on-white lettering) but which is actually the Federal Triangle stop opening on to Wilson Plaza behind the Reagan Building where agents (Linney and Phillipe) have a crucial late-night rendezvous.

At one point, there is a purposeful "traffic jam" caused on the length of the Potomac Parkway leading up to Lincoln Memorial. However, as the principals talk and fence at length in the street (the Potomac River is in view), there is absolutely no movement of any traffic behind them, and most of the vehicles around seem to be riderless (there are two lanes of parking here). Such a dialogue would be unbelievable at the site, as the street is a busy one-way drive up to the Memorial Bridge. Location manager Pridemore said that the filmmakers wanted to shoot this scene in Georgetown, but it required two days, too long a disruption for that neighborhood.

50 CHARLIE WILSON'S WAR

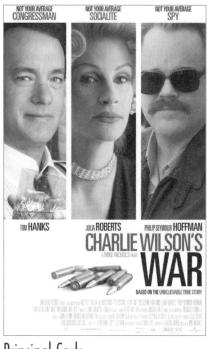

2007. Relativity Media and Participant Productions, distributed by Universal Pictures, 100 minutes, color.

Director: Mike Nichols.

Screenplay: Aaron Sorkin.

Cinematography: Stephen Goldblatt.

Editing: John Bloom and Paul Rubell.

Original Music: James Newton Howard.

Principal Cast:

Tom Hanks	Charlie Wilson	Peter Gerety	Larry Liddle
Amy Adams	Bonnie Bach	John Slattery	Cravely
Philip Seymour Hoffman	Gust Avrakotos	Denis O'Hare	Harold Holt
Julia Roberts	Joanne Herring	Om Puri	President Zia-ul-Haq
Ned Beatty	Cong. Doc Long	Ken Stott	Zvi Rafiah
Emily Blunt	Jane Liddle	Jud Tylor	Crystal Lee

Synopsis: "Good Time" Charlie Wilson is an obscure Democratic congressman from Texas's second district, better known for the babes he hires for his office (Charlie's "angels") than for his legislating. He likes coke, booze, and the ladies, paying just enough attention to his district to keep his seat. By 1980, he takes an interest in the Soviet occupation of Afghanistan, especially after being urged to act on the issue by wealthy Houston socialite Joanne Herring. He is particularly moved by the Afghans' plight after visiting an Afghan refugee camp in Pakistan, whose officials also urge more assistance for their fellow Muslims. Wilson finds that the US has no official policy on the Afghan situation, while the CIA is content to have the Soviets waste their treasure on their occupation.

Looking for help within the CIA, Wilson connects with Gust Avrakotos, a committed and feisty operative working with the Agency's Afghanistan group. While Charlie gains funding for the under-equipped mujahedeen, Gust tackles strategic planning, which results in a major covert operation which challenges the Soviets. Pushed by Wilson, funding levels for the Afghan insurgents rise from paltry levels to a billion dollars, allowing their fighters to challenge Soviet helicopter gun ships with Stinger missiles. This proves a crucial turning point in the war. With Afghanistan triumphant in 1989, Charlie and Gus urge support for a post-Soviet occupation to stabilize the country, but by then American policy makers have moved on. Wilson himself receives an award for his work from the American clandestine services.

Background: The film, adapted from George Crile's 2003 book *Charlie Wilson's War: The Extraordinary Story of the Largest Covert Operation in History*, a book that fascinated producer Tom Hanks, who, with his co-producer Gary Goetzman, worked to get the film made. It was also a project that screenwriter Aaron Sorkin actively sought. Sorkin had earlier written two other major films with Washington settings, *A Few Good Men* (q.v.) and *The American President* (q.v.), as well as creating the long-running NBC series *The West Wing*. The picture was director Mike Nichols' last work to date. *Charlie Wilson's War* eventually did adequate business, earning over $100 million in box office worldwide.

Though elements of the story may seem hard to believe, most of them were, in fact, portrayed as they happened. Wilson himself, after seeing the film, felt that the filmmakers had captured the events correctly and entertainingly. In comments on a History Channel documentary released at the time of the film, Wilson praised the film's accuracy and Tom Hanks' portrayal of him, demurring only in saying that the girls he actually hired for his office staff were, if anything, prettier than the lovelies used in the movie.

Comment: The film was critically well received, and Sorkin's script was praised, although some reviewers felt he pulled too many punches. *Charlie Wilson's War* received one Oscar nomination, that of Best Supporting Actor for Philip Seymour Hoffman. Most critics, in fact, focussed on Hoffman's energetic Gust as the soul and linchpin of the film. In his review in *The New Republic*, reviewer Christopher Orr offered fairly typical praise:

> *From the moment he appears onscreen, however, this is Philip Seymour Hoffman's movie. His rumpled, cranky spy is hilarious–George Smiley by way of Jack Black–but with an edge of quiet ferocity that makes every scene he's in play a little sharper. He's the funniest character in the film, but also seems the most real, a man whose terse wit and don't-give-a-s*** demeanor might easily have been forged by a career of unseemly, spookish deeds.*

DC/Hill Notes: Though with significant scenes that take place in supposed Washington settings (notably Wilson's congressional staff office, a corridor off the House chamber, and CIA offices), the production did no shooting in DC. It did, however, use some aerial backdrops of the city, especially showing Washington at night from Wilson's apartment building (apparently located in high-rise Rosslyn, Virgina, on the west side of the Potomac River).

Goofs: When Wilson returns to Washington to cast a vote, he enters the House floor from an adjoining room which appears to have a direct connection to his office, which would be impossible (the office would be in one of the House buildings across Independence Avenue).

51 TALK TO ME

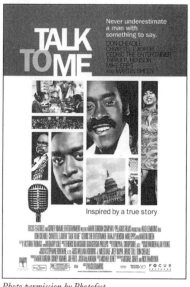

2007. Focus Features, 118 minutes, color.

Director: Kasi Lemmons.

Screenplay: Michael Grant and Rick Famuyiwa.

Cinematography: Stephanie Fontaine.

Editing: Kenny Marsten.

Original Music: Terence Blanchard.

Photo permission by Photofest

Principal Cast:

Don Cheadle .... Ralph "Petey" Greene	Vondie Curtis-Hall......... Sunny Jim Kelsey
Chiwetel Ejiofor .... Dewey Hughes	Richard Chevolleau .... Poochie Braxton
Martin Sheen .... E.G. Sonderling	Alison Sealy-Smith .... Freda
Taraji Henson .... Vernell Watson	Herbert L. Rawlings, Jr. ....James Brown
Mike Epps............................. Milo Hughes	Damir Andrei. .... Fred De Cordova
Cedric the Entertainer..."Nighhawk" Terry	Jim Malmberg.....................Johnny Carson

Synopsis: DC, mid-1966. Ralph Waldo "Petey" Greene, a jailbird with the gift of gab, comes to the attention of Dewey Hughes, the station programmer for WOL Radio in Washington, who is seeking new on-air talent to revive his moribund station. Petey goes almost straight from Lorton Penitentiary to a spot as a morning deejay on WOL. More than a deejay, he becomes an on-air philosopher, a "brother" who gains a whole new audience for his station and its uneasy manager E.G. Sonderling. He becomes a hero to many in DC in April 1968, when—observing the rioting going on in the aftermath of the Martin Luther King, Jr. assassination—he appeals to his loyal listeners to back off from violence. The height of his influence comes when he launches a citywide rally, introduces James Brown, and pleas for his brethren to "Put your anger away."

As Petey's fame grows, Hughes, who becomes his manager, rides the wave with him, aiming for a payoff which represents Hughes' own show business dream: a shot on his idol Johnny Carson's *The Tonight Show*. Petey gets the dream gig on the show's stand-up spot, but he can't bring it off–he feels inauthentic before the white audience–and Dewey's dreams are dashed. Years pass before the two men can, uneasily, reconcile before Greene's early death at 53.

Background: The film's script is one of those that is "inspired by" a true story. Liberties are taken with many details of Greene's actual career for dramatic effect. Among the film's adjustments to reality:

Greene was not a disc jockey; he had a Sunday morning talk show.

He never introduced James Brown to a crowd in DC; Brown did a post-riot show in Boston which was televised widely.

Petey never appeared on *The Tonight Show*.

Dewey Hughes never delivered a eulogy at Greene's funeral. He did not attend the funeral, and he and Greene did not reconcile.

At the time of the film's release, *The Washington Post*'s Neely Tucker wrote a story about how estranged the Greene family was from the whole movie project, claiming they were never asked to contribute to or participate in it. They felt that the finished film was misleading about Greene and his legacy, and that it was, instead, a story positively focussed on Dewey Hughes.

The film, though well reviewed generally–especially Cheadle's performance–did tepid business, only a bit above $4 million worldwide.

Comments: *Talk to Me* is an intriguing blend: a slice of Washington life shown through the work of radio personality Greene and a character study matching him–a man of the "street"–with his station programmer Dewey Hughes, representing the assimilated Negro.

Cheadle carries off the role with panache. He is a mix of threat and pathos, a guy who can lash out then tear up. He presents both the bristling side and the bantering side of the charismatic Greene, a man who could rap before its time and who never forgot his grim upbringing. He's very much in period, too, with a perfect Afro and sporting a stunning parade of Sixties threads. Ejiofor, as Hughes, proves an assured, intelligent performer, playing a man "from the Anacostia projects" who remakes himself as a respectable company man, one who has repressed his tough background but still recognizes its potency.

Ejiofor's steady poise is a great counterbalance to Cheadle's flash. The two find a mutual dependency: Dewey says: "I need you to say all the things I'm afraid to say," and Petey counters with "I need you to do all the things I'm afraid to do." Director Kasi Lemmons, in only her third film, is solidly in command with *Talk To Me*, telling her story effectively and handling her actors beautifully.

Cedric the Entertainer (smart) and Vondie Curtis-Hall (smooth) give solid support as other station on-air talent, as does Martin Sheen, playing against character here as the flapping, insecure station manager. However, Taraji Henson (a rising actress who comes from Southeast DC) seriously overplays Greene's tenacious girlfriend Vernell. Her presence is used for facile laughs as the giddy, dumb sidekick who sports an Afro that seems to grow like a Chia pet throughout the film. She stands out as a gross stereotype in a picture whose chief characters are more than stock ones.

DC Notes: *Talk to Me* is another one of those Washington movies that doesn't really feature much of our mean or clean streets. It was mostly filmed, probably for budgetary reasons, in Toronto, and uses little local footage. There are only a few fleeting shots on the Mall (a standard establishing shot which duly gets the Capitol in the picture), and there is a quick flash of the outside of the iconic Ben's Chili Bowl on U Street, NW.

52 BURN AFTER READING

2008. Relativity Media and StudioCanal, released by Working Title Films, 96 minutes, color.

Director and screenplay: Joel and Ethan Coen.

Cinematography: Emmanuel Lubezki.

Editing: Roderick Jaynes.

Original Music: Carter Burwell.

Principal Cast:

Frances McDormand	*Linda Litzke*	J.K. Simmons	*CIA Director*
John Malcovich	*Osborne Cox*	Jeffrey DeMunn	*Cosmetic Surgeon*
George Clooney	*Harry Pfarrer*	Elizabeth Marvel	*Sandy Palmer*
Tilda Swinton	*Katie Cox*	Olek Krupa	*Attaché Krapotkin*
Brad Pitt	*Chad Feldheimer*	J.R. Horne	*Divorce Lawyer*
Richard Jenkins	*Ted Treffon*	Kevin Sussman	*Tuchman Marsh Man*
David Rasche	*Palmer*	J.R. Horne	*Divorce Lawyer*

Synopsis: Osborne Cox, a CIA analyst, resigns from the agency when accused of a drinking problem. His wife, Katie, aiming to divorce him, secretly copies his financial data onto a CD. She is having an affair with US Marshall Harry Pfarrer, a playboy disaffected from his own wife. The Cox CD finds its way to a local gym, Hardbodies, where staffer Chad Feldheimer is convinced it contains classified government secrets. Linda Litzke, another gym employee, suggests they use the disk to blackmail Cox, so she can pay for extensive cosmetic surgery. Cox rebuffs their blackmail, so they try peddling their disc to the Russian embassy. Harry, who dates women on the Internet, hooks up with Linda, and they begin seeing each other. Osborne is locked out of his Georgetown townhouse by Katie.

Chad breaks into Cox's house for more classified dirt but is found in a closet by Harry, who shoots him dead. Harry then learns his wife has also begun divorce proceedings. In a park, Harry meets Linda, who expresses concern about the missing Chad. Harry realizes that Chad was the man he killed, questions Linda, and flees in terror. Linda's manager, Ted Treffon, is sweet on her and agrees to help her get more info from the Cox house. At the same time, Cox, in a rage, breaks into his own house, encounters Ted, and kills him with a gun and a hatchet. At CIA headquarters, Osborne's former boss and the latter's chief try to sort out what happened but can only find bafflement.

Background: *Burn After Reading* was a massive turn-about in tone for the Coen brothers, who had just previously made the Oscar-winning Western noir *No Country for Old Men*. This spy spoof/farce was their first original screenplay since their 2001 movie, *The Man Who Wasn't There*. Ethan Coen compared *Burn After Reading* to the Allen Drury political novel *Advise and Consent* and called it "our version of a Tony Scott/Jason Bourne kind of movie, without the explosions." There are no explosions, just one botched enterprise after another.

While writing the script, the Coens had actors Frances McDormand (Joel Coen's wife), George Clooney, Brad Pitt, John Malkovich, and Richard Jenkins in mind for the parts, with Tilda Swinton being added later.

Comment: The Coens are aiming at black, absurdist farce in *Burn After Reading*, but only occasionally pull it off. They have had a tendency in their films to condescend to their characters, to look down on them as manipulative figures, and that's what basically happens here. The general stupidity—and sometimes orneriness—of the characters wears thin over the course of the film and makes them hard to sympathize with. Frances McDormand, as the makeover-obsessed Linda, too quickly dances a one-note samba with her needy demands and cluelessness. Brad Pitt, as the witless Chad, may seem amusing in his haplessness at first, but his dumbness comes to grate. His getting blown away in a closet is raw, but you don't miss him. Clooney's many tics pile up but don't amuse. Tilda Swinton, irritable from the beginning as Malkovich's scheming wife, never gets beyond sour, etc., etc.

The exception in this line-up is John Malkovich's Osborne, hilarious out of the box as an affronted CIA man who sustains a barely controlled rage as he's confronted by all the "idiots" around him. While a narcissistic snob, the trials that befall him—the loss of his job, his wife's animosity, his father's sad state—gain him some real sympathy and the right to strike out at the lesser beings. Malkovich, appearing in his first Coen brothers film, was very positive about his experience. He said of the shooting, "The Coens are very delightful: smart, funny, very specific about what they want but not overly controlling, as some people can be."

DC Notes: Although the film narrative takes place wholly in Washington, DC, most filming was done in and around New York City, as the Coens wanted to be close to their families. Scenes were filmed in Brooklyn Heights, the Bronx, New Rochelle, and Paramus, New Jersey. Washington locations were in Georgetown, on the side of the reflecting pool of the Lincoln Memorial, and on the ramp on the Potomac Parkway (also used in *Murder at 1600* and *Breach*, q.v).

In the film, the Cox's house, though it has something of the Georgetown look, was actually shot in Brooklyn.

George Clooney's character, Harry, is an inveterate jogger, and he takes off for one long, convoluted run during the film. Starting at the Potomac Parkway below the Lincoln Memorial, he is next seen running around the rim of the Tidal Basin, then over the Key Bridge from the Rosslyn side, to finally end up on 35th Street, NW, in Georgetown, a distinctive cobbled street that has a nice view back down to the Key Bridge.

53 STATE OF PLAY

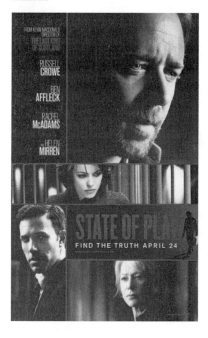

 2009. Made by Working Title Films, *inter alia*, distributed by Universal Pictures, 128 minutes, color.

Director: Kevin Macdonald.

Screenplay: Matthew Michael Carnahan (re-writes by Tony Gilroy, Peter Morgan, and Billy Ray) from the television story by Paul Abbott.

Cinematography: Rodrigo Prieto.

Editing: Justine Wright.

Music: Alex Heffes.

Principal Cast:

Russell Crowe	*Cal McAffrey*	*Michael Berresse*	*Robert Bingham*
Ben Affleck	*Cong. Stephen Collins*	*Jeff Daniels*	*Cong. George Fergus*
Rachel McAdams	*Della Frye*	*Rob Benedict*	*Milt*
Helen Mirren	*Cameron Lynne*	*Harry Lennix*	*Det. Donald Bell*
Jason Bateman	*Dominic Foy*	*Viola Davis*	*Dr. Judith Franklin*
Robin Wright Penn	*Anne Collins*	*Sonia Baker*	*Maria Thayer*

Synopsis: The film contrasts the trajectories of two college buddies, crusty reporter Cal McAffrey of the "Washington Globe," and ambitious young Congressman Stephen Collins of Pennsylvania. Cong. Collins is a rising star and on the side of the angels in probing a defense contractor, PointCorp. An apparent suicide by Sonia Baker, a key staffer of Collins, devastates the congressman, who was her lover. In investigating the suicide, McAffrey begins to suspect Collins and hopes to bag a big story. His editor, Cameron Lynne, insists that he work with a young blogger colleague, Della Frye.

The two very different journalists eventually form a testy alliance as they jointly begin piecing together stories about both Baker and PointCorp. Cal comes to see the Baker case as connected to another incident, a street killing in Georgetown. They also discover that a PR man with connections to PointCorp, Dominic Foy, knew Sonia, and Foy is forced into revealing that Sonia also worked for PointCorp and, indeed, was paid to spy on Collins. As the story drives to its conclusion, Collins's relative innocence fades as his murky motivations and suspect past are revealed.

Background: Based on an esteemed 2003 British television mini-series of the same name, *State of Play* was the subject of a bidding war among several studios for the original property written by Englishman Paul Abbott. It became associated with director Kevin Macdonald early on, and Brad Pitt was long interested in the lead. Pitt was set to play the part of Cal in 2007, but that prospect foundered about the time of the 2007-2008 Writers' Guild of America strike. Ben Affleck's role was originally cast for Edward Norton, who also had to bow out.

Production Notes: Most of the production was shot in Los Angeles' studios, where the filmmakers reproduced a cavernous newsroom for the Washington Globe newspaper. As with *All the President's Men* (q.v.), production and costume design looked to *The Washington Post*'s newsroom as a model, and the paper was acknowledged in the end credits.

Comment: *State of Play* offers the relative rarity of a solidly crafted motion picture that is truly about Washington, DC–a film that takes pains to incorporate numerous elements of the city into its narrative. In plot, however, it rings familiar changes on some of the old clichés of politics in film. It offers the familiar Hollywood portrayal of congressional politics as a thoroughly corrupt and venal process. Comparatively, journalism, though its purposes and personnel may be flawed, remains relatively heroic and humane. The filmmakers clearly looked to *All the President's Men* as a model in many ways, including shots of the Watergate complex and incorporating a tense sequence in a parking garage. This sense of homage continued right up to the conclusion, which ends, as does the earlier picture, with revelatory scandal headlines being typed out full frame--though this time it's on a computer screen instead of a teletype machine.

Even with its shining a bright light on the underside of our politics and fiddling a bit with DC geography, *State of Play* remains a briskly-paced, smartly written, and entertaining thriller, with some deft performances. The story is easy to get caught up in and challenging to follow—and it uses much of a DC that many will recognize.

DC/Hill Notes: The film had one of the longest Washington shooting schedules among recent films, about a month, and used an unusual number of DC locations and local set-ups.

Washington-area film buffs will have fun picking out local sights such as The District Line shop in Georgetown, K Street, NW and the underside of Key Bridge, Ben's Chili Bowl on U Street, NW, the steps of the Scottish Rite Temple on 16th Street, NW, Heller's Bakery in Mount Pleasant, the Market Inn and the Maine Avenue Fish Market in Southwest, and the Americana Hotel in Crystal City, as well as other spots in town. The Department of Housing and Urban Development in SW doubles as a city hospital.

The Kennedy Center gets one of its rare moments in DC movies, with sequences inside and out. McAffrey (Crowe) confronts Congressional whip Cong. Fergus (Daniels) within the Center's sumptuous foyer (with a Millennium Stage performance in the background) and then confronts him outside the front of the building (the only other use of the Center is in *True Colors*, q.v.).

In the film, Cong. Collins (Affleck) and his wife (Wright Penn) are seen fleetingly on a TV screen while they are at a press conference. The stately room, seen only fleetingly, is actually the Great Hall of the Library of Congress. The film originally had an extended sequence on this press conference, but it was dropped from the final cut (it appears in "Deleted Scenes" in the DVD version).

An important early sequence leading up to the Baker suicide/murder was shot at the Rosslyn Metro station, a rare use of the subway in commercial movies. Metro officials carefully vetted the script, limited what actions could be shot, and confined the hours of filming so as not to disrupt the system.

Local DC-area references are also sometimes tossed in for authenticity, as when the Globe's editor, a feisty Helen Mirren, cracks that the paper's burgeoning story is "not just gossip over drinks at The Monocle!" (The Monocle being a venerable restaurant and watering hole near the Senate office buildings on Capitol Hill.)

Goofs: For Hillites, it's amusing to see how congressional elements are treated in *State of Play*. Since the filmmakers were not permitted to shoot near the Capitol itself, they used surrogate buildings to indicate legislative gravitas and architecture.

One example shows Cong. Collins (Affleck) coming down the steps of the Library of Congress' Jefferson Building standing in for a House office building.

Later, when Collins supposedly heads to his "office," he instead runs into the Mellon Auditorium at 1301 Constitution Avenue, NW. It even has a sign with "Cannon" near the entrance to refer to one of the actual House office buildings.

Also, when Cal is seen quizzing Collins in an "official" colonnade on the Hill, they are actually cruising the 12th Street side of the Federal Triangle downtown.

In other slips, young Sonia Baker leaves her apartment building in the Adams-Morgan section of Northwest Washington and–swiftly–walks to the Rosslyn Metro station, some two miles away across the river in Virginia (a strange way to go to Capitol Hill).

Also, in the scene mentioned above played outside the Kennedy Center, McAffrey, leaving the scene, runs south down the main walkway, which leads nowhere except to a driveway.

54 NIGHT AT THE MUSEUM: BATTLE OF THE SMITHSONIAN

2009. 20th Century Fox, 105 minutes, color.

Director: Shawn Levy.

Screenplay: Robert Be Grant and Thomas Lennon.

Cinematography: John Schwartzman.

Editing: Dean and Don Zimmerman.

Music: Alan Sivestri.

Principal Cast :

Ben Stiller .... *Larry Daley*	Ricky Gervais .... *Dr. McPhee*
Amy Adams .... *Amelia Earhart*	Bill Hader .... *General Custer*
Hank Azaria .... *Kahmunrah/Lincoln*	Jon Bernthal. .... *Al Capone*
Owen Wilson................................. *Jedediah*	Patrick Gallagher................*Attila the Hun*
Robin Williams................. *Teddy Roosevelt*	Jonah Hill.......... *Brandon (Security Guard)*
Christopher Guest .... *Ivan the Terrible*	Jake Cherry....................................... *Nicky*
Alain Chabat.............. *Napoleon Bonaparte*	Rami Malek.............................*Ahkmenrah*
Steve Coogan .... *Octavius*	Mizuo Peck................................ *Sacajawea*

Synopsis: When New York's American Museum of Natural History is scheduled for renovation, several of its exhibits are shipped to the Smithsonian Institution in Washington, DC to be archived. The magic tablet of Ahkmenrah, which has allowed the exhibits to become animated at night, was to remain, but Dexter, a capuchin monkey, steals it and brings it to the Smithsonian. Once in Washington, the tablet re-animates Ahkmenrah's evil brother Kahmunrah, who is housed in a secret chamber of the Smithsonian's Federal Archives and looks to take back the Egyptian throne.

Larry Daley, ex-night watchman at the American Museum, now has his own security company. When he learns that his museum friends, including the toy soldiers Jedediah and Octavius, have been captured by Kahmunrah, he goes to DC to help them escape. He takes on the identity of a security guard and teams up with new historical figures, such as Amelia Earhart and General George Custer, to challenge Kahmunrah and his army and retrieve the magic tablet. Kahmunrah answers Larry's challenge by recruiting famous villains of the past: Ivan the Terrible, Napoleon Bonaparte, and Al Capone. The two forces contend in the Smithsonian Castle, the National Air and Space Museum, and the National Gallery, and Larry successfully duels the Egyptian with his glow-in-the-dark flashlight.

Background: This comedy/fantasy is a spin-off from the highly successful *Night at the Museum* (2006) which was set in the American Museum of Natural History. The gimmick of the original story, replicated here, is that a magic Egyptian artifact–a tablet–allows the museum's exhibits to come alive at night and roam the building, a phenomenon discovered by the amiable museum guard Larry Daley, who comes to identify with his roaming night companions.

The picture was a money maker, though just barely, because it was so expensive to produce. It cost about $150 million and returned somewhat over $177 million, this compared to the first *Night at the Museum,* which cost approximately $110 million and earned over $250 million. Critically, too, the film was received more tepidly than its predecessor, though Amy Adams was roundly praised for her lively portrayal of the famous 1930's aviatrix.

Production Notes: While some establishing shots of the Smithsonian were actually used, the bulk of the picture is a special effects extravaganza (mostly done in a massive Vancouver sound stage) throwing a whole mess of differing historical, technical, and cultural objects into a fizzy mix (see **Goofs** on next page).

The actual shooting on the Mall was done in front of the Smithsonian Castle and the Air and Space Museum. An extra on those scenes noted that star Ben Stiller was always accompanied by two large body guards, walking him to and from the set. Yet, between takes the actor was congenial, walking over to the ropes that kept on-lookers at bay and chatting with fans.

DC Notes: The film, like much of the country, assumes that there is a "Smithsonian Museum," rather than the complex of entities that make up the Institution. Even though the young kid Jack informs his dad Larry (Stiller) that there are "19 different parts to the Smithsonian," the film proceeds as if they are all on the Mall. Legitimate shots in Washington involve exteriors of the Mall, the Smithsonian Castle, and the Lincoln Memorial. There is also an actual shoot inside the Air and Space Museum, though a later action sequence has the spunky Amelia Earhart flying the Wright biplane inside the building–the purest fantasy. An amusing element of the film involves both Rodin's "The Thinker" and the Lincoln statue in the Memorial coming alive in digitized animation (both figures are voiced by Hank Azaria).

Goofs: A favorite device in DC movies, usually less serious ones like *Battle of the Smithsonian*, involves super secret underground facilities in the bowels of official Washington (such invention feeds all those inveterate conspiracy theorists). This contrivance figures in movies like *Dave, Murder at 1600*, and *True Lies* (q.v.), and *Get Smart*. It shows up again here with the special "Federal Archives" in DC contained in a "deep storage" facility right under the Mall.

Larry Daley enters buildings whose interior nature changes. For example, he leaves a taxi on the Mall and runs into the real Smithsonian Castle but then encounters a mysterious chamber with a large window like a medieval chapel. When Daley comes up again on the Mall, he goes to what is supposed to be the National Gallery but is called instead the "Washington Art Museum."

Larry approaches a large structure clearly labeled "Air & Space Museum" It is, indeed, the actual museum, but the large lettering–added using special effects–does not exist on the front of the building.

A lengthy, and often clever, special effects sequence in the Washington Art Museum includes several blatantly mistaken Gallery holdings including a large version of "The Thinker" (original in Paris) and two iconic paintings, Grant Wood's "American Gothic" and Edward Hopper's "Nighthawks," both of which reside in the Art Institute of Chicago.

The film mixes up the holdings of the Air and Space Museum (biplanes, rockets) with artifacts from the Museum of American History (*Wizard of Oz* slippers, Archie Bunker's chair, etc.)

55 CASINO JACK

2010. Hannibal Pictures and Rollercoaster Entertainment, distributed by ATO Pictures, 108 minutes, color.

Director: George Hickenlooper.

Screenplay by Norman Snider.

Cinematography: Adam Swica.

Editing: William Steinkamp.

Music: Jonathan Goldsmith.

Principal Cast:

Kevin Spacey	Jack Abramoff	Yannick Bisson	Oscar Carillo
Barry Pepper	Michael Scanlon	Eric Schweig	Chief Poncho
Kelly Preston	Pam Abramoff	Maury Chaykin	Big Tony
Jon Lovitz	Adam Kidan	Christian Campbell	Ralph Reed
Rachelle Lefevre	Emily Miller	Spencer Garrett	Tom DeLay
Graham Greene	Bernie Sprague	David Fraser	Karl Rove
John David Whalen	Kevin Ring	Ruth Marshall	Susan Schmidt

Synopsis: Washington über-lobbyist Jack Abramoff believes fervently that "influence is the most important currency in Washington" and can fulfill one's wildest dreams. But his influence peddling leads to hubris and ruin. His major scheme, carried out with the help of his colleague Michael Scanlon, involves defrauding a group of Native Americans out of millions of dollars after being hired to lobby for casinos on their land. Together with Scanlon and small-time shyster businessman Adam Kidan, Abramoff also gains a partial interest in a line of illegitimate casino cruises out of Miami. While working these schemes, he hobnobs with Washington heavies such as Tom DeLay, Karl Rove, Ralph Reed, and others. Throughout his hustling, however, he remains weirdly devoted to his family and his Jewish faith. When his lobby empire crumbles, his wife is clueless. In the end, Abramoff fantasizes about blowing the whistle on the whole world of corruption he has inhabited and he ends up, after a plea, behind bars.

Background: The film is somewhat surprising in one respect: the script is full of actors playing real-life characters still in or around the world of Washington. Another recent Washington-based movie, *Fair Game* (q.v.) also incorporated some real figures in its true-life story of Valerie Plame, but it fudged many of them, particularly those involved with intelligence. Casino Jack names names and renders real scandal-tinged people and Washington players, like notorious Rep. Tom Delay, indicted Rep. Bob Ney, Sen. John McCain, Abramoff colleague Kevin Ring, conservative icons Grover Norquist, Karl Rove, and Ralph Reed, Post journalist Susan Schmidt, inter alia. Frankly, some of these impersonations are better than others.

The director, George Hickenlooper, died a few weeks before the film was released.

Coincidentally, *Casino Jack* came out just months after a serious documentary film called *Casino Jack and the United States of Money* which carefully outlined the stunning rise and abrupt fall of Abramoff. That film, made by documentarist Alex Gibney, gave a vigorous, warts and all, portrayal of this super-hustler as he suborned officials and legislators, feathered his luxury nest, and offered a calamitous model of hard-ball politics.

Comment: *Casino Jack* aims at sardonic wit and knowing snideness, confirming to filmgoers just how unbelievably crass our political process has become. Call it a comedy of bad manners. Kevin Spacey, as it turns out, looks nothing like the real Abramoff, but it hardly matters (especially to viewers outside Washington, who have little sense of the man as a public figure) because, while the real Jack was coarse and fat, the actor is cool and slim. However, to his credit, Spacey is appropriately oily and smooth, the very picture of a well-dressed operator who could say just the right things to a beleaguered Congressman or a cowed bureaucrat. He gets to deliver smart-alecky lines like: "Washington is like Hollywood, but with uglier faces."

The one time the film tries to duplicate the actual Abramoff is in using the television image of the man under indictment, somber under a black flat-brim fedora and pinched double-breasted coat. The costumers put Spacey in the same wardrobe, but, frankly, rather than evoking the original, it just looks silly. Abramoff's partner in lobbying crime, Michael Scanlon, is played by a wired Barry Pepper as a hyper, even manic character, apparently paralleling the real life Scanlon. Thus, Spacey offers a becalmed Ying that fits nicely with Pepper's frenzied Yang. Jon Lovitz, the old Saturday Night Live regular who plays the sleaze ball Kidan is woefully out of place here, mugging up a storm as if he belongs in another movie. It aims to be a crackling, tart exposé, and it achieves it only half-way. Sometimes incidents happen too fast, with too little explication, and some of the building pressures on the harried lobbyists just seem like flapdoodle.

DC Notes: Washington insiders should get a mild kick out of *Casino Jack*, though they will look in vain for a film featuring the physical Washington. The bulk of the movie was shot in Toronto and Hamilton, Ontario. To indicate DC, there is only the occasional establishing shot, such as the façade of Abramoff's "Signatures" restaurant (once on the 800 block of Pennsylvania Avenue), the Grant Memorial (below the Capitol), and the Washington Monument.

Quote: At the beginning of the picture, Spacey as Abramoff, looking in the mirror in a restroom, offers his own fierce credo, an outpouring of Washington, DC invective at its most brutal:

People look at politicians and celebrities on the TV and the newspapers, glossy magazines—what do they see? "I'm just like them." That's what they say. "I'm special. I'm different. I could be any one of them." Well guess what, you can't. You know why? Cause in reality, mediocrity is where most people live. Mediocrity is the elephant in the room. It's ubiquitous. Mediocrity in your schools. It's in your dreams. It's in your family. And those of us who know this—those of us who understand the disease of the dull—we do something about it. We do more because we have to. The deck was always stacked against us. You're either a big leaguer, or you're a slave clawing your way onto the "C" train. Some people say Jack Abramoff moves too fast. Jack Abramoff cuts corners. Well, I say to them, if that's the difference between me and my family having the good life and walkin' and using the subway every day, then so be it. I will not allow my family to be slaves. I will not allow the world I touch to be vanilla.

56 FAIR GAME

 2010. River Road Entertainment and Participant Media; distributed by Summit Pictures, 108 minutes, color.

Director: Doug Liman.

Screenplay: by Jez and John Butterworth, based on the memoir *Fair Game* by Valerie Plame.

Cinematography: Doug Liman and Robert Baumgartner.

Editing: Christopher Tellefsen.

Musical Score: John Powell.

Principal Cast:

Naomi Watts	Valerie Plame	Sam Shepard	Sam Plame
Sean Penn	Joseph Wilson	Tom McCarthy	Jeff
Noah Emmerich	Bill	Khaled El Nabawy	Hammad
Ty Burrell	Fred	David Denham	Dave
David Andrews	Scooter Libby	Liraz Charhi	Dr. Zahraa
Bruce McGill	Jim Pavitt	Nassar	Mr. Tabir
Brooke Smith	Diana	Geoffrey Cantor	Ari Fleischer
Michael Kelly	Jack	Adam LeFevre	Karl Rove

Synopsis: Valerie Plame is an undercover CIA operative, based in Washington but involved in sensitive operations in the Middle East, where she is charged with investigating Saddam Hussein's nuclear capability. Her husband is Joe Wilson, a retired State Department officer with past service in Niger. He is approached by Plame's CIA colleagues to travel there to check out an intelligence report on nuclear material supposedly destined for Iraq. Wilson finds no evidence for the report, but the White House discounts his findings. After President Bush, in his 2003 State of the Union address, links the Niger nuclear material to Iraq (as partial justification for the Iraqi invasion), Wilson denounces the Niger connection in a *New York Times* op-ed.

The administration, in evident retaliation, smears Wilson by linking him to his wife, Plame, an undercover officer. Plame is then "outed" in leaked news accounts originating from the Vice President's chief of staff, Scooter Libby, whereupon she is dismissed from the Agency and her career effectively ended. Her dismissal leaves some of her contacts in exposed positions. Her marriage is also tested when she and Wilson disagree on whether to go public with their inside information. In a final effort to address the actions against her, Plame agrees to testify about what she knows before a Congressional committee, while Libby is eventually convicted of perjury and sentenced to jail.

Background: This is a movie based on Valerie Plame's memoir, *Fair Game: My Life As a Spy, My Betrayal by the White House.* "Based on" in Hollywood terms means, of course, that some license was taken by the screenwriters to heighten the drama. One important example of invention for dramatic effect (and to humanize Plame) concerns a subplot wherein she urges an Iraqi exile to contact her family (which includes an Iraqi scientist) then tries to extricate them from Baghdad only to have them come under bombardment from US forces. The script also takes understandable liberties with the real events, though the happenings are basically told in sequence. Incidents and meetings are collapsed in time to keep the pace moving.

As was done with *All the President's Men* (q.v.), the filmmakers saved themselves some fuss and attained a more documentary feel by not having actors stand in for the principal political presences–like George W. Bush and Dick Cheney in this case. The latter two do appear as themselves but only in genuine television images.

Interesting Washington background fact: the father of the film's director, Doug Liman, was the distinguished New York lawyer Arthur Liman, chief counsel at the Senate's Iran-Contra hearings in 1986.

Comment: The film effectively intersperses the fast-moving political events of the Plame affair with the ongoing personal struggles of the Wilsons, as they try to balance work pressures and family duties. What works best about *Fair Game* is, however, the acting.

Naomi Watts is impressive as Valerie Plame. Her appealing yet intense mien, with a tincture of sadness, seems just right for her character, a sympathetic spook who has to worry about babysitters for her twins. She's all business when it counts, yet caring at home. It helps, too, that you can see a clear resemblance between Watts and the real Plame (who appears in footage during the end credits). Sean Penn, though physically similar to the real Joe Wilson only in the center part of his hair, displays much of the testy spirit of the diplomat-turned-protester, and he is good at portraying both the weary but accepting stay-at-home dad and the fire-breathing defender of his wronged wife.

Among a bevy of sound character performances, one stands out: David Andrews as Lester "Scooter" Libby. While it could be argued that he is over-the-top in his imperiousness, he makes for a great villain, smarmy and supercilious at once. He is wonderfully nasty in one chilling scene where he grills a cowed CIA analyst about questionable Iraqi intelligence which he wants the White House to endorse.

DC/Hill Notes: A miscellany of Washington locations were used during filming *Fair Game* in the spring of 2009. There are standard shots: the White House (which still shows traffic moving on Pennsylvania Avenue), an overhead shot of the Memorial Bridge, and Pennsylvania Avenue with the Capitol in the background.

Several sequences concentrate around the Ellipse and the Mall. At one point Plame (Watts) walks on to the Ellipse (the Washington Monument is in view) and finds a seat on a bench to meet with her colleague Jim (Bruce McGill); the Old Executive Office Building and the White House are in the background. Later, she attends a parade along Constitution Avenue, with the Monument (again) and the American History Museum in view. Finally, Plame gets a cab on the bridge near the Jefferson Memorial on her way to the Hill, then her cab crosses the Mall, and, in the next shot, she is walking up the steps of the Russell Senate Office Building to her committee hearing.

Goofs: Valerie and Joe (Penn) supposedly meet in a DC park to talk things out, but the scene was shot in Cobble Hill Park in Brooklyn.

When Joe leaves a lunch with some African clients, he exits the Willard

Hotel at 14th and Pennsylvania Avenue, NW. He gets a cab and asks to be taken to the Palisades, a neighborhood in upper Northwest DC, but he ends up at the Grant Memorial (with the Capitol in the background), in the exact opposite direction from his destination.

HOW DO YOU KNOW

2010. Gracie Films, distributed by Columbia Pictures, 121 minutes, color.

Writer/Director: James L. Brooks.

Cinematography: Janusz Kaminski.

Editing: Richard Marks.

Music: Hans Zimmer.

Principal Cast:

Reese Witherspoon	Lisa Jorgenson	Andrew Wilson	Matty's Teammate
Paul Rudd	George Madison	Shelley Conn	Terry
Owen Wilson	Matty Reynolds	Tony Shalhoub	Psychiatrist
Jack Nicholson	Charles Madison	Ron McLarty	George's Lawyer
Dean Norris	Tony	Lenny Venito	Al
Kathryn Hahn	Annie	Mark Linn-Baker	Ron
Yuki Matsuzaki	Tori	Molly Price	Coach Sally

Synopsis: Star softball player Lisa Jorgenson is left off the Team USA roster but is comforted by Matty Reynolds, a relief pitcher for the Washington Nationals. She decides to move in with him in his luxurious downtown DC penthouse. She likes the fun-loving ballplayer but not his affairs with other women. Business man George Madison is indicted for securities fraud at a company run by his father, Charles Madison, and is fired. His fiancé walks out on him, and he is abandoned by everyone but his father and his devoted secretary, Annie. Via mutual friends, George invites Lisa to a dinner which turns out to be a disaster when he unloads his troubles on the unsuspecting Lisa.

Under the gun, George could face prison time, but loyal Annie tries to give him inside information to help him. Irresponsible Matty tries to reform but offends Lisa, who moves out and ends up tipsy at George's apartment. Charles then confesses to his son that it was he who committed the illegal act for which George is being charged. Because of a previous conviction, Charles could get 25 years, whereas George would only have a short prison term. Lisa reconsiders her previous reluctance to settle down and must decide between Matty and George. George, now smitten with Lisa, makes a proposition to his father: if Lisa agrees to be with him, Charles must do time. If she won't, George will take the rap for his dad.

Background: James Brooks works slowly: *How Do You Know* was only his sixth film in a bit less than 30 years. He began the script in 2005 with a story idea of a young woman athlete. This line was eventually combined with one involving a business executive in a dilemma. The production, especially for a "dramedy," was expensive–roughly $100 million–with half of that coming from hefty salaries for the stars and the director. Nicholson, for example, received $12 million for his supporting role (he replaced Bill Murray on the picture).

Released in December 2010 during the Christmas overload of new films, the film did poorly at the box office. Overall, it did not earn back one-half of its costs. Critically, too, it was mostly panned. A fairly representative slam came from Anthony Lake of *The New Yorker:*

> *(The characters) swim into one another's ken and then veer off again, into the solo arc of their itchy ditherings, pausing only to pass weird, superfluous judgment on what has occurred. "Good phone call!" says one. "Nice visit!" says another. Bad movie!*

Comment: In a way, *How Do You Know* is a neat 25-year follow-up to Brooks' stellar 1987 comedy, *Broadcast News* (q.v.): an attractive triangle–composed of hot youngish Hollywood stars–perform a will-she or won't-she fandango in the world of contemporary Washington. Instead of TV journalism, the context this time is sports and business, but it provides a similar kind of male competition: the blonde-locked, semi-studly entertainer (Owen Wilson viz. William Hurt) and the dark-haired, semi-nerd (Paul Rudd viz. Albert Brooks) vying for the diminutive sweetie (Reese Witherspoon viz. Holly Hunter). Whoa! You even have the indomitable Jack Nicholson as a commanding figure in both films. What has changed, however, is the chemistry.

How Do You Know simply does not get the traction from its script or the chemistry among its characters that *Broadcast News* exhibited in spades. Big credibility questions arise early when, though two of the principals are professional athletes, we get almost zero sense of their physical competence. Paul Rudd also, winsome as he is, doesn't seem believably cut from corporate cloth. If you have trouble getting past these flaws, the whole screenplay takes a nosedive.

In fact, the screenplay is another problem. While there are some nice touches–a mini-essay on package-opening is one–the material is really overly familiar and predictable. For example, there is the required best buddy/support gal, in this case two of them, one for each lead. The film frankly feels long (it runs 121 min.), as some of the obligatory "relationship" talk is strung out and repetitive (such as a treatise on Play-Doh, of all things). The writing this time basically lacks the zip and rhythm that Brooks has shown in other works.

DC/Hill Notes: A few Washington locations are used, but a good bit of the film was also shot in Philadelphia, especially in its downtown urban settings. As he did, quite calculatingly in *Broadcast News,* Brooks again eschews the standard, iconic images of the District for more pedestrian places. Prominent among the film's locations is the Bowen Building in the 800 block of 15th Street, NW, which stands in for a downtown apartment building where Matty (Wilson) lives in high style. Other DC settings include Dupont Circle and a Metro bus stop. A handsome, shiny Metro bus, in fact, floats through the film like a transportation leitmotif. For the very first time in a Hollywood movie, the Nationals' Park in Southeast is used–for scenes involving ballplayer Matty.

A reporter from *Washingtonian* magazine worked as an extra on the movie and gave a detailed account of its location shooting. Her notes are interesting for what they reveal of the monumental boredom for extras (also called "backgrounders") on a Hollywood film and the painstaking pace of director Brooks (one scene she observes requires 26 takes).

Goofs: In that sequence at Nationals' Park, Matty is shown in the pitcher's bullpen, but he is in the wrong one. He's in the visitor's bullpen (not the home team's) in left-center field, used perhaps because it had better light at the time of shooting.

58 J. EDGAR

2011. Produced by Imagine Entertainment and Malpaso Productions, distributed by Warner Brothers Pictures, 137 minutes, color.

Director: Clint Eastwood.

Screenplay: Dustin Lance Black.

Cinematography: Tom Stern.

Editing: Joel Cox and Gary D. Roach.

Original Music: Clint Eastwood.

Principal Cast:

Leonardo DiCaprio	*J. Edgar Hoover*	Ed Westwick	*Agent Smith*
Armie Hammer	*Clyde Tolson*	Ken Howard	*Harlan F. Stone*
Naomi Watts	*Helen Gandy*	Stephen Root	*Arthur Koehler*
Josh Lucas	*Charles Lindbergh*	Denis O'Hare	*Albery S. Osborn*
Judi Dench	*Anna Marie Hoover*	Geoff Pierson	*A. Mitchell Palmer*
Damon Herriman	*Bruno Hauptmann*	Lea Thompson	*Lela Rogers*
Jeffrey Donovan	*Robert F. Kennedy*	Christopher Shyer	*Richard M. Nixon*

Synopsis: The film intercuts the mature J. Edgar Hoover in the 1960's, dictating his memoirs to a series of young FBI agents, with flashbacks to his work as a young officer with the Justice Department and his later years with the Federal Bureau of Investigation, officially formed in 1935. The 1960's narrative includes segments showing J. Edgar dealing with Robert F. Kennedy during his brother's presidency and with Richard Nixon during their stormy relationship. The flashback coverage includes Hoover's involvement as a young man with the Palmer Raids right after WWI, with the founding of the Bureau, and with the crucial hiring of Hoover's life-long aides and intimates, FBI Associate Director Clyde Tolson and personal secretary Helen Gandy.

The historical elements also highlight Hoover's pursuit of gangster John Dillinger and his participation in the search for the Lindbergh baby's kidnapper after 1932. Also treated is his disquieting relationship with his difficult mother, Anna Marie, and his complicated bond with Tolson. Late in the story it is revealed, in a conversation between Tolson and Hoover, that the latter's reminiscences recounting his triumphs (such as "his" capture of Dillinger and "his" taking of kidnapper Bruno Hauptman) are mostly self-serving. Tolson, it turns out, has read the draft memoirs and found them full of grandiose lies and exaggerations meant to confirm the Hoover legend.

Comment: The film could be taken as the psychological study of a very public man overcompensating like mad because of his own personal inadequacies, many of them caused by an absent father and a demanding mother. It proves an elaborate but finally unsatisfying effort. Leonardo Di Caprio struggles to give some psychological dimension to his character and succeeds in the main, but the overall picture weakens the profile. Most importantly, *J. Edgar,* while serious and earnest, is finally turbid in intent and look. The film has an unfortunate dankness, an element which may be true of Hoover's life, but which is mainly dispiriting. The photography heightens the turbidity, with scenes that look like they are dipped in a grey syrup.

Also, Eastwood, so often great with actors, has a script (by Dustin Lance Black) which doesn't give his leads enough to do. Tolson and Gandy, for two, are mere presences in the film rather than real motors that help to drive Hoover's behavior. Watts, a fine actress with the right material (as in *Fair Game,* q.v.), does little more than shuttle people into and out of Hoover's office. Hammer, as Tolson, portrays a smooth and glib figure, but we learn nothing about what he really contributed to the FBI and have little sense of why he was so attracted to Hoover (and he has to suffer one of the worst make-up jobs in memory). Sadly, too, the film is marred by impersonations of RFK and Nixon that are unconvincing. *Fair Game* (q.v.) solved this problem of incorporating prominent political figures (in that instance, Bush and Cheney) by only showing them on screen in real television images.

DC/Hill Notes: J. Edgar Hoover was born in the heart of Capitol Hill, in a house on the south side of Seward Square where the United Methodist Church now stands. There are sundry Washington locations in the film, the most authentic of which were those at the Library of Congress, where the real Hoover worked for five years as a young man before joining the Justice Department. For a scene in the film where J. Edgar shows Helen the Library's card catalog, Eastwood and his crew spent a weekend in late

March 2011, a shoot described in the Library of Congress's house weekly, *Gazette* (see photo insert).

The *Gazette* describes how Eastwood, his two cast members and a crew of about 100 took over the Great Hall and the Main Reading Room of the Library, with "giant, helium-filled balloons floated about the floors... illuminating the scene." The article says "the crew also installed two rows of specially constructed card catalogs–more than 5 feet high and roughly 25 feet long but with only eight drawers that actually opened..." It is in Alcove 6 of the Main Reading Room where the boyish Hoover makes a marriage proposal to Gandy that she smartly spurns.

Goofs: Young J. Edgar is seen riding his bike from his home to the scene of a crime in 1919, but rather than showing him close to the Capitol (where he lived), the glowing dome is seen far off in the distance at a downward angle. Similarly, his house on Seward Square, shown from the outside, looks nothing like a Capitol Hill row house.

Some shots supposedly around the Capitol are obviously fake, particularly a funky driveway at the base of the Senate side steps.

Finally, a chronological goof. Hoover is seen looking out his office window at the top of the Justice Department as Roosevelt's Inauguration Day motorcade (in 1933) passes below him on Pennsylvania Avenue. When he goes to the window, however, we see the grand National Archives looming outside his office on 9th Street. Trouble is, the Archives building wasn't finished until 1935, two years later.

Addendum–*The FBI Story*: It is instructive to compare this mainstream Hollywood film of the 21st century with an artifact from another era: the Warner Brothers film *The FBI Story*, released in 1959. Those 50 intervening years show how much American attitudes about government, about the FBI, and, especially, about J. Edgar Hoover, had changed.

This film appeared several years before revelations about Hoover's willfulness and paranoia, before he was deemed a threat to presidents and other higher-ups. The film is a paean to one of America's most esteemed civil servants and a commercial for the enterprise he built. The film's story is told as a kind of FBI's "greatest hits," with stalwart Jimmy Stewart in full stalwartness, representing a mature FBI agent who tells about his own 35-year career with the Bureau, thus covering the highlights of the Bureau's crime-fighting over that span.

Unlike *J. Edgar*, where no particular FBI cooperation was likely or solicited, *The FBI Story* was given almost carte blanche to cover the agency, but at a cost. In commentary after a showing of the film on Turner Classic Movies in November 2011, host Ben Mankiewicz noted that the FBI had "complete creative control" over the project with approval over the script, the director (Mervyn Leroy), and, especially, the cast, Hoover himself picking Stewart for the lead as Agent Hardesty. Everybody who worked on the film was vetted by the Bureau, according to Mankiewicz, and "two agents were on the set at all times; they were there to show the Agency in the best possible light."

Filmed in the era before the new FBI Building, the movie shows the full panoply of Bureau operations at the time, including the vast file rooms and fingerprint collections, the entries and the hallways (in the Justice Department), the gun rooms and the crime labs—all seen under the earnest over-voice of Stewart intoning the virtues of the FBI. The film is a unique Hollywood document in that it includes a 25-second sequence showing none other than the Director himself, sitting in his own office in Washington (the narration does not actually identify him) and soberly receiving a file from his long-time deputy Clyde Tolson. No dialogue humanizes the Great Man for us.

The FBI Story had access to the Bureau that no studio has had before or since. Besides the many elements indicated above, the film ends with a sequence inside the inner courtyard of the Justice Department (where the Department was headquartered for decades) where Stewart and his family get in their car and drive out. They then tour DC a little, driving north across the Mall with the Agriculture Department, the Smithsonian Castle, and the Capitol in view. The car then drives in front of the Lincoln Memorial—with a fabulous shot out onto the reflecting pool and the Washington Monument taken from the right shoulder of Daniel Chester French's Abe Lincoln—before passing the Iwo Jima Memorial (in Arlington).

SELECTED SHORT SUBJECTS

Wherein is discussed all those myriad movies which didn't entirely focus on Washington or its institutions, but which featured the city or its political life as a plot or background element.

I. Movies in Wartime Washington

If Washington, DC had a general image during World War II, it was as the bureaucratic beehive of the war effort, where eager patriots of all regions and all stripes gathered, packed into a slightly sleepy Southern town that, all of a sudden, hosted big matters. Hollywood studios recognized this wartime Washington, both as a source of drama and comedy, and produced a series of films that reflected its new status. They were strictly studio productions with no time or budget for real Washington locations. The best by far was George Stevens' comedy *The More the Merrier* (q.v.), but there were enough of them to almost constitute a genre.

Typical of them was the melodrama *Ladies of Washington* (1944), in which an embittered young woman is forced to move into a DC rooming house packed with other girls, then meets a dashing foreigner (Anthony Quinn, in an early role) who turns out to be an enemy agent.

Another total studio effort was *Without Love* (1945), the third film in which Spencer Tracy and Katherine Hepburn starred together. Tracy is a scientist coming to DC to further the war effort and, due to the city's crowded conditions, takes a room in Hepburn's house, where she eventually becomes his helpmate. There are standard establishing shots of Union Station and the Capitol. Hepburn's house is located at "481 Connecticut Avenue", which would place it roughly on the Ellipse.

So This Is Washington (1943) has a popular radio comedy team of the era, Lum and Abner, as hick inventors who come to DC with a synthetic rubber formula to aid in the war effort. They become instant "rural sages," dispensing advice on agricultural policy to senators on a bench in "Jackson Park" just off the Tidal Basin. There are numerous process shots of the Capitol, the Lincoln Memorial, and the Washington Monument. Most interesting for Washingtonians is a sequence from a restaurant which has process footage showing moving traffic on Pennsylvania Avenue at about 15th Street, NW–including the city streetcars.

The wartime comedy *Government Girl* (1943) stars Sonny Tufts as an industrialist in town on defense business and, as his flighty secretary, Olivia de Havilland, in a role quite at odds with that actress's usually demure style. The film is, in the immortal words of W.C. Fields, a "mere bagatelle," notable only for an extended motorcycle sequence which liberally mixes actual location shots by a second unit in DC (with doubles) and process shots (behind the two leads). This odyssey starts near a circle at Massachusetts Avenue and 16th Street, NW (a street car can be seen) but then jumps all over the place to incorporate views of Pennsylvania Avenue, New Jersey Avenue, Constitution Avenue, and North Capitol Street, before finally cutting across the Capitol's East Lawn then onto the grounds of the Washington Monument! Whew! *Government Girl* is not much of a movie, but it offers the viewer an intriguing time capsule of our city in the early 1940's.

In the Bob Hope comedy *They Got Me Covered* (1943), DC embodies the place to fight the enemy. Hope plays a foreign correspondent visiting his girl, Dorothy Lamour, who works in the Washington, DC office of Hope's newspaper. The plot involves a secret meeting at the Lincoln Memorial at midnight which Hope, the dummy, gets mixed up with the Washington Monument by mistake!

The espionage element is used again in *Sherlock Holmes in Washington* (1943) where Holmes and Watson, played by Basil Rathbone and Nigel Bruce, somehow leap from Victorian London to take up a case which leads to DC. The film uses a number of process shots of the city, including the Capitol, Union Station, National Airport, amd Pennsylvania Avenue. There is also, most interestingly, an aerial of the Washington Monument which shows the WWII temporary buildings–built for the war effort–on the north side of the Mall.

Most prominent of the Washington-set pictures that treated enemy espionange was *Watch on the Rhine*, which was nominated for the Best Picture Oscar in 1943 and whose lead, Paul Lukas, won that year's award for Best Actor. Lukas plays a German refugee living in DC with the family of his American wife played by Bette Davis. Based on a hit play by Lilian Hellman, the film was scripted by her lover Dashiel Hammett. Though set in Washington, it was entirely studio made with no DC filming (a pasted-in Washington Monument shows in the rear view of one car).

Perhaps the best of the spy-themed World War II movies was *The House on 92nd Street* (1945), a documentary-style thriller conceived by producer Louis de Rochment and directed by Henry Hathaway. The concept was to diligently follow a true crime story mingling real-life footage with fresh fictionalized material. In this case, the film followed FBI agents trailing and apprehending a nest of German spies whose activities centered in New York City (thus, 92nd Street, their hangout), but it did include significant Washington scemes.

The FBI offered complete cooperation for a film which lauded their competence, and the producers showed numerous aspects of Bureau operations, then located in the Justice Department. There are scenes showing the FBI's file rooms, offices, and research facilities, as well as a gigantic hangar-like space holding the massive fingerprint collections. Perhaps most tellingly, the film also included some actual footage (from a Bureau hidden camera) that showed real German espionage figures moving in and out of the German Embassy in Washington.

II. Science Fiction Sites

Washington has been treated in science fiction films over many years, its iconic monuments being a tempting subject for destruction. Some invasions have already been highlighted in the regular chapters of this book, such as *The Day the Earth Stood Still* and *Earth vs. the Flying Saucers*. Others could be mentioned.

Washington gets invaded by a giant bug in *The Deadly Mantis* (1957), a B-picture so bad that it was mocked as schlock years later by the comedy TV show *Mystery Science Theater 3000*. The praying mantis of the title, unleashed from hibernation at the North Pole, speeds down the East Coast to settle in DC. It flies over the Capitol (of course) then inexplicably lands on the Washington Monument, where two terrorized night guards watch it climb up the structure.

The Capitol makes a surprise appearance in the futuristic fantasy *Logan's Run* (1976), which takes place in a 2274 when no one is permitted to live beyond 30. However, the hero and his girlfriend want to live and escape their pristine domed city to end up in a chaotic jungle which turns out to be–the Capitol Grounds! Peter Ustinov–as a left over legislator–leads them around the weed-infested House chamber.

In the science fiction blockbuster, *Independence Day* (1996), the capital comes under fire from invading aliens, with the most spectacular sequence being a wholesale frying of the White House. Luckily for the president (Bill Pullman), he is whisked out of the Oval Office prior to the attack and, being a jet pilot, is able to lead a glorious charge against the invaders and save the nation. The White House, poor thing, was also obliterated in *Superman II* (1978), when bad guys from the planet Krypton (Superman's home) destroy the building with their smash rays.

In Tim Burton's fantasy-farce, *Mars Attacks!* (1996), it's the Capitol that gets creamed. The Martians, initially welcomed by the earthlings (led by President Jack Nicholson), are invited to address the Congress. But once in the House chamber, they zap all the legislators with ray guns, and leave a smoking dome. Burton was a big admirer of Ray Harryhausen's effects in *Earth vs. the Flying Saucers* and other 50's science fiction films and mod-eled his flying saucers in the film quite precisely after the earlier picture.

In an exception to the standard wicked alien invasion, *Contact* (1997) tells the tale of a committeed astronomer (Jodie Foster) who believes she hears signals from extraterrestrial life and struggles to get funding from the National Science Foundation to confirm her views. In the key Washington scene, she testifies in an enormous congressional committee room (actually the Mellon Auditorium on Constitution Avenue, NW) then leaves the Capitol, supposedly down its West Front steps but only to emerge right on the Mall, facing a crowd with the Washington Monument in the distance, at about the level of 4th Street.

In the 2001 remake of *Planet of the Apes,* a simian-ruled Washington receives astronaut Mark Wahlberg when his space capsule lands on the Lincoln Memorial's reflecting pool and skips like a stone down to the Memorial's entrance. When he gets out and climb's the grand steps, he is greeted most appropriately–said a *Washington Post* wag: "by a statute of the Great Emancipator...Ape Lincoln!"

Apparently the aliens don't give up easily, because they keep coming. Most recently, in *The Invasion* (2007), Washington is invaded by the insidious body snatchers (who have invaded American towns in at least three earlier versions). The snatchers are able to make robots of humans by invading them in their sleeping state, and this time, Washington psychologist Nicole Kidman tries to keep them away from her young son. The film was mostly shot in Baltimore, as so many other "local" movies, but it does mark a milestone in DC filming: the first time a Hollywood camera crew was able to shoot fully within a Metro station, this one at Cleveland Park. Being chased by zombies who have already been snatched, Kidman and her son run into the station and all the way down the escalators to the bottom platform (they end up, of course, in Baltimore).

Aliens from outer space are not the only things that can threaten our nation's capital: sometimes just the quirks of the solar system become our nemesis.

Take, for example, *Meteor,* where the earth is threatened with extinction by a big rock from outer space. Its Washington element has acerbic scientist Sean Connery (going through the motions in this sleeper) exasperated by panicking generals at the Defense Department. While in DC, he hangs out at an apartment hotel just below the House Office Buildings in SE.

Then there is *Deep Impact* (1998), a disaster picture whose peril is a giant comet which will vaporize the earth. Part of the picture is set in DC, where the heroine, a reporter played by Tea Leoni, lives. Sequences in the picture were shot at the Key Bridge, at the Hay-Adams Hotel, the Sequoia

Restaurant on the Georgetown waterfront, and on the roof of the Robert C. Weaver Building (HUD headquarters) in Southwest. A piece of the comet does eventually land in the Atlantic, creating a megatsunami that pretty much wipes out the East Coast. All is not lost, however, because the movie ends with the surviving President (Morgan Freeman) standing in front of a devastated Capitol being reconstructed.

In the film entitled *2012* (released in 2009), scientists learn that the earth's core is heating up so fast that the crust of the earth is becoming unstable, endangering life on earth. Here again, DC gets hit–rather, inundated, as President Wilson (Danny Glover) tries to save the capital. But he and his staff, stranded in a refugee camp under a giant cloud on the South Lawn (covered in ash), are finally washed away when a tsunami hits the city and crashes an aircraft carrier into the White House. (ouch!)

A one-off variation on disaster pictures is *Raise the Titanic* (1980). This is not strictly a "disaster" picture, but it is certainly about a famous disaster. As a thriller, the film is ho-hum but it does incorporate a mix of diverse DC locations, including Dulles Airport, the Mayflower Hotel (scene of a press conference), the yacht Sequoia, and Meridian House International off 16th Street, NW (a stand-in for the Embassy of the USSR).

III. DC for Laughs

While one may be disappointed that so many Hollywood filmmakers just can't seem to get our Washington right, one should not be too surprised that film comedies take more liberties with our nature and geography. In fact, that same kind of looseness with the facts helps define them as comedies, after all. Several comedy films have been highlighted in this volume, including several goofy ones, like *D.C. Cab, Dick, The Distinguished Gentleman*, and *Legally Blonde 2: Red White and Blonde, The Man with One Red Shoe, Protocol*, which were never meant to be taken seriously. A number of others merit at least a passing mention.

An innocuous role-reversal comedy from 1964 was *Kisses for My President*, starring Polly Bergen as the first female president and Fred MacMurray as the "First Husband." This is a gentle farce which ribs the husband, as he inherits a frilly bedroom, must attend women's social events, and is frustrated trying to romance a too-busy chief executive. The reconciliation of the plot is very 1964: the president becomes pregnant and renounces her office.

One misbegotten comedy was the 1968 travesty *Wild in the Streets,* a psychedelic cheapo very much of its time. Its silliness included a hippie takeover of the government when LSD is secreted into the city's water supply and the Congress trips out in its own chamber, giddily voting for enfranchising 14-year olds! That chamber, by the way, was about the size of a high school gym and just about as plausible. The film starred the otherwise esteemed Hal Holbrook as a fervently ambitious congressman in a role he probably hopes everyone has forgotten.

Then there was *The Werewolf of Washington* (1973), a bottom-of-the barrel affair where a presidential press aide (Dean Stockwell) becomes a wolfman who attacks a woman in a phone booth at the bottom of the Capitol and who goes all hairy during a session of the Joint Chiefs of Staff. The film also includes some actual, but purely random, DC shots, among the most notable being the (now defunct) Sans Souci restaurant on 17th Street, NW.

The First Family (1980) is tepid satire from comedy writer Buck Henry (who also directed–badly), with Bob Newhart as wimpy President Manfred Link trying to establish diplomatic relations with a fictional African country, Upper Gorm. Comic talents like Madeline Kahn, Gilda Radner, and Fred Willard are wasted in this misfire. Its one pleasant location surprise is when the presidential limo drives down Pennsylavania Avenue with the Apex Liquor building (now housing the National Council of Negro Women) in the background.

Similarly lame is the little-known 1980 comedy, *Nothing Personal,* with Donald Sutherland as a professor objecting to seal slaughter and Suzannne Somers as a Harvard-educated lawyer (!) who allies with him. Its single memorable Washington sequence is a car chase which begins at an Exxon station in Georgetown and is supposed to end with the vehicle being driven into the Tidal Basin (shades of Wilbur Mills and Fanne Foxe in 1974), but the splash actually happens at Jones Point in Alexandria.

A comedy with much more dramatic intent is *Heartburn* (1986), based on the memoir of Nora Ephron and written for the screen and directed by

A Street SE to represent the fixer-upper in the film.

Three for the Road (1987) is a brainless comedy with Charlie Sheen as the naive staffer for a vile Senator who is willing to exile his upstart child to save his very thin political skin. The film is a travesty, typified by the credit sequence showing Sheen gunning his motorcycle towards what is supposed to be the U.S. Capitol but is actually the State Capitol of Little Rock, Arkansas!

The raucous, *Naked Gun 2 1/2: The Smell of Fear* (1991) is a good-spirited comedy which treats DC geography with the same lack of respect it treats everything else: The view from "The Police Station" looks out on the Capitol, the city has a "Little Italy," and the "National Press Club" is apparently located at the site of St. John's Church on 16th Street, NW. Also, there is a crucial dock scene–with a clear view of a San Francisco bridge in the background. In this kind of flick, nobody cares.

In *Loose Cannons* (1990), another Washington "port" is displayed. The leads are tough homicide cop Gene Hackman and his partner Dan Aykroyd, with a brilliant deductive mind and a serious multiple personality disorder. One chase sequence has our heroes riding into an "industrial area" off South Capitol Street and ending up at a major port (perhaps Baltimore) with a large ship and container hoists in view. The film also used locations at the DAR building and the lobby of the National Museum of Women in the Arts on New York Avenue, NW. In a blatant appeal to Washington filmgoers, Hackman wears a Redskins jacket a good part of the movie.

The obscure Robert Townsend comedy *Meteor Man* (1993), about a high school teacher from DC's inner city Washington D.C. who becomes a super-powered hero, was almost wholly shot in Baltimore with little to indicate Washington. Just as obscure, and rightly so, is *National Lampoon's Senior Trip* (1995), where the trip in question is by ditzy Ohio high schoolers to the Nation's Capital. The humor is no subtler than any other Lampoon film. It features, for example, a grotesque scene where randy kids critique J. Edgar Hoover by lighting farts at his "eternal flame" in Arlington National Cemetery–when all Capitol Hillites know that Hoover is, in fact, buried at Congressional Cemetery!

Whether Warren Beatty considered his film *Bulworth* (1998) a "comedy," or just a sardonic tirade against both liberal pieties and corporate influence in politics, it does treat a US senator who, totally disullusioned about politics, decides to arrange his own assassination. While the film opens in Bulworth's Senate office (the inevitable Capitol dome outside the window), the focus quickly shifts to his campaigning back in California, where he is shaken out of his stupor by discovering the raw "authenticity" of black street folk and hip-hop. Locals will perk up when they hear the senator crack wise about the prestigious Sidwell Friends and St. Albans schools in a debate performance. This uneven film, with plenty of hit and missed targets, does have one fully convincing peformance: Oliver Platt as Bulworth's chief aide is a wonderful incarnation of the ever-adapting Hill staffer.

More recently, there is *Evan Almighty* (2007) with Steve Carrell as a clueless congressman from Buffalo to whom God (not surprisingly, Morgan Freeman) speaks so that he might become a new Noah and build an ark to protect the environment of Northern Virginia. The preposterous finale has Evan's ark gliding down the Potomac, sloshing down the Mall, and crashing into the Capitol during a committee hearing. One caustic critic had it about right when he said of this film that: "There are more jokes in any chapter of the Book of Job than in the whole of *Evan Almighty*."

IV. Washington in Name Only

There are a number of movies that supposedly take their setting in the Washington area but which barely acknowledge the city in their scripts or imagery. One early example is the important post-war police procedural *Crossfire* (1947), which seriously treats anti-Semitism. Though it "takes place" in Washington, DC, there is no recognizable physical evidence of the city anywhere in this somber, but effective film.

Stars and Stripes Forever (1952) is a biopic of John Phillip Sousa, long time leader of the US Marine Band. Sousa, in fact, was born on Capitol Hill (on the 600 block of G Street SE), spent most of his life in Washington, and was buried in Congressional Cemetery, but there are no DC scenes in the picture, which was shot on 20th Century Fox's sound stages in Hollywood.

In 1964, two major doomsday movies appeared within nine months of each other: the pitch-black comedy *Dr. Strangelove or: How I Learned to Stop Worrying and Love the Bomb* and *Fail-Safe*, based on a popular thriller novel. Both had long sequences in Washington, DC bunkers as a president (Peter Sellers and Henry Fonda, respectively) contemplated a nuclear option but neither needed to be shot in Washington. Kubrick's *Dr. Strangelove*, in fact, had its war room constructed in Shepperton Studios in England.

Another kind of doomsday figured in Darryl Zanuck's elaborate (but turgid) re-creation of the Japanese attack on Pearl Harbor, *Tora!, Tora!, Tora!*. The film had numerous Washington "settings" but almost all took place in "offices" that were shot in studios. Only minimal "postcard" shots of the Capitol, the Lincoln Memorial, and the Mall were used.

The second of the Bruce Willis action/suspense franchise, *Die Hard II* (1990), supposedly takes place at Dulles National Airport. However, airport exteriors were principally filmed at Denver International Airport. Keen eyes will also notice that when hero John McClain (Willis) calls his wife from the airport, one can see "Pacific Bell" on the pay phone.

Oliver Stone is a major director pointedly concerned with political matters, enough so to produce a controversial trilogy of films on contemporary US presidents: *JFK* (1991), *Nixon* (1995) and *W.* (2008). Though strongly committed to these film stories concerning the Presidency, Stone used almost no DC location material in their telling. The first, of course, was actually about Jim Garrison (Kevin Costner) and his assassination conjectures rather than about JFK, and the second was more of an attempt to plumb the mysterious Nixon's mind rather than to depict him in a political context. *W.* bordered on farce. The first two had minimal Washington scenes, while *W.* had none–it was mostly shot in Shreveport, Louisiana.

The War of the Roses, a black comedy of 1999 with Michael Douglas and Kathleen Turner as the ultimate feuding couple, was supposedly set in Washington, but the single evidence of DC is a dim view of the Capitol dome seen through the window of Douglas's divorce lawyer played by Danny De Vito. The more recent *Wedding Crashers* (2005), has its two comic leads (Vince Vaughan and Owen Wilson) as Washington bon-vivants, but almost all the film was shot on Maryland's Eastern Shore.

Man of the Year (2006) is a rather lame Robin Williams comedy about a TV news satirist who decides to run for president for a lark and ends up being elected when a national computer voting system malfunctions. Another made-in-Canada movie, its lone concession to DC locations is limo shots around Lafayette Square.

V. Playing the Spy Game

Beyond WWII espionage films, the spy genre has long used Washington as a setting because the intelligence community and general officialdom are based there. A few of these spy films appear in this book (to note: *Breach, Burn After Reading, Enemy of the State, Fair Game, The Man With One Red Shoe, No Way Out, True Lies*), but many more have dipped into DC for comic or dramatic effect.

An interesting early example is the espionage thriller *The Thief* (1952) which stars Ray Milland as a nuclear scientist with the Atomic Eneregy Commission clandestinely filming top secret documents and passing them on to an unnamed enemy with the drop point being–where else–the Main Reading Room of the Library of Congress! He uses both the card catalog of the Library as well as a reference book for his secret stash. Mostly shot in New York, *The Thief* was an odd studio experiment in that the film had no dialogue, only music, live sound, and sound effects. It was not a hit.

A trivial post-war example is *The 49th Man* (1953), a cheesy, cheap anti-commie thriler wherein the "U.S. Security Service" is looking for bombs being sumuggled into the U.S. The plot at one point has its hero being driven down Pennsylvania Avenue as a hostage, with a poor process shot showing a dim Capitol dome in the rear view mirror.

Scorpio (1973) is a routine Cold War thriller starring Burt Lancaster as a CIA officer. One sequence shows the front entrance to the CIA Building in Langley, with an obvious stand-in for the "lobby" of the Agency (with a reproduction of the CIA's logo). Another sequence involves a surveillance tape which shows a woman both entering and leaving the Library of Congress, performing a suspected "drop." That same footage is replayed near the end of the picture, but this time the camera closes in for a "reveal." P Street, NW in Georgetown (with remaining trolley tracks) is used for a staged accident, and Georgetown serves also as a site for an assassination by Burt in a car.

Three Days of the Condor (1975), directed by Sydney Pollack and starring Robert Redford, is one of that decade's more interesting examples of paranoid cinema. Mostly based in New York City, it has only cursory scenes in DC, one where a smooth hitman (Max von Sydow) is seen chatting with a corrupt CIA official in a night shot on the Memorial Bridge. The film is based on a 1974 novel by James Grady (a young Hill staffer at the time) entitled *Six Days of the Condor*, and intriguingly, the book takes place in DC and uses as a prime location a rowhouse on 3rd and A Street, SE.

The In-Laws (1979) is a spy spoof with Alan Arkin as a hapless New York dentist and Peter Falk as a scruffy CIA agent. The opening sequence (a heist of a Department of Treasury truck) ends up with Falk lounging on the roof of a building in near NW, with a view (north) of Union Station as well as (south) to the Capitol. In *Spies Like Us* (1985) comics Chevy Chase and Dan Ackroyd play an odd couple from Washington who are unwittingly groomed by the Defense Intelligence Agency to act as expendable decoys to draw attention away from a serious mission in Soviet Central Asia. Not enough laughs ensue. Yet another CIA spoof, *Company Man* (1999) opens with a Senate hearing on the Bay of Pigs in 1962, where a blowhard senator is questioning, in a too tiny hearing room, an "accidental" agent (actually a grammar professor). A bad JFK impersonator appears in one late White House scene.

In *The Good Shepherd* (2006), directed by Robert DeNiro and starring Matt Damon as CIA agent Edward Wilson, the film opens in 1961 at the time the Bay of Pigs invasion is being planned by the Agency. One sequence shot on Capitol Hill has the Damon character leaving the Capitol Hill Valet (on the 400 hundred block of East Capitol Street, SE) with a laundry box containing a secret "drop" whose contents are later revealed in a hotel room. *(Personal Note: I witnessed this shoot in my own neighborhood and after the final cut at the laundry, both DeNiro and Damon, along with crew members, had a nice break socializing with a US senator who lived on the same block.)*

Body of Lies (2008) was an ambitious project directed by Ridley Scott which pitted two American spies at loggerheads: Leonardo Di Caprio as a principled, on-the-ground agent in the Middle East contending with terrorists, while amoral, tech-happy Russell Crowe carps at him back at CIA headquarters in Langley. For Capitol Hill folks, the most interesting sequence was in September 2007 at the venerable Eastern Market in the midst of the Hill, representing, believe or not, Amsterdam! *The Washington Post* reporter Gene Weingarten described the scene:

> *The stars of the day were the 220 "extras" earning about $150 apiece, wandering the street, gamely wearing furs, parkas, gloves and overcoats in 85-degree weather. Evidently, this was to be a winter scene. To avoid inconvenient faintings, location aides were assigned to spray the extras with water mist and wipe their faces with tissues. A team of demolition experts was working on a gray Volvo, which was going to blow up.*

The car was, indeed, blown up "real good," and the two-day shoot eventually took up about five seconds of screen time. As it turned out, you couldn't even recognize the Market: the explosion was shown only on a TV screen in the movie.

The violent action-thriller *The Shooter* (2007) has a rogue element of the CIA (in cahoots with a grotesquely corrupt senator) challenged by–as usual–a lone marksman, played by Mark Wahlberg. The Justice Department and the Grant Memorial figure in the few Washington scenes, as does Freedom Plaza, the latter as a potentail site for a presidential assassination attempt.

Most recently in the spy genre, there is *Salt* (2010) starring Angelina Jolie as Evelyn Salt–perhaps the most fetching and best dressed CIA agent ever–who works undercover in DC for a petroleum firm. The film is mainly hogwash but is notable for a chase sequence which begins when Salt runs into the Metro station at Archives, then exits Metro at L'Enfant Plaza, only to leap from the Plaza Promenade to land on top of trucks running on the Southeast/Southwest Freeway. The chase goes up and down the Freeway, with trucks doubling back against themselves, until Salt somehow escapes on a motorcycle and grabs a Bolt Bus to New York.

ADDENDUM

One film genre that has bypassed Washington, DC almost entirely is the musical. (It's just hard to "get down" with politics). The only movie that has a full DC context is *Damn Yankees* (1958), where Washington Senator baseball fan Joe Boyd makes a pact with the devil for a chance for his team to beat the hated Yankees. The film, however, featured no DC footage and did not use Griffith Stadium, the Senators' park at the time, but a little-used minor league stadium in South Los Angeles.

Only two other musical films have even a minimal Washington connection. One is Irving Berlin's *Call Me Madam* (released as a film in 1953), which has its DC toastmistress Sally Adams (Ethel Merman) giving herself a send-off at her lavish digs in the city (with the requisite Capitol view) before leaving for her ambassadorial assignment in "Lichtenburg." Another is the film adaptation of *Hair* (1979). While *Hair* is essentially a New York story, the film's climax includes a gathering of the principals at a grave in Arlington Cemetery followed by a rousing rendition of "Let the Sunshine In" sung by thousands of happy hippies bouncing on the Ellipse in view of the White House.

CANNING'S TOP TEN WASHINGTON MOVIES
(in chronological order)

1. *Mr. Smith Goes to Washington* – Still the indelible classic, the film that introduced Capitol Hill to millions.

2. *Born Yesterday* (1950 original) – A brisk comedy which still stands up after 50 years and opens a window to DC in the process.

3. *The Day the Earth Stood Still* (1951 original) – An inspired science fiction fable tinged with intriguing philosophical overtones.

4. *Seven Days in May* – Outstanding cinema of paranoia, with powerful tensions worked out among a stellar cast.

5. *All the President's Men* – One of the greatest film docudramas, tense and tight as any classic thriller.

6. *Being There* – An almost viciously sardonic take on Washington and celebrity but played out with a gentle inevitability.

7. *Broadcast News* – Crafty and convincing take on TV journalism as witnessed through a delightful romantic triangle.

8. *A Few Good Men* – Court martial as riveting courtroom drama, contesting security issues of real moment.

9. *In the Line of Fire* – One of the best Washington heroes takes on one of the best Washington villains.

10. *Slam* – One DC movie which gets into all the cracks and crevices of our city, which other movies mostly ignore.

Plus, one more for the road...

11. *State of Play* – A crisp and compelling political drama which uses contemporary DC locations with expertise and pertinence.

END NOTES

POLITICS AND FILM

1   In his comprehensive study... Terry Christensen, *Reel Politics: American Political Movies from Birth of a Nation to Platoon,* New York: Basil Blackwell, 1987, p. 8.

2   In reviewing American... James Monaco, *How to Read a Film: The Art, Technology, Language, History, and Theory of Film and Media,* New York: Oxford University Press, 1981, p. 219.

2   A number of observers has... Paul Boller, Jr., *Congressional Anecdotes,* (chapter II), New York: Oxford University Press, 1991, p. 12.

2   American had "a culturally ingrained..." James Sterling Young, *The Washington Community,* 1800-1828, New York: Harcourt, Brace and World, 1966, p. 59.

4   "...playing to the crowd"... Gregg Easterbrook, "What's Wrong With Congress?", *The Atlantic,* December 1984, p. 64.

4   ...the likes of Sonny Bono... Fred Grandy has suggested just how close these two old professions have become. "What I really wanted to do was act," he once said, "Eventually, I split the difference and went into politics." (cited in Michael Barone and Grant Ujifusa, *The Almanac of American Politics 1994,* Washington DC, National Journal, Inc., 1993, p. 485).

5   "...both the commander-in-chief"... Jason Killian Meath, *Hollywood on the Potomac,* Arcadia Publishing, Charleston, SC, 2009, p. 33.

5   Long-time political practitioner... Hedrick Smith, *The Power Game: How Washington Works,* New York: Random House, 1988, pp. 94-95.

6   "Much of the real Washington..." Jonathan Alter, "True Colors" (review), *Esquire,* May, p. 96

6   In their 1995 study... John R. Hibbing and Elizabeth Theiss-Morse, *Congress as Public Enemy: Public Attitudes Towards American Political Institutions.*, New York: Cambridge University Press, 1995, p. 157.

7   "If we fail to teach... Ibid., p. 161.

LOCATION, LOCATION, LOCATION

8   One of the city's long-time... Lynn Rothman, "Location Shots," *Action* magazine, July/August 1978, p. 13.

9   "The National Park Service doesn't..." Orrin Konheim, "Benefit of a Scout," *Washington City Paper,* June 20, 2012.

11   According to an informed... Interview with Peggy Pridemore, location manager, February 7, 2012.

11   He claimed there was... Rothman, op. cit.

11   ...the Capitol jurisdiction... Pridemore, op. cit.

12   In a front-page article... Steve Hendrix, "For D.C. film industry, a Capitol hassle," *The Washington Post,* January 31, 2012, p. A1.

12   As Crystal Palmer.... Palmer quoted on radio broadcast "How to Make a Movie in Washington, D.C., *The Kojo Nnamdi Show,* February 23, 2012.

12   In 1978, the film *F.I.S.T.*.... Location manager Stuart Neumann was particularly

proud of a sequence obtained for that film. With the help of a Senate staffer, the film company had a good portion of Capitol Hill closed down (especially Constitution and Delaware Avenues) on a Sunday so that, when Stallone strode down the SW steps of the Russell Building, he saw–in a wide panorama–literally hundreds of period (1950's) trucks and cars in all directions. The shoot produced a giant traffic jam all the way down Constitution to about 3rd Street, NW, and to Union Station down Delaware. Today, Neumann noted, such an elaborate sequence would be done in studio by using CGI. (from telephone interview with Stuart Neumann, location manager, May 29, 2012).

13   Another significant exception... On *Quiz Show*, Redford wanted to shoot both inside and outside the Capitol. Two of his assistant producers came to Washington to request such permission, where they met with Speaker Tom Foley's press spokesman, Jeff Biggs. Biggs was delegated the task of telling the producers that the rules did not allow any filming for a commercial project. Unhappy with this response, they wondered whether it would make any difference if Redford himself were to make the request. Biggs indicated that the Speaker's Office did not have separate rules for Redford. The next day Redford himself came to Washington, met with the Speaker and–*voila*! he received permission to shoot outside the Capitol (but not the inside shots). (Email from Jeff Biggs, April 11, 2012.)

14   One noteworthy refusal... Catherine Eisele, "Spielberg Denied Close Encounter at Capitol," *The Hill*, Washington, DC, March 19, 1997, pp.1+.

15   The production team for... Michael Feeney Callan, *Robert Redford: a Biography*, New York: Alfred A, Knopf, 2011, p. 231.

15   According to one veteran... Neumann, op. cit.

15   "...we're as gracious as... Linda Lee, "Oval Offices, by Way of Hollywood," *The New York Times*, April 13, 1997.

16   In just one case... "'The Contender'–filmed on Location in Virginia..." (press release), Virginia Film Office, September 28, 2000.

16   One recent estimate... Hendrix, op. cit.

16   January 2012 article... Ibid.

16   A similar piece... Carol Ross Joynt, "Why Movies and TV Shows Set in DC Aren't Usually Filmed in DC," *The Washingtonian*, February 2012.

16   Brooks was quoted... Ibid.

18   ...Metro's rigid rule... Lena H. Sun, "Rail to Reel," *The Washington Post*, April 1, 2008, p. B1. This article gives both good background on how the Metro system now assesses Hollywood shoots as well as a short history of location shooting in and around Metro.

19   They have even taken... Interview with Crystal Palmer, DC Office of Motion Picture and Television Development, February 15, 2012.

19   Palmer accentuates the positive... Palmer radio interview, op. cit.

SOFT FOCUS

1. MR. SMITH GOES TO WASHINGTON

23   In his biography... Frank Capra, *The Name Above the Title*, New York: The MacMillan Company, 1971, p. 261.

23   ...which one magazine.... *Life* , "Movie of the Week: Mr. Smith Goes to Washington," October 1939, p. 72.

23   Much of the authentic... Robert C. Byrd, "The Senate in Literature and Film" (Chapter 21), *The Senate 1789-1989: Addresses on the History of the Senate*, Washington DC: U.S. Government Printing Office, p. 484-5.

24 To achieve the appropriate effect... Capra, op. cit., p. 276.

24 Capra cracked... Ibid., p. 280.

24 Film Historian... Daniel D. Fineman, "Mr. Smith Goes to Washington" in *Magill's*

24 A more serene assessment... Robert H. Ferrell, *Dear Bess: The Letters from Harry to Bess Truman, 1910-59* (New York: W.W. Norton and Co., 1983), p. 426.

25 As *The New York Times* reviewer... Frank Nugent, "Mr. Smith Goes to Washington" (review), *The New York Times*, October 20, 1939.

25 More contemporarily... Christensen, op cit., p. 47.

2. THE MORE THE MERRIER

28 "we had fun on that picture..." George Stevens, *George Stevens: Interviews*, (edited by Paul Cronin), Jackson, MS: University Press of Mississippi, 2004, p. 112.

28 Arthur's biographer... John Oller, *Jean Arthur: The Actress Nobody Knew*, New York, Limelight Editions, 1997, . 141.

28 *They...sit down...* Ibid.

28 The venerable *New York Times*... Bosley Crowther, "The More the Merrier" (review), *The New York Times*, May 14, 1943.

3. BORN YESTERDAY

31 Columbia Pictures' Harry Cohn... Citation from "Trivia" section, *Born Yesterday*, *IMDb* database.

31 According to a biographer... Patrick McGilligan, *George Cukor: A Double Life*, New York: St. Martin's Press, 1991, p. 202.

31 Cukor turned it down... Gene D. Phillips, George Cukor, Boston: Twayne Publishers, 1982, p. 109.

31 Cukor praised Kanin's work... Gavin Lambert, *On Cukor*, New York: G.P. Putnam's Sons, 1972, p. 214-15.

31 For two weeks, the cast... *IMDb* database, op. cit.

4. THE DAY THE EARTH STOOD STILL

35 Claude Rains has been... Richard C. Keenan, *The Films of Robert Wise*, Lanham, MD: The Scarecrow Press, 2007, p. 72.

35 "Rennie's face has the gaunt..." Ibid.

35 As Kennan elaborates... Ibid.

35 Principal outdoor photography... Paul Laffoley, "Disco Volante (the Flying Saucer)", 1998 essay (web site).

35 The saucer itself looked ... Kennan, op. cit., p. 73 (quoting John Brosnan).

35 According to one commentator... Ibid.

36 ...period reviews were not that laudatory... Bosley Crowther, "The Day the Earth Stood Still" (review), *The New York Times*, September 19, 1951.

36 All the location shooting... Robert Wise audio commentary from DVD of *The Day the Earth Stood Still*, 20th Century Fox, 2002.

5. WASHINGTON STORY

39 After reviewing Pirosh's script... James H. Graham, "Movie-makers Finishing Film About Capitol," *Washington Times-Herald*, September 1952.

39 The director remarked... Ibid.

39 Although the filmmakers agreed... Ibid.

39 The reporter bemoaned... Ibid.

40   Critics found it... John Walker, (ed.), *Halliwell's Film Guide* (eighth edition), New York: Harper Collins Publishers, 1992, p. 1,203.

6. A MAN CALLED PETER
43   Filming was done... "A Man Called Peter," *Turner Classic Movies (TCM)* website, "Notes" page.
43   Richard Burton was originally... *TCM* website, Ibid.

7. EARTH VS. THE FLYING SAUCERS
46   Harryhausen described... Ray Harryhausen audio commentary from DVD of *Earth vs. the Flying Saucers,* Columbia Pictures, 2007.
46   In his autobiography... Ray Harryhausen (with Tony Dalton), *An Animated Life,* New York: Billboard Books, 2004, p. 84.
46   Some stock footage... Citation from *Earth vs. the Flying Saucers* entry in *Wikipedia,* December 2011.

8. HOUSEBOAT
49   It was during the shooting... Marc Eliot, *Cary Grant: A Biography*, New York: Three Rivers Press, 2004, p. 307.
49   Grant kissed a beautiful... Ibid.
49   Later that evening... Ibid.

9. ADVISE AND CONSENT
52   Laughton's preparation for his role... Otto Preminger, *Preminger: An Autobiography*, Garden City, New York: Doubleday and Company, 1977, p. 150.
53   ...was Burgess Meredith... Ibid. p. 159.
53   Preminger offered Dr. Martin Luther King... Ibid., p. 158.
53   Senator Robert Byrd... Byrd, op. cit. p. 487.
53   *Time* magazine's reporter... "Advise and Dissent." *Time*, March 30, 1962, p. 13.
54   ...Senator Stephen Young... Preminger, op. cit., p. 159.
54   The most influential movie critic... Bosley Crowther, "Point of Order–Objection to Filmed 'Advise and Consent'," *The New York Times,* June 17, 1962.
55   ...the shooting of a lavish... Willi Frischauer, *Behind the Scenes of Otto Preminger: An Unauthorized Biography,* New York: William Morrow and Company, Inc., 1974, p. 202.
55   Assessing the film in the 1980's... Byrd, op. cit., p. 488.

10. SEVEN DAYS IN MAY
58   The facsimile of that Oval... Fletcher Knebel, "Seven Days in May: The Movie the Military Shunned," *Look*, November 19, 1963, p. 91.
59   After rehearsal... Kate Buford, *Burt Lancaster: An American Life*, New York: Alfred A. Knopf, 2000. P. 231.
59   Frankenheimer recalled... Gerald Pratley, *The Films of John Frankenheimer*, Bethlehem, PA: Lehigh University Press, 1998, p. 46
59   Salinger then arranged for the film's... Ibid.
59   ...Knebel offered a lively... Knebel, op. cit.

LOW ANGLE

11. THE EXORCIST

63 Warners considered a number... Citation from *The Exorcist* (film) entry in *Wikipedia*, November 2011.

63 The shoot began... Ibid.

63 The casting also went through... Ibid.

64 The Blatty novel... Ibid.

12. ALL THE PRESIDENT'S MEN

68 He bought the rights... Callan, *Robert Redford,* op. cit., p. 218.

68 William Goldman's original script... Ibid., p. 219.

68 *The Washington Post* itself covered... Tom Shales and others, "When Worlds Collide: Lights! Camera! Egos!", *The Washington Post*, April 11, 1975.

68 Redford, in a recent biography... Callan, op. cit., p. 228.

69 Before fleeing the fabled newsroom... Shales and others, op. cit.

69 ...the shoot in DC was difficult... Callan, op. cit., p. 231.

69 Coblenz also reported that... Ibid.

69 ...an argument over the film's ending... Ibid., 232.

70 The film was universally lauded... Vincent Canby, "All the President's Men" (review), *The New York Times,* April 8, 1976.

70 The apartment where Woodward... Lloyd Grove, "Hooray for Hollywood: A Starstruck Stroll Through the Streets of Washington," *The Washington Post* (Weekend section), January 16, 1981.

71 ...the production "devoted ... Rothman, op. cit.

71 *Forty-eight hours before the shoot...* Kathleen Maxa, "Hollywood on the Potomac," *Business & Real Estate Washington*, 1980, p. 86.

71 ...recalled the event... Neumann, op. cit.

13. BEING THERE

74 He saw its inclusion... Ed Sikov, *Mr. Strangelove: A Biography of Peter Sellers*, New York: Hyperion, 2002, p. 373.

74 "It breaks the spell..." Ibid.

75 Critic Frank Rich... Ibid., p. 361.

75 After being ejected... Grove, op. cit.

75 Here he encounters... Maxa, op. cit. p. 93.

75 The interiors of the house... Citation from "Film Locations" section, *Being There*, *IMDb* database.

14. THE SEDUCTION OF JOE TYNAN

78 One critic compared her... Eugene E. Pfaff, Jr. and Mark Emerson, Meryl Streep: A Critical Biography, Jefferson, NC: McFarland and Company, Inc., 1987, p. 35 (quoting *Time* critic Frank Rich).

79 *Joe Tynan...more than...* Christensen, *Reel Politics*, op. cit., p.171.

79 Stanley Kauffman, for example... Pfaff, Jr., op. cit.

80 Also, the office of Senator Birney... Grove, op. cit.

15. FIRST MONDAY IN OCTOBER

82 Henry Fonda was unavailable... Pat Dowell, "Filming 'October' in January," *The Washington Star*, January 6, 1981, p. C-3.

82 Matthau's biographers... Rob Edelman and Audrey Kupferberg, *Matthau: A Life*, Lanham, MD, 2002, p. 228.

82 The film was originally... Citation from "Trivia" section, *First Monday in October*, *IMDb* database.

19. ST. ELMO'S FIRE

94 In the DVD of the film... Joel Schumacher audio commentary from DVD of *St. Elmo's Fire*, Columbia Pictures, 2001.

94 Having read the script... Ibid.

95 The exterior shots... Ibid.

20. BROADCAST NEWS

97 James L. Brooks wrote... Citation from "Trivia" section, *Broadcast News*, *IMDb* database.

97 ...rather than shoot on an LA set... Pridemore, op. cit.

98 ...Ebert found it...There was praise... Roger Ebert, "Broadcast News" (review), *The Chicago Sun-Times*, December 16, 1987.

98 ...the three principals... Vincent Canby, "Broadcast News" (review), *The New York Times*, December 16, 1987.

98 Richard Corliss of *Time*... Richard Corliss, "Broadcast News" (review), *Time*, December 16, 1987.

98 The anchor desk... *IMDb* database, op. cit.,

21. GARDENS OF STONE

101 *The son of movie director*... "Coppola's Son Killed, O'Neal's Injured" (unsigned), United Press International filing, May 27, 1986.

101 The report noted... Ibid.

101 Fairly typical of the critical tone... Vincent Canby, "Gardens of Stone," *The New York Times*, May 8, 1987.

102 According to location manager... Pridemore, op. cit.

22. NO WAY OUT

104 The Pentagon was featured... Neumann, op. cit.

104 Robert A. Nowlan and Gwendolyn Wright Nowlan, *The Films of the Eighties*, Jefferson, NC: McFarland & Company, Inc., 1991.

23. SUSPECT

108 ...Cher's outburst... Roger Ebert, "Suspect" (review), *Chicago Sun-Times*, October 23, 1987.

109 In director Yates' somewhat sour... Peter Yates audio commentary from DVD of *Suspect*, Tri-Star Pictures, 2006.

109 His vinegary remarks... Citation in email letter from Bren Landon, Director of Public Relations, Daughters of the American Revolution, August 1, 2012.

24. CHANCES ARE

112   ...Cybil Shepherd was effective... Roger Ebert, "Chances Are" (review), *Chicago Sun-Times*, March 10, 1989.

112   *The Washington Post's*... Rita Kempley, "Chances Are" (review), *The Washington Post*, March 10, 1989.

112   The film's two courtroom... Citation from "Film Locations" section, *Chances Are*, *IMDb* database.

TRACKING SHOT

25. TRUE COLORS

118   ...a cameraman on the shoot... Interview with Stuart Stein, second assistant cameraman on film, March 10, 2012.

26. THE DISTINGUISHED GENTLEMAN

121   ...found it a sad chapter... Tom Rosenstiel, "When Hollywood Comes to Washington: An Insider's Look at the Movies That Have Put Congress on the Silver Screen," *Roll Call* (Constituent's Guide), April 8, 1996, p. 27.

121   The impressive congressional office... Citation from "Film Locations" section, *The Distinguished Gentleman, IMDb* database.

27. A FEW GOOD MEN

124   Sorkin got the inspiration... Citation from London blog ThisisTheatre.com, January 2006.

124   The Kaffee character... Citation from "Trivia" section, *A Few Good Men, IMDb* database.

28. DAVE

127   It was occupied again... Linda Lee, op. cit.

128   The exterior of the hospital... Stein, op. cit.

29. IN THE LINE OF FIRE

130   Jeff Maguire's script... Citation from "Trivia" section, *In the Line of Fire, IMDb* database.

130   Some movie magic... Jane Galbraith, "'Line of Fire' Gives Crowd Control a New Meaning," *Los Angeles Times*, July 11, 1993, p. 26.

131   A cameraman who worked... Stein, op. cit.

134   In the dramatic wind-up... Wolfgang Peterson audio commentary from DVD of *In the Line of Fire*, Columbia Pictures, 2006.

30. THE PELICAN BRIEF

136   The rights to... Citation from "Trivia" section, *The Pelican Brief, IMDb* database.

136   Grisham wrote the part... Ibid.

137   ...Ebert...used his review... Roger Ebert, "The Pelican Brief " (review), *The Chicago Sun-Times*, December 17, 1993.

31. TRUE LIES

141   ...the first Lightstorm Entertainment... Citation from *True Lies* entry in *Wikipedia*.

141   Upon its release... Citation from "Trivia" section, *True Lies*, *IMDb* database.
142   This hotel, however... *IMDb* database, Ibid.
142   ...the film's writers... *IMDb* database, Ibid.
142   ...according to a....police source... Interview with Quintin Peterson, retired Metropolitan Police Department officer, May 11, 2012.

32. THE AMERICAN PRESIDENT
144   For the convincing... Linda Lee, op. cit.
144   Sorkin later adapted... Citation from *The American President* entry (section "Influence on *The West Wing*") in *Wikipedia*.
144   The last sequence... Citation from "Trivia" section, *The American President*, *IMDb* database.

33. ABSOLUTE POWER
148   Screenwriter William Goldman... Citation from *Absolute Power* entry in *Wikipedia*.
148   Insider's Note... Quintin Peterson, op. cit.
149   The Sullivan mansion... Citation from "Trivia" section, *Absolute Power*, *IMDb* database.
149   ...the headquarters of DC's MPD... Quintin Peterson, op. cit.

34. MURDER AT 1600
151   The production's most ambitious... Linda Lee, op. cit.

35. WAG THE DOG
154   The credit for the film... Citation from *Wag the Dog* entry in *Wikipedia*.
154   Some commentators... Ibid.
154   In a *Newsweek* article... "Double Takes," *Newsweek*, March 2, 1998.
154   Hoffman himself... Dustin Hoffman audio commentary from DVD of *Wag the Dog*, New Line Pictures.
155   In the commentary... Barry Levinson audio commentary, Ibid.

36. ENEMY OF THE STATE
157   One is the "Ruby" lingerie store... Citation from "Trivia" section, *Enemy of the State*, *IMDb* database.

37. SLAM
160   Director Marc Levin came... Michael Canning, "Slam: A New Film," *Washington Review*, April/May 1999, p. 18.
160   Levin said the film's... Ibid., p. 19.
160   It was while working.... Ibid.

38. RANDOM HEARTS
164   Pollack gave himself... DVD audio commentary, *Random Hearts*, Columbia Pictures.

QUICK CUTS

40. THE CONTENDER
170 Born in Israel... Information from *Rod Lurie* entry in *Wikipedia*, April 11, 2012.
170 In 2005, Lurie created... Information from *Commander in Chief* (TV Series) entry in *Wikipedia*, May 21, 2012.

41. THIRTEEN DAYS
173 Robert F. Kennedy wrote... Citation from *Thirteen Days* (film) entry in *Wikipedia*.
173 ...McNamara criticized the film... Interview (Forum) with Robert McNamara, *The PBS Newshour*, March 1, 2001.
173 In commentary on the film... Roger Donaldson audio commentary from DVD of *Thirteen Days*, New Line Cinema.
174 Donaldson felt the two... Ibid.
175 One interesting use of documentary... Ibid.

42. ALONG CAME A SPIDER
178 Cross carries an officer's... Quintin Peterson, op. cit.

43. MINORITY REPORT
180 Philip Dick's short story... Information from *Minority Report* (film) entry in *Wikipedia*.
180 The film also has... Ibid., (under "Style").
181 ...LaSalle...raved... Mike LaSalle, "Spielberg's Return to Form" (review), *The San Francisco Chronicle*, December 20, 2002.
181 Lisa Schwarzbaum...felt... Lisa Shhwarzbaum, "Minority Report" (review), *Entertainment Weekly*, July 12, 2002.
181 J. Hoberman...offered... J. Hoberman, "Private Eyes" (review), *The Village Voice*, June 25, 2002.
181 ...news sources continued... Charles Arthur, "Why 'Minority Report' Was Spot On," *The Guardian*, June 16, 2010.
183 According to veteran location manager... Pridemore, op. cit.

45. SHATTERED GLASS
189 The actual restaurant... Citation from "Trivia" section, *Shattered Glass*, IMDb database.

46. NATIONAL TREASURE
191 For a period shot... Landon email, op. cit.
193 An extra on the film... Email exchange with Nancy Leroy, February 29, 2012.

47. THE SENTINEL
195 Most caustic was... Bill Gallo, "The Sentinel" (review), *The Village Voice*, April 18, 2006.
195 According to director... Clark Johnson audio commentary from DVD of *The Sentinel*, 20th Century Fox, 2007.
196 There is also an elaborate... Pridemore, op. cit.
196 The final scene shot... Ibid.

196 The final scene shot... Ibid.

48. THANK YOU FOR SMOKING
198 The movie rights to... Citation from *Thank You for Smoking* (film) entry in *Wikipedia*.

49. BREACH
202 The FBI allowed... Pridemore, op. cit.
203 Phillippe and Linney also have... Ibid.
203 ...then he is apprehended... Billy Ray audio commentary from DVD of *Breach*, Universal Pictures, 2008.
203 Planning to film on the actual street... Pridemore, op. cit.
203 Pridemore said... Ibid.

50. CHARLIE WILSON'S WAR
205 In comments on... "The True Story of Charlie Wilson's War" (documentary), *The History Channel*, December 22, 2007.
205 In his review... Christopher Orr, "Charlie Wilson's War" (review), *The New Republic*, December 21, 2007.

51. TALK TO ME
208 Dewey Hughes never delivered... Neely Tucker, "Left Out of the Picture," *The Washington Post*, August 20, 2007.
208 At the time of the film's... Ibid.

52. BURN AFTER READING
211 Ethan Coen compared... Susan Wloszczyna, "Fall Movie Review: Coens Dumb It Down with 'Burn,'" *USA Today*, August 28, 2008.
211 While writing the script... Citation from "Trivia" section, *Burn After Reading*, *IMDb* database.
212 He said of the shooting... John Malkovich cited in "Burn After Reading," *Empire* magazine, Autumn 2008.
212 ...the Cox's house... Pridemore, op. cit.

53. STATE OF PLAY
214 It became associated with... Information taken from *State of Play* (film) entry in *Wikipedia*.
215 The film originally... Under "Deleted Scenes" in DVD of *State of Play*, Universal Pictures, 2009.

54. NIGHT AT THE MUSEUM: BATTLE OF THE SMITHSONIAN
218 A extra on those scenes... Leroy, op. cit.
219 ...but the large lettering... Pridemore, op. cit.

55. CASINO JACK
221 That film, made by... A complete review of Alex Gibney's *Casino Jack and the United States of Money* can be found at my website "wwwmikesflix.com" under "Reviews" (May 2010). In my own words, it "recounts one of the more egregious episodes of lobbyists run amok, the slimy rise and ignominious fall of Jack Abramoff, champion defiler of our

politics."

56. FAIR GAME
225　Valerie and Joe...meet... Pridemore, op. cit.

57. HOW DO YOU KNOW
228　He began the script in 2005... Information from *How Do You Know* entry in *Wikipedia.*
228　A fairly representative slam... Anthony Lane, "Couple Trouble" (review), *The New Yorker,* December 28, 2010.
229　A reporter from... Carolyn Presutti, "Camera? Action!" (in "People and Politics"), *Washingtonian,* February 2010.

58. J. EDGAR
232　The *Gazette* describes... Mark Hartsell, "Bright Lights, Big Names: Eastwood Films at Library," *Library of Congress Gazette,* April 1, 2011, p. 1.
233　In commentary after a showing... Ben Mankiewicz commenting on "The FBI Story," *Turner Classic Movies (TCM),* aired November 19, 2011.

SELECTED SHORT SUBJECTS

237　Burton was a big admirer... Citation from *Mars Attacks* ("Production") entry in Wikipedia.
238　...he is greeted most... Richard Harrington, "The Movies Go To Washington," *The Washington Post* (Weekend section), July 13, 2007, p. 25.
240　...but the splash... Grove, op. cit.
242　One caustic critic... Richard Roeper, "Evan Almighty" (review), *Chicago Sun-Times,* June 22, 2007.
245　...a night shot on Memorial Bridge... Stuart Neumann, DC location manager for this film, recalls he witnessed a near disaster at this scene. The set-up was ready around midnight, but, at about 12:15 am, the lights on the backdrop–the Memorial itself–suddenly went out (the crew had been told they would function well into the night). Luckily, a clever technician found the correct electrical panel near the Memorial and got the juice turned on again about a half-hour later and saved the day (or night).
246　*The Washington Post* reporter... Gene Weingarten, "Boom Town: How Hollywood Came to Town and Really Blew It" *The Washington Post Magazine,* September 30, 2007.

NOTE: In this volume, almost all box office information about contemporary films (after 1980) comes from the website Box Office Mojo (www.boxofficemojo.com) which now forms part of the International Movie Database (IMDb).

ACKNOWLEDGEMENTS

To Jack Wennersten, for suggesting the idea for this book in the first place, and Neal Gregory, for providing sound advice and support towards its completion; and to Karen Falk, for her vigilant editing and creative design-work on all aspects of the project.

To Crystal Palmer, of the DC Office of Motion Picture and Television Development, for her enthusiastic personal support for this book; Marci Brennan and Doug Fallone of the Everett Collection and Ron Mandelbaum and Todd Ifft from Photofest, for their help with illustrations for this volume; Quintin Peterson, for his perceptive cop's eye view of D.C. movies; Zoran Sinobad of the Moving Image Section of the Library of Congress for invaluable research assistance; Paul Hogroian of the Duplication Services of the Library of Congress; Faye Haskins, Photo Librarian in the DC Public Library's Washingtoniana Division, for photo acquisition; location managers Peggy Pridemore and Stuart Neumann, for essential insights and details on DC locations; Stuart Stein, local cameraman, for useful tidbits about his local shoots; Nancy Leroy, for views on life as an extra; Bren Landon of the DAR, and also Jeff Biggs, Cheryl Adams, Sheridan Harvey, and Hazel and Bob Kreinheder.

Also, thanks to my colleagues Jean-Keith Fagon, Melissa Ashabranner, and Andrew Lightman, Publisher, Executive Editor, and Managing Editor, respectively, of the *Hill Rag* newspaper on Capitol Hill, all of whom have allowed me an outlet for both seeing and reviewing films for almost 20 years.

Most especially, I want to thank my wife, Judy (of the clear blue eyes), for her generosity and encouragement in every aspect of this project, including her adroit editing, her unerring taste, and her unflagging companionship of almost half a century (a lot of it spent at the movies).

INDEX OF FILM TITLES

INDEX OF WASHINGTON AREA LOCATIONS

PHOTO CREDITS

Posters

Mr. Smith Goes to Washington, The More the Merrier, Born Yesterday, The Day the Earth Stood Still, Washington Story, Advise and Consent, Seven Days in May, The Exorcist, All the President's Men, Along Came a Spider/all Courtesy: Everett Collection

Being There,© United Artists/Courtesy: Everett Collection

Broadcast News, True Lies,© 20th Century Fox/Courtesy: Everett Collection

No Way Out,© MGM/Courtesy: Everett Collection

The Distinguished Gentleman,© Buena Vista/Courtesy: Everett Collection

A Few Good Men, In the Line of Fire, The American President, St. Elmo's Fire,© Columbia Pictures/Courtesy: Everett Collection

Dave, The Pelican Brief,© Warner Brothers Pictures/Courtesy: Everett Collection

Thirteen Days, Wag the Dog,© New Line Cinema/Courtesy: Everett Collection

Minority Report,© DreamWorks/Courtesy: Everett Collection

Shattered Glass,© Lions Gate/Courtesy: Everett Collection

Thank You for Smoking,© Fox Searchlight Pictures/Courtesy: Everett Collection

Breach, Charlie Wilson's War, State of Play,© Universal/Courtesy: Everett Collection

Fair Game,© Summit Entertainment/Courtesy: Everett Collection

The Contender, National Treasure, Talk to Me/Courtesy: Photofest.

Insert

Page 1–*Mr. Smith Goes to Washington*, Courtesy: Everett Collection; inset/Courtesy: Everett Collection; *The More the Merrier*/Courtesy: Library of Congress

Page 2–*Born Yesterday, Washington Story*/both Courtesy: Library of Congress

Page 3–*Seven Days in May*, reprinted with permission of the DC Public Library, Star Collection© The Washington Post; *Advise and Consent*/Courtesy: Photofest

Page 4–*The Exorcist* (1)/Courtesy: Everett Collection; (2) Reprinted with permission of the DC Public Library, Star Collection© The Washington Post

Page 5—*All the President's Men*,© Warner Brothers Pictures/Courtesy: Everett Collection; inset reprinted with permission of the DC Public Library, Star Collection© The Washington Post; *First Monday in October*, reprinted with permission of the DC Public Library, Star Collection© The Washington Post

Page 6—*Broadcast News*/Courtesy of the Library of Congress, *In the Line of Fire*,© Columbia Pictures/Courtesy: Everett Collection

Page 7—*The American President*,© Columbia Pictures/Courtesy: Everett Collection, *Minority Report*, Mike Canning

Page 8—*J. Edgar*/Courtesy: Cheryl Adams (Library of Congress); *Being There*,© United Artists/Courtesy: Everett Collection

USEFUL WEBSITES FOR FILM REVIEWS

Rotten Tomatoes (www.rottentomatoes.com) is a website which assesses movies based upon a "film review aggregator." Its staff collects online reviews from certified critics and compiles an average score as a percentage of positive ("fresh") reviews as against negative ("rotten") ones. "Fresh" films are those with over 60 percent positive reviews; those with less than 60 percent are "rotten," with the scale going from 0 to 100. To be rated, films must have a least 40 certified reviews. The number of reviews varies widely, from just a handful to more than 250 for top films. The site name stems from the practice of audiences throwing rotten tomatoes at a poor stage performance. Officially launched in April 200, its ownership has changed over the years (it is currently owned by a subsidiary of Warner Brothers).

Metacritic (www.metacritic.com) summarizes entertainment reviews of movies (and other media). The site was launched in January 2001 and distills many critics' views into a single Metascore, a weighted average of the most respected critics writing reviews online and in print. The number of reviewers ranges from less than ten (for more obscure offerings) to around 40 for a mainstream picture. Metascores are on a 0 to 100 (worst to best) scale, with basically "positive" reviews starting at 60. As a relatively late start-up, Metacritic has few reviews of films released prior to 1990.

NOTES ON VIDEO SOURCES

Almost all of the movies mentioned in this book are available in video, mostly in DVD format, though a few exist only in VHS tape. The vast majority of the titles are available by rental through Netflix (www.Netflix.com) or by purchase through Amazon (www.amazon.com) or Movies Unlimited (www.moviesunlimited.com). Among all the Washington movies identified, only a small group of relatively obscure films from the 1930's and 1940's have never been issued in video formats, i.e., *Washington Masquerade, Washington Merry-Go-Round, The President Vanishes, Ladies of Washington,* and *Government Girl.* Among all of the film's given in-depth treatment in this volume, only one, *Washington Story* from 1952, has never come out on video. The only way readers can currently get a look at these relative rarities is to hope they show up some time on the Turner Classic Movies (TCM) cable channel.

ABOUT THE AUTHOR

Mike Canning has long been fascinated by Hollywood's foibles, making his first visit to the "flickers" in Fargo, North Dakota at the precocious age of four, hence inspiring his second career–going to the movies. Here he opens up a world beyond Washington's tourist friendly monuments and museums, exposed by moviedom's love-hate affair with the city. Mike has reviewed movies for the *Hill Rag* newspaper in Washington, DC for almost 20 years. He is also a freelance writer on film, public affairs, and politics and has written often on the depiction of Washington, DC and the U.S. Congress in American feature films. In his first life he was a Foreign Service Officer for 28 years, working as a press and cultural officer in eight countries on four continents. He lives on Capitol Hill, surrounded by many of the scenes he writes about.